ALTRUISTIC LOVE

PUBLICATIONS OF
THE HARVARD RESEARCH CENTER
IN ALTRUISTIC INTEGRATION AND CREATIVITY

ALTRUISTIC LOVE

A Study of American "Good Neighbors"
and Christian Saints

IN PREPARATION

EXPLORATIONS IN ALTRUISTIC LOVE
AND BEHAVIOR: A SYMPOSIUM

TYPES, TECHNIQUES, AND FACTORS
OF ALTRUISTIC EXPERIENCE

ALTRUISTIC LOVE

A Study of American "Good Neighbors" and Christian Saints

PITIRIM A. SOROKIN

THE BEACON PRESS

Boston · 1950

Copyright, 1950

THE BEACON PRESS

Printed in U.S.A.

PREFACE

There are times when mankind most urgently needs an upsurge of scientific discoveries and technological inventions. And there are times when the paramount need is a release of aesthetic or religious or philosophical creativity. Finally, there are periods when the greatest need of humanity is ethical creativity at its noblest, wisest, and best.

An exuberant blossoming of ethical creativity seems to be the most desperate need of humanity today. Mankind will survive if there are no great scientific or philosophical or artistic or technological achievements during the next hundred years. But this survival becomes doubtful if the egotism of individuals and groups remains undiminished; if it is not transcended by a creative love as Agape and as Eros—love as a dynamic force effectively transfiguring individuals, ennobling social institutions, inspiring culture, and making the whole world a warm, friendly, and beautiful cosmos.

From the tragic experience of the last few decades we have begun to learn that without a minimum of love no social harmony, no peace of mind, no freedom, and no happiness are possible. Partly in this book, but more fully in a series of forthcoming studies of the Harvard Research Center in Altruistic Integration and Creativity, it will be shown that love is literally a life-giving force; that altruistic persons have on the average a far greater duration of life than ordinary, and especially egotistic, persons; that love annuls loneliness and is the best antidote to suicidal and morbid tendencies; that love-experience is true cognition; that love-experience is beautiful and beautifies anything it touches; that love is goodness itself; that love

PREFACE

is freedom at its loftiest; that love is fearless and is the best remedy for any fear; that love is a most creative power; that it is an accessible and effective means to a real peace of mind and a supreme happiness; that it is the best therapy against hate, insanity, misery, death, and destruction; that, finally, it is the only means of transcending the narrow limits of our Lilliputian egos and of making our true self coextensive with the richest Manifold Infinity.

Even from a purely utilitarian and hedonistic standpoint, these verities are so significant that an intensive study of love—of its how and why, of the techniques of its "production," "accumulation," and "circulation"—can no longer be neglected if humanity wants to survive and to continue its creative mission.

The field of this study is infinite, consisting of a host of difficult problems, and requiring the concerted work of the best minds of several generations. One of these problems is that of learning about the altruistic type of personality, its forms, traits, and the causes of its altruism. Strange as it may seem, we know little about the altruistic person. We have studied the negative types of human beings sufficiently—the criminal, the insane, the sinning, the stupid, and the selfish. But we have neglected the investigation of positive types of Homo sapiens—the creative genius, the saint, the "good neighbor." We know a great deal about the general characteristics of the subsocial types. But we know precious little of the general or typical properties of creative persons. What, if any, are the typical characteristics of altruistic persons? Taken as a nominal group, what is their sex and age composition, their health and duration of life, their occupation, economic status, and social position, their education and other biological and psychosocial characteristics? What are their types, and how did they happen to become altruistic?

The subsequent studies of American "good neighbors" and of Christian-Catholic saints try to answer tentatively some of these questions. The American "good neighbors" represent persons somewhat more altruistic than the rank and file. The majority of Christian saints are likewise altruistic, even though the categories of sainthood and altruism are not identical, and even though some of the saints do not display a notable altruism toward other human beings. Both of these investigations are preliminary: preliminary in one sense because they will be used as material for a further study of altruistic man by other investigators and myself (in a forthcoming monograph, *Types, Techniques, and Factors of Altruistic Experience*); and preliminary in another sense because of the very simple statistical procedures used in the study. Being one of the first statistico-sociological studies of "good neighbors" and saints, and dealing with material (especially in the case of the saints) that is far from precise, the study hardly warranted an application of more refined statistical techniques than mere arithmetical summaries and percentages. In the simplest way these seem to give all the important quantitative results which the material contains.

In conclusion I want to thank all my collaborators in these studies. Their co-operation and their share is so important that the real author of the book is a collective body of persons: they include, for "American Good Neighbors," C. Woodson, J. H. Maddox, John Manfredi, and Dr. J. Fichter; for "Christian-Catholic Saints," Marcia L. Alpert; and for "Russian-Orthodox Saints," Dr. S. G. Pushkarev. I am greatly indebted also to Herbert Landon, Kenyon & Eckhardt, Inc., and the late Tom Breneman, for their generous help in the study of American "good neighbors."

PITIRIM A. SOROKIN

Cambridge, Massachusetts

CONTENTS

Preface   v

PART I
AMERICAN "GOOD NEIGHBORS"

1. The Need for a Positive Emphasis 3
2. The Selection of Our "Good Neighbors" . . . 6
3. Activities of "Good Neighbors" 11
4. Opinions about Good-Neighborliness 17
5. Sex Distribution 19
6. Age Distribution 22
7. Parental Families 25
8. Marital Status and Families 30
9. Social, Occupational, and Economic Status . . . 35
10. Rural-Urban and Nationality Distribution . . . 38
11. Education and School Intelligence 39
12. Attitudes toward the World at Large 41
13. Religious Attitudes and Affiliations 42
14. Political Ideologies and Affiliations 50
15. Affiliations with Other Organizations 52
16. Other Characteristics 54
17. Factors in Good-Neighborliness 57
18. Two Routes to Good-Neighborliness 59
19. Recipients of Help 64
20. "Good Neighbors" and Their Dearest Persons . . 68
21. Happiness and Peace of Mind 77
22. "Good Neighbors" as Deviants 81
23. The Meaning of Good-Neighborliness 85

CONTENTS

PART II
CHRISTIAN–CATHOLIC SAINTS

24. The Sources of This Study 91
25. Sex Distribution 94
26. Age Distribution 100
27. Months of Death and Canonization 106
28. Countries of Birth and Death 108
29. Class Origins 122
30. Parental Influences 136
31. Types of Entrance on the Road to Sainthood . . 138
32. Routes to Sainthood 146
33. Marriage Status 151
34. Socio-occupational Status 154
35. Adaptation to Environment 169
36. Techniques of Self-control 177
37. Fluctuation of the Number of Saints throughout the Centuries 179
38. The Saint in Sensate, Idealistic, and Ideational Cultures 185

PART III
ALTRUISM AND THE PERSONALITY

39. Good-Neighborliness and Saintliness: Summary . . 197
40. The Meaning of Altruistic Love 213

APPENDIX

A. Sample American "Good Neighbors" 215
   1. Letters Received by the "Breakfast in Hollywood" Program 215
   2. Sketches of "Good Neighbors" 218
B. Russian-Orthodox Saints 240

Index 248

PART ONE

AMERICAN "GOOD NEIGHBORS"

1. THE NEED FOR

A POSITIVE EMPHASIS

In its declining sensate phase Western culture has become increasingly negativistic. In papers and magazines it devotes the front page to hair-raising murder stories, to sex scandals or perversions, to hypocrisy or insanity, hardly ever mentioning any good deed or anything truly positive. It does the same in fiction; in cinemas and plays; in operas and songs; in painting and sculpture; in radio and television. Sex, insanity, and crime constitute roughly from 80 to 90 per cent of the topics in these fields of contemporary Western culture. The situation is no different in other fields. Our sensate culture there also dwells mainly in the region of subsocial sewers; breathes mainly their foul air; and drags down into their turbid muck everything heroic, positive, true, good, and beautiful.[1]

In the sensate social sciences this concentration on the pathological has manifested itself in several ways. One of these is a proliferation of various "debunking" interpretations of man, culture, and values: mechanistic, reflexological, biological, materialistic, organismic, endocrinological, behavioristic, etc. These interpretations have deprived man and his culture and values of everything divine, spiritual, supermaterialistic, or human. They equate man and his culture and values with atoms, electron-protons, reflex mechanisms, reflex organisms, the libido, and so on. Another manifestation of

---
[1] For evidence of this, see my *Social and Cultural Dynamics*, 4 vols. (New York, 1937–1941); also my *Crisis of Our Age* (New York, 1941).

this pathological bent in the social sciences has been their concentration on a study of the negativistic and pathological types of human beings and human actions, and their reluctance to study the positive types of *Homo sapiens* and human relations.

For decades Western social science has been cultivating, *urbi et orbi*, an ever-increasing study of crime and criminals; of insanity and the insane; of sex perversion and perverts; of hypocrisy and hypocrites. A vast set of special disciplines has been developed for these purposes: criminology and penology, with their subdivisions and branches; psychiatry, psychoanalysis, and mental hygiene, with still more numerous branches and proliferations.

In contrast to this, Western social science has paid scant attention to positive types of human beings, their positive achievements, their heroic actions, and their positive relationships. The criminal has been "researched" incomparably more thoroughly than the saint or the altruist; the idiot has been studied much more carefully than the genius; perverts and failures have been investigated much more intensely than integrated persons or heroes. In accordance with the total nature of our negativistic culture, our social science has been semi-blind about all positive types and actions and very sharp-eyed about all negative types and relationships. It seems to have enjoyed moving in the muck of social sewers; it has been reluctant to move in the fresh air of high social peaks. It has stressed the pathological and neglected the sound and heroic.

The result is that our social science knows little about positive types of persons, their conduct and relationships. Not having studied these, it lacks also a more adequate knowledge of the negative phenomena: for a knowledge of the positive is necessary in order to have a full knowledge of the negative.

The time has come when this one-sidedness of sensate social science must be corrected. For a fuller knowledge, we must concentrate increasingly on a study of positive values, personalities, relationships, and phenomena. The study of American "good neighbors," together with those of saints, great altruists, and creative geniuses, is one of numerous studies to stress the positive. As we shall see, these studies throw light even on negative phenomena.

2. THE SELECTION OF

OUR "GOOD NEIGHBORS"

The total sample of our "good neighbors" is made up of three groups. The first and largest group consists of more than one thousand persons selected as "good neighbors" and sent an orchid by a committee for the late Tom Breneman's "Breakfast in Hollywood" radio program.[1] The selection by the committee was made on the basis of letters of recommendation sent to Tom Breneman by various individuals. In his letter of recommendation for a "good neighbor," the radio listener described concisely the good deeds that had made someone he knew eligible for the title of "good neighbor," the receipt of an orchid, and a citation on the radio program. The number of such letters of recommendation received by Tom Breneman was far greater than could be cited on "Breakfast in Hollywood." Therefore a selection of these letters was made by Tom Breneman's committee. Only a part of these letters were accepted and read on the program. In other words, only a fraction of the persons recommended as "good neighbors" were granted this distinction. These one thousand and more letters of recommendation were "selected" letters: their "recommendees" were those that were chosen, sent an orchid, and granted the title of "good neighbor."

[1] I am grateful to the late Tom Breneman, Herbert Landon, and Kenyon & Eckhardt, Inc., for supplying me with more than one thousand letters of recommendation and for their generous help in the collection of additional autobiographical and questionnaire material. In all these respects, their help has been invaluable.

From among these one thousand letters we made a second selection: we chose some five hundred letters that seemed to describe greater and more genuine good deeds than the other letters. Through this double selection, some five hundred persons were chosen to constitute our first group of "good neighbors." They are not notable altruists; but all in all they are seemingly above the average in their altruistic activities and good-neighborliness.

The examples in Appendix A give an idea of the letters of recommendation and of the "good neighbors" they proposed. These typical letters show that each of five hundred "good neighbors" of this group is a "good neighbor" indeed. This group will be referred to as the "Letters" group.

Our second group of "good neighbors" is made up of 93 members from our first group. In addition to the information given in the letters recommending them, these 93 members wrote their autobiographies and answered a questionnaire. In this way we have much fuller information about these 93 persons than about the rest of our five hundred "good neighbors." This group will be referred to as the "Biographies" group.

Our third group consists of 112 persons who were selected by Harvard graduate and undergraduate students, and by some social workers, as the most altruistic persons among those whom each of them knew. All of these 112 persons answered a fairly detailed questionnaire; some wrote their autobiographies; some were carefully interviewed and studied. Here is a sample of the kind of questionnaire used.

1. Age.
2. Nationality.
3. Sex.
4. Race.
5. Economic status (lower, middle, upper).
6. Height and weight.
7. Married or single? If married, is your marriage happy or unhappy? Why?

8. Should you be willing to marry a person of a different religion, race, or nationality?
9. What do you cite as the cause for such a condition?
10. Native stock.
11. Number in your family.
12. Number of children.
13. Religion.
14. Education (elementary, high-school, college).
15. What grades did you receive in your elementary, high-school, and college education?
16. How would you describe your attitude toward your teachers?
17. Occupation.
18. In your occupational work what position do you occupy (executive, journeyman, etc.)?
19. Political affiliation.
20. Hobbies.
21. From what books do you receive your greatest inspiration toward good-neighborliness?
22. Enumerate societies with which you are associated.
23. Give the type of songs and music you like best. State briefly why.
24. What is your favorite sport?
25. Number of persons in parental family.
26. Was your childhood a happy one?
27. Who influenced you most in your family (father, mother, or both)?
28. Which did you love more? Explain why.
29. What are the family troubles, if any, of your immediate family?
30. What were they in the family of your childhood?
31. To what do you attribute your good-neighborliness?
32. Did you ever have any unusual experience (event, crisis, illness, or meeting of another person) which changed your outlook on life?
33. What do you believe to be the basis of man's goodness or badness?
34. By what techniques have you become a "good neighbor"? And by what techniques would you seek to make others good?
35. Indicate in decreasing order twelve persons who are

dearest to you. Give their nationality, religion, age, sex, occupation, and relationship to you.
36. Have you been extending good-neighborliness in your deeds toward persons other than friends or relatives? If so, in what manner?

In Appendix A are included several abbreviated sketches of the "Questionnaires" group, prepared by members of my seminar in the course of their investigation of these "good neighbors."

The examples in the Appendix give a fairly good idea of the kind of "good neighbors" we have dealt with. Most of them do not look heroic in their good deeds. Their altruism is plain and fairly ordinary. It is, however, real. Each of our "good neighbors" has rendered real help to his fellow men and has done so freely, without any legal duty or even moral obligation. In many cases these deeds were done without expectation of any advantage or profit. While the actions and persons are not heroic, in their totality these ordinary "good neighbors" and their plain good deeds make the moral foundation of any society. Great altruists alone cannot supply even the very minimum of love and mutual help necessary for any surviving society: the heroic apostles of love and their great actions are too few to supply this minimum. It is furnished mainly by thousands and millions of our plain "good neighbors." Each giving a modest contribution of love, in their totality they produce an enormous amount of "love energy."

If a society has the necessary quota of these "good neighbors" and of their actions, it is fortunate indeed. With the solid moral foundation of these good deeds, such a society is insured to a considerable degree against lawlessness, anarchy, and great inner tensions. Relationships among its members will be decent; their feeling of oneness and community will be alive; the misfortunes of this or that member will be alleviated.

Without this moral foundation of the deeds of the "good

neighbors," no society can be satisfactory. No matter how enlightened its official law, how democratic its political regime, how successful its economic production, the society is liable to be disorderly, full of tensions, unhappy members, and criminals. Without this moral foundation, fine laws, democratic institutions, and economic well-being are likely to be significant chiefly on paper. Herein lies the basic significance of the ordinary good deeds and of the plain "good neighbors." Their plain deeds are more important than a few cases of heroic altruism or the official laws of politicians and statesmen. *Quid leges sine moribus!* Without "good neighbors" and their actions, any "welfare state" or socialist or communist or fascist state will turn out to be a soulless and formal machinery, incapable of rendering real welfare services and often becoming a hate-filled bureaucracy enjoying its position through exploitation of the laboring classes and the majority of the people. Such states and organizations are mere sham-welfare, sham-democratic, sham-Christian organizations.

Now let us turn to an analysis of the graspable traits of our "good neighbors."

3. ACTIVITIES

OF "GOOD NEIGHBORS"

In societies where there are few institutionalized social-service agencies, "good neighbors" fill the greater part of the basic requirements of its needy members. In societies where the basic needs of its members are taken care of either by kinship groups or by official social-service agencies, the main activities of the "good neighbors" tend to supplement the activities of kinship groups or official agencies. In the United States, we have a well-developed set of federal, state, municipal, community, religious, educational, and other—public and private—institutionalized agencies that take care of all the basic needs of the population. For this reason the bulk of altruistic activities of American "good neighbors" supplements the relief activities of our institutionalized social-service agencies.

Even well-developed institutionalized agencies in a "welfare state" like ours cannot meet all the needs of the population. Through their inevitable standardization and bureaucracy these agencies do not meet many needs considered socially superfluous. They do not supply either a wedding or graduation dress to a poor bride or a high-school girl. It is often a most important need for such girls to have the proper wedding or graduation dress. The helping hand of a non-bureaucratic "good neighbor" brings sunshine into the lives of such needy persons.

In other cases the institutionalized agencies meet a given

need inadequately. Such is the case with almost all the needs, especially with those considered superfluous. "Too late and too little" or "not prompt and less than needed" may be said of almost all the needs met by the institutionalized agencies. A big-hearted "good neighbor" alleviates the situation through his *immediate* and *generous* help. It is a "good neighbor" who steps in to heal the sore spots of day-to-day existence and does something about them immediately. "Do something quick!" —the motto of one of our "good neighbors"—is applicable to all of them. When Maine forest fires destroyed many homes, some amount of help eventually was rendered by the official agencies—the Red Cross and state and local agencies. But the help was slow in coming and inadequate. In several cases, members of the local A. F. of L. carpenters' union came to the rescue: voluntarily, without any remuneration, in their after-labor hours, they rebuilt several houses of their neighbors. In this way they supplemented the utterly inadequate relief rendered by official agencies. What is the distinction? Their work was really the main help, while the official relief was a mere supplementation.

Moreover, under certain circumstances, the institutionalized agencies are forbidden to render help to persons and groups that are declared criminal, subversive, questionable, and so on. Jean Valjean, in Victor Hugo's *Les Misérables*, was persecuted rather than helped by the official agencies. The unofficial good heart of the truly Christian bishop came to his rescue and saved his body from hunger and prison, and his soul from perdition. Official agencies do not help the crowd of "disreputable people" who are welcomed in the house of Miss H. (see Appendix A). Individualistic Protestants or atheists in our group have their own sets of values, often different from the official norm. Accordingly, they often help people in positions officially considered subversive or objectionable. In all such cases the shortcomings of the official set of values and of the institutionalized agencies are supplemented and corrected by the free, unbureaucratic and intuitively ethical activities of "good neighbors."

Their good deeds fill also the gap created by the formality and bureaucracy of the agencies. Institutionalized help is ordinarily cold, formal, soulless, and heartless. Recipients of their "relief" are but numbered cases to officials. As a result, a few dollars given to the needy often amount to less than the warm-hearted, sincere sympathy, good words, and few pennies given by a "good neighbor." A quest for sympathy, understanding, and encouragement—the desire to find a co-sympathizer in either despair or loneliness—is just as strong in human beings as the need for food or clothing. Official agencies can rarely fill this sort of need. Only a true "good neighbor" can meet, and does meet, these needs. In these and similar ways our "good neighbors" supplement the activities of the official social-service agencies and fill the void left by them. This explains almost all the concrete forms of the good deeds of our groups.

Table 1 gives a detailed classification of the good-neighborly activities. *Twenty-four per cent of their deeds alleviated boredom and empty time by furnishing recreation, amusement, and sympathetic company.* This is the largest or most frequent form of neighborly activities in our group. It points to the existence in our nation of a considerable amount of painful boredom, and the inability of many to enjoy their own company and to fill their time by creative or pleasurable activities. This need seems not to be met by the institutionalized agencies. Even when they do something along these lines, their entertainment is so standardized that it does not attract many. In contrast to this, the help offered by "good neighbors" along these lines is well adapted to the individual tastes of the benefited persons. Hence the large place this sort of deed occupies in all the activities of "good neighbors."

Related to these deeds are the activities that *help loneliness and grief and even romantic love. They make up some 5 per* cent of all the deeds of "good neighbors." This re-enforces the foregoing conjecture about the prevalence of considerable boredom and lonesomeness in our society. The industrial, urban, and highly mobile character of our life generates these incessantly and profusely. For the reasons given above, the

Table 1

Problems Alleviated by "Good Neighbors"

	Number of cases	Percentage
Amusement, recreation, and alleviation of boredom	120	23.7
A combination of the other problems with varying degrees of emphasis	70	14.0
Health and physical problems	45	9.0
Education	35	7.0
Clothing	28	5.5
Problems arising out of face-to-face relationships except grief	28	5.5
Housing	27	5.4
Substitution for parents	24	4.7
Loneliness	22	4.3
Problems arising out of contact with an impersonal society	18	3.5
Temporary lodging	16	3.1
Money	15	3.0
Food	15	3.0
Transportation	9	1.7
Disaster services	6	1.1
Jobs	6	1.1
Toys	5	1.0
Communication	4	.8
Authority (conflicts with)	3	.6
Food and clothing	3	.6
Counseling and guidance	3	.6
Romantic love	2	.4
Grief	1	.2
Status symbols	1	.2
Total	506	100.0

institutionalized agencies are ill adapted to meet these needs. Real sympathy and warm and direct co-experiencing are necessary for alleviating grief, banishing loneliness, and helping in romantic love. "Good neighbors" solve these tasks much more successfully than the bureaucrats of agencies. Hence the conspicuous place these activities occupy in the total deeds of our neighbors.

Nine per cent of the good deeds helped in meeting and alleviating various troubles of those aided: troubles with authorities, with members of the family (especially in husband-wife relationships), with friends and acquaintances, and with various institutions. Here, again, the warm heart of a "good neighbor" eases many a problem and brings some sort of peace to those who cannot be helped by the institutionalized agents. A concrete example of this sort of help was described in the case of Miss H. Here, again, the deadening formalism and the cold and heartless official "relief" of our mechanized social machinery are vitalized by the living sympathy and warm friendship of "good neighbors."

Of other problems solved by the deeds of our neighbors: 5 per cent of the deeds helped to solve housing and lodging problems which were acute in the years of the war and immediately after it; 7 per cent, the education of needy persons; 9 per cent, health and sickness problems; 5 or 6 per cent, clothing needs; 2 or 3 per cent, transportation and communication difficulties; 3 per cent, food needs; 3 per cent, money requirements; and 4.7 per cent of the deeds consisted in substituting for parents. The rest of the activities met diverse needs ranging from toys to jobs, disaster services, and so on.

Only from 3 to 10 per cent of these activities were performed once. From 80 to 97 per cent were carried on for some time, occasionally for years. The altruistic activities of our group were thus continual or continuous for a period of some duration.

This brief analysis clarifies the supplementary nature of the

AMERICAN "GOOD NEIGHBORS"

activities of "good neighbors." The limitations of the institutionalized agencies become understandable; the existence of a great deal of loneliness, boredom, and grief in our highly industrialized and mobile society comes clearly to the surface; and the need for living, warm, elastic, heart-to-heart helping activity proves to be paramount. *If all the good deeds of all "good neighbors" are considered, their vitalizing, moralizing, beautifying, and encouraging effects are likely to be more important than all the official relief of the institutionalized agencies.* Real sympathy, a warm heart, unquestioning friendship, all-forgiving love—these free gifts of "good neighbors" can hardly be granted by official agencies. These gifts are in the long run possibly more valuable than any number of dollars or material goods supplied. *In this role the social functions of "good neighbors" are perennial and immortal. Their forms may change; their substance remains unchangeable.*

4. OPINIONS ABOUT GOOD-NEIGHBORLINESS

Characteristics of good-neighborly activities are well indicated by our "good neighbors." They define good-neighborliness as *acts and attitudes that realize the Golden Rule* (41 per cent), *"unselfish interest in others"* (17 per cent), *"tolerance and patience"* (7 per cent), *"love of humanity and friendliness"* (19 per cent), *"belief in God and faith"* (9 per cent), *"desire to be of help"* (4 per cent), *the rest giving a combination of these principles and values.* It is significant that practically all "good neighbors" stress the fact that genuine good-neighborliness means not so much knowledge and preaching of the Golden Rule, love, friendship, and so on, as applying these principles in one's overt behavior and natural attitudes toward others and the world at large. "Good deeds speak louder than good words"; "the road to Hell is paved with good intentions but is devoid of good deeds"; "preaching love without practicing it is sheer hypocrisy"— such are some of the comments of our "good neighbors." Some of them candidly remark that even the incessant invocation of the name of God or Jesus Christ, or repetition of prayers, or regular attendance at church services is also phariseeism if these are not followed by good deeds. Spontaneity of good efforts, informality, and warm-heartedness versus the cold formality and red tape of official relief; kindness versus the obligatory duty of legal help; individual practice of good deeds versus standardized rules of official relief—these traits

17

of good-neighborly actions are well emphasized by our group. Eighty-two per cent of them define their attitude toward the recipients of their help as "love-fellowship co-operation"; 12 per cent as "heartfelt compassion and pity"; 6 per cent as "a freely taken responsibility, duty, or obligation." All this shows that our "good neighbors" are well aware of what kind of actions are good-neighborly; that these must be not mere abstract preachments but a consistent practice of these preachings; and that good-neighborly actions differ from those of official relief by various agencies and from obligatory help prescribed by official law.

5. SEX DISTRIBUTION

The sex composition of our three groups is as follows:

Table 2

	"Letters" group		"Biographies" group		"Questionnaires" group	
	Number	Per cent	Number	Per cent	Number	Per cent
Male	36	7.2	6	6.4	26	23.2
Female	376	74.0	73	78.5	85	75.9
Groups and couples	94	18.8	14	15.1	1	.9

These figures indicate that in the United States the overwhelming majority of "good neighbors" doing non-institutionalized good deeds are women. In all our three samples they make up roughly 75 per cent of the "good neighbors," whereas men make up from 6 to 23 per cent. In contrast, among those who were recipients of the help of "good neighbors," men were about three times as prevalent as women. There are 25 and 9 per cent, respectively, in the first group; 10 and 2 per cent in the second; and 4 and 1 per cent in the third group (the rest being mixed groups).

It is interesting to compare these percentages with other groups. Among American criminals the ratio of male to female offenders ranges between 19 to 1 and 3 to 1, in practically all violations of law (except a few that can be committed only by women).[1] Women thus are much more good-neighborly and much less criminal than men in America. Women also

---

[1] See H. von Hentig, *Crime* (New York, 1947), chap. v, or any competent text on criminology.

show a lower ratio of mental disease and suicide than men.[2] On the other hand, among Catholic and Russian-Orthodox Christian saints women make up only from 5 to 16 per cent.[3] Likewise their percentage among the great altruists is about 5 to 10 per cent. Among all British geniuses women represent only 5.3 per cent; among eminent American scientists, 1.8 per cent; among American labor leaders and leaders of radical movements, 6.4 per cent; among the leaders of American farmers, 3.2 per cent;[4] among one thousand world-wide persons of genius, women constitute about 29 – or 2.9 per cent.[5]

These data suggest that women's range of variability seems to be narrower than that of men. Women show a smaller percentage than men in both of the extreme types of human beings: criminals, the insane, those with suicidal tendencies, as well as the great geniuses in science, philosophy, technology, the fine arts, religion, altruism, saintliness, and practically all other fields. Whether this narrower range of women's variability is due to biological or to sociocultural conditions still remains unclear. Probably both factors, somatic and sociocultural, are responsible.

How shall we explain the notable prevalence of women among our samples of American "good neighbors"? It is mainly due to three specific sociocultural factors. First, our data were collected mainly during the war years, when millions of men were drafted into the armed forces. Neighborly activities were exercised mainly by women; and American soldiers,

---

[2] See B. Malzberg, *Social and Biological Aspects of Mental Diseases* (New York, 1940); A. Scheinfeld, *Women and Men* (New York, 1944).
[3] See Part Two.
[4] See P. Sorokin and C. Zimmerman, "Farmer Leaders in the United States," *Social Forces*, September, 1928, pp. 34–35; P. Sorokin, "Leaders of Labor and Radical Movements in the United States and Foreign Countries," *American Journal of Sociology*, November, 1927, p. 393; J. McKeen Cattell, *American Men of Science* (New York, 1910), pp. 583ff.; E. L. Clarke, *American Men of Letters* (New York, 1916), pp. 48ff.
[5] W. G. Bowerman, *Studies in Genius* (New York, 1947), p. 260; H. Ellis, *A Study of British Genius*; J. McKeen Cattell, *American Men of Science* (2d ed.).

sailors, and airmen were one of the principal groups that received their help. This reason alone explains a large part of the prevalence of women in our total group, and the prevalence of men among the recipients of help. Another reason is strictly sociocultural: in this country, good-neighborly activities of men are channeled into the institutional forms of social-service agencies more than those of women. Financial and other contributions of men to charity and good-neighborliness are made predominantly through writing checks and giving donations to institutional agencies. These financial contributions are one of the chief forms in which men manifest their altruistic actions. For other forms of altruistic activity that require time and energy many busy men simply do not have the time. Women, on the other hand, are less able to help financially but are available for direct action. They have more time and more energy for these non-institutional forms of action.

Finally, non-institutionalized kindness and unselfishness in our culture seem to be stimulated mainly in women. If boys show these tendencies (considered "feminine" by our culture), the traits are discouraged in early childhood as being "sissified." In the adult life of our highly competitive world, men would have difficulty in supporting their families and in successfully rising from the status of office boy to bank or corporation president, if they were highly unselfish, altruistic, and self-sacrificing. In girls and women, on the other hand, these tendencies, in a moderate and conventional form, are encouraged and stimulated. They begin to practice them early in the home, with neighbors and members of the family; and they continue to do so in various forms during their adult age.

With the emancipation and equalization of the sexes, this difference is possibly weakening, but it still is tangible and operating. This peculiarly American situation leads to the prevalence of women among our "good neighbors." These factors together seem to explain their prevalence satisfactorily.

6. AGE DISTRIBUTION

Other conditions being equal, for obvious reasons very young and very old persons are in greater need of being helped than adult, middle-aged persons. Babies, young children, and old folks are less capable of helping others than are the intermediary age groups. Therefore, out of 556 "good neighbors," 498, or some 90 per cent, are adults; 49, or 9 per cent, are aged; 8, or a little more than 1 per cent, are adolescent; and 1 is at the age of ten years. In a more detailed form the "Questionnaires" group gives the following percentages: 0.89 per cent at the ages from 10 to 19; 8.93 per cent from 20 to 29; 8.0 per cent at 30 to 39; 21.42 per cent at 40 to 49; 32.14 per cent at 50 to 59; 15.18 per cent at 60 to 69; the remaining 13 per cent at the age of 70 and above. The ages from 30 to 59 show about 70 per cent of all "good neighbors."

These data mean that good-neighborliness is not something that comes by itself, without the effort, talent, and time necessary to develop the art, and to become socially recognized for it. Like any other creative activity—in science, the arts, or technology—altruism, or good-neighborliness, is moral creativity in the field of goodness. Like creativity in the fields of art and thought, it requires an appropriate talent, and incessant effort to cultivate and develop it. Therefore it is not strange that the age composition of our group, and especially the age at which a person is recognized as a "good neighbor," are similar to the age composition and to the age of social recognition of scientists, thinkers, artists, money-makers, and other creative groups. Thus the median age of 4,204 eminent scientists at the "time of their chief work" is 43 years, with 9 per cent of the whole group under 30 years; 37 years for mathematicians, 38 years for bacteriologists and chemists, 40 for physiologists and physicists, up to 45 and 46 years for psychologists, geologists, botanists, zoologists, and anthropologists.[1]

It took an average of 48.5 years for 62 non-hereditary monarchs to become monarchs, the age of 29 years being the earliest age of an upstart's ascent to the throne, and the age of 80, the oldest.[2]

The majority (86 per cent) of American millionaires who were born poor became millionaires at the age of from 31 to 60; only 2.2 per cent arrived at the age of 20 to 30. The average age of ascent to the elective position of the Roman Catholic Pope is 61.3 years; of presidents of France, Germany, and the United States, 55 to 59 years. Likewise the median age of United States senators, representatives, secretaries, and other statesmen, Supreme Court justices, the supreme commanders of the armed forces, and so on, is between 50 and 67 years; that of eminent composers, painters, literary men, inventors, and other creative persons is between 34 and 44 years. Only a minority of these got their first social recognition at an age of below twenty-four years.

These data bear out the above contentions: good-neighborliness is real creativity in the field of goodness; as any genuine creativity it requires the proper talent and then careful training and effortful cultivation; for all that, as in any other creativity, time is necessary; therefore only at about the same age at which creators in other fields become socially prominent, do creative "good neighbors" become socially recognizable.

---

[1] C. W. Adams, "The Age at Which Scientists Do Their Best Work," *Isis*, Nos. 105 and 106, 1946, pp. 166–169.
[2] For these and other data, see my "Monarchs and Rulers," *Social Forces*, March, 1926, p. 530; H. C. Lehman, "The Age of Eminent Leaders," *American Journal of Sociology*, January, 1947; Lehman, "Age of Starting to Contribute versus Total Creative Output," *Journal of Applied Psychology*, October, 1946; P. Sorokin, *Society, Culture, and Personality*, pp. 192–193; E. B. Gowin, *Correlation between Reformative Epochs and the Leadership of Young Men* (New York, 1909).

The age composition of all creative groups contrasts sharply with that of criminals and semi-criminals. Among these groups the most criminal age in this country is between 14 and 25 years, the years 18 to 21 being the most dangerous.[3] The contrast is comprehensible. Going down is always easier than going up. To rise creatively or socially always requires effort, not to mention many other factors. No effort or talent or time is needed to sink to the bottom of the social sewers. When young people are not integrated morally and socially; when inner self-control is not inculcated; when the structure of youth personality is unintegrated or undermined; when social and cultural conditions tempt young people to satisfy their biological and other egoistic conditions—they easily sink to the rank of juvenile delinquents and, finally, criminals.

Here again we see that our group of "good neighbors" sharply differs from the "pathological" social groups and individuals. Its character puts into relief the contrasts between its age and sex composition, and those of criminal and other "pathological" groups.

Though the age composition of the recipients of the aid of our "good neighbors" has not been systematically studied, and the categories of the infants, adolescents, and the aged were noted side by side with the poor, the ill, soldiers, and so on (whose age was not registered)—even under these conditions, the percentage of the infants, adolescents, and aged (who were helped as "infants, adolescents, and the aged") is considerably greater than their proportionate number among the good neighbors: 2.3 per cent of infants, 3.45 per cent of the aged, and some 30 per cent of adolescents and young soldiers were among the numbers of those helped. This only substantiates the above statement that, other conditions being equal, it is the very young and the very old who need to be helped, rather than being able to help others.

---

[3] See the details in von Hentig's work, mentioned above, chap. vi; W. C. Reckless, *Criminal Behavior* (New York, 1940), pp. 103ff.

7. PARENTAL FAMILIES

The size of the parental families of the "good neighbors" is depicted by the following data:

Table 3

Number of children	Number of families	Percentage
One	9	6.6
Two	13	9.6
Three	18	13.3
Four	21	15.9
Five	12	8.8
Six and over	62	45.8

Thus almost one half of the "good neighbors" came from large families with six and more children; only 6.6 per cent came from one-child families. The parental family of "good neighbors" seems to have been considerably larger than the size of the present average American family, as well as that of a few decades ago. Thus, in 1930, Chicago and farm families had respectively 39.8 per cent and 16.3 per cent childless families; 22.9 and 20.5 per cent with one child; and only 1.9 and 21.4 per cent had four or more children. Thus even the farm families happened to have a smaller number of children than the families of our "good neighbors." In 1920 and 1910 the average size of the American family was slightly larger than in 1930; but even then, the average size of the American family was notably smaller than the parental families of our group.[1]

---

[1] For the size and the number of children in American families see W. Ogburn (ed.), Recent Social Trends (New York, 1933), Vol. I, pp. 681ff.; C. V. Kiser and P. K. Whelpton, "Social and Psychological Factors Affecting Families," The Milbank Memorial Quarterly, Vol. XXII, January, 1944; E. Burgess and H. J. Locke, The Family (New York, 1945), pp. 494ff.

This means that large families, when they are in good shape morally and socially, are a better school for the true socialization of human beings than small families. The parental large families of "good neighbors" happened to be in a good shape indeed. Of the "good neighbors," 70.6 per cent state they had a very happy childhood; an additional 18 per cent had a fairly happy childhood; and only eleven per cent had an unhappy childhood. Later on we shall note that most of the happy did not have any sudden "conversion" to altruism, while most of the unhappy had such a conversion. The reasons for their happy childhood are, in the opinion of "good neighbors," "understanding and loving parents" (42 per cent of the reasons), "love and respect in home" (32 per cent), "being kept busy with useful and interesting activities" (14 per cent), "absence of financial troubles" (3 per cent), the rest giving no specific reasons. Thus some 74 per cent of all the reasons for happiness in childhood point explicitly to loving parents and to love, respect, and harmony in the home. Only 3 per cent are assigned to lack of financial troubles. All in all, these answers look valid: harmony, love, and respect in the home are indeed the most important components of happiness in childhood. Without them no real happiness is possible. With them, even a poor family of children are happy.

The sound and integrated state of most of the parental families of "good neighbors" is revealed also by the fact that 46 per cent of the parental families of the "Questionnaires" group had no troubles (in the opinion of these "good neighbors"); the remaining percentage of the parental families had difficulties, caused mainly by such unavoidable events as serious illness (37 per cent in the "Biographies" group and 8 per cent in the "Questionnaires" group), financial trouble (29 and 16 per cent respectively), death of parents and children (65 and 10 per cent respectively). Only 7 per cent of the "Questionnaires" group report some troubles of delinquency (while the "Biographies" group report no trouble of that kind); and 17 and 6 per cent report some incompatibility among their parents. Since there is hardly any family that does not have some troubles or tensions throughout its life, the parental families had their share of troubles. But the amount of these troubles, and especially their kind, seem to have been comparatively insignificant and mainly unavoidable, such as death and illness.

Thus an overwhelming majority of the comparatively large parental families of our neighbors were indeed well integrated and harmonious. As such, they were the most important agent in shaping the personality of our "good neighbors."

These data throw light on somewhat contradictory evidence in regard to the size of the parental family of criminals: in some samples the small, in others the large, parental families produced a higher quota of criminals. Some criminologists ascribe the fact to the largeness, others to the smallness, of the parental family of criminals. In the light of our data, the real culprit seems to have been not the size, but the discordance and misery, the demoralized and unintegrated character of these families. The crime-breeding large families bred the delinquents not because the families were large, but because they were in poor shape, morally, mentally, socially, and economically.

In questionnaires and autobiographies special attention was called to several details of the relationship of "good neighbors" to their parents in childhood. The first observation is that hardly any "good neighbor" (even those that had an unhappy childhood) mentions anything of the kind of relationship (Oedipus complex, etc.) which Freud and Freudians unduly generalize from their observations of pathological or subnormal families and persons. Less than 1 per cent of our neighbors indicated harshness or unjust punishment on the part of the parents.

The second observation is that 18 per cent of "good neighbors" loved the father somewhat more, 28 per cent loved the mother more, and 54 per cent loved both equally. Some 18 per cent thought that the father was more influential in the family; 32 per cent viewed the mother as more influential; the remaining percentage stated that the two parents were equally influential.

As to the reasons for the choice of most-loved parent, the most common reason (25 per cent of all the reasons given) is that a "good neighbor" was most loved by the parent selected; an additional 2 per cent are made up of the similarity of interests of a "good neighbor" and his most loved parent; 10 per cent of the reasons are due to the death or absence of the less-loved parent; 6 per cent to the dominant personality of the most-loved parent; less than 1 per cent (.99%) are due to the harshness or punitive inclination of the less-loved parent; about 7 per cent of the reasons refer to a specific trait of a preferred parent: equanimity, wisdom, sacrifice, higher intelligence, etc.

The above data indicate that in the parental families of "good neighbors" there occurred hardly any of the situations stressed by Freudians and the partisans of a "mom" theory. Hardly any "good neighbor" mentions any hatred toward his parents. Fifty-two per cent of them stated that they loved the two parents equally. Considering that women form the overwhelming majority of our sample, we see that among those who loved one of the parents more, the greater part of them loved their mother more than their father; this is an additional repudiation of the Oedipus and similar complexes. Nay, more: the most important reason for loving one parent more than the other was the greater love of this parent for the "good neighbor"; only less than 1 per cent of the reasons is accounted for by the negative factor of a comparative dislike of one of the parents for his harshness and punitiveness. Here again we have a corroboration of a general rule: love generates love, dislike and harshness generate dislike and aloofness. The data show also that the mother is not only more loved but also more influential than the father in the parental families of "good neighbors." If the father is possibly more influential as a "secretary of foreign affairs," the mother, as a "secretary of the interior," has been more influential than the father. This is often forgotten by those sociologists of the family who depict almost all types, except the disintegrating modern one (or "the companionate family," as they call it euphemistically), as institutions in which mothers and women generally have been slaves, suppressed by the tyranny of the father or husband, and having no real influence upon the formation of the personality of the children. Real facts are very different from this all too simple and one-sided picture. Not only in the case of our neighbors, but in many other cases, including the patriarchal family of the past, the mother was much less suppressed and much more influential than these authors depict.

These and many other deductions from this study are substantiated by further studies to be published in this series.

8. MARITAL STATUS

AND FAMILIES

From the parental family let us turn to the families of the "good neighbors" themselves. Some 76.7 per cent of "good neighbors" are married; 15.4 per cent are single; 6.9 per cent are widowed; and 1 per cent are divorced. In view of the peculiar sex-and-age composition of our group, different from that of the total American population at the age of fifteen years and more, an exact comparison of the marital status of "good neighbors" with that of the total population is impossible. A very rough comparison suggests, however, that our group has a somewhat higher proportion of married, and a lower proportion of divorced people, than the total population of the United States at the age of fifteen years and over.

In this respect our group differs sharply from the negative groups of criminals, the mentally diseased, and the suicides. Among these, the proportion of the single and of the divorced is higher than among the total population. On the other hand, the divorced show the highest rate of criminals, of psychoneurotics, and those inclined to suicide; next come the single and the widowed, and the smallest quota is given by the married. Thus both sets of data—given by our "good neighbors" and by the criminal, insane, and suicide groups—suggest that the divorced are in greater danger of becoming members of these negative groups than are the married (undivorced) and the single. On the other hand, the divorced and the single have a somewhat smaller chance of becoming "good neighbors" than the married. These results agree with what we know about the causes of crime, insanity, and suicide.

The size of the family of the typical "good neighbor" may be seen from the following figures. In the groups of "Biographies" and "Questionnaires":

18 and 14 per cent are childless;
18 and 14 per cent have one child;
31 and 29 per cent have two children;
10 and 15 per cent have three children;
10 and 7 per cent have four children;
 4 and 11 per cent have five children;
 9 and 10 per cent have six and more children.

In comparison with 6,551 Indianapolis white couples whose reproductive cycles were almost over, our group is very similar in its fertility status.[1] But in our group, the reproductive cycle is not quite over. In comparison with other samples studied,[2] our group has a notably lower proportion of childless marriages and marriages with one child, and a notably higher proportion of families with five and more children. Like their parental family, which was larger than an average family of their contemporaries, the families of our group seem to be also somewhat larger than those of their contemporaries. Here again, the noted positive relationship between a strong, large family and good-neighborliness emerges. Like their parental families, the families of good neighbors are well integrated, and in comparison with the rank and file of other families, function harmoniously. Of the "Biographies" group 4 per cent, and of the "Questionnaires" group 69 per cent, explicitly state that their families have no difficulties or troubles. If even such an explicit statement has to be taken with reservations

---

[1] See Clyde V. Kiser and P. K. Whelpton, "Social and Psychological Factors Affecting Families," *The Milbank Memorial Fund Quarterly*, Vol. XXII, January, 1944.
[2] See W. Ogburn, *Recent Social Trends* (New York, 1933), p. 687.

(especially when it comprises 69 per cent), it points, nevertheless, to the highly satisfactory state of the family. Only one family reports delinquency trouble among its offspring. An overwhelming proportion of the troubles are caused by the biological factors of death and illness on the part of the members of the family. Thus in the "Biographies" and "Questionnaires" groups, respectively, 11 and 9 per cent of all the difficulties are caused by illness; 54 and 6 per cent by the death of the spouse or children (the notably lower rate of the second group being due to the 69 per cent having no troubles); 26 and 9 per cent by financial difficulties; and 11 and 5 per cent by the incompatibility of spouses.

Thus only a small percentage of all the troubles are due to a psychosocial maladjustment of the spouses or to financial difficulties. With the exception of the 11 and 5 per cent of the families with some incompatibility on the part of man and wife, the rest of the families have a harmonious life and are comparatively strong in the face of the prevalent instability and disharmony of the contemporary American family. This is additionally corroborated by the statements of "good neighbors" about their happiness or unhappiness in marriage. Some 83 per cent state without any qualification that their marriage is happy; an additional 6 per cent evaluate their marriage as happy, but with some reservations; only 9 per cent state that their marriage is unhappy. Thus some 90 per cent are satisfied with their marriage and the family. Such a percentage is quite high and speaks for itself.

As to the reasons for happiness in marriage, 44 per cent of the "good neighbors" see it in "similar interests," 21 per cent in "love," 14 per cent in "congeniality," 5 per cent in "religious beliefs." "Similar interests," "love," and "congeniality," though different terms, probably point to the same factor. If so, then some 80 per cent ascribe their married happiness to love and congeniality.

As in the case of the parental families, the inner strength

of the families of "good neighbors" turns their comparatively larger size into a factor for true socialization of the members, instead of making it the negative factor of delinquency as is found in disharmonious, unstable, or unintegrated families.

As a significant detail, it may be mentioned that 50 per cent of our neighbors would marry a person of different *faith* and 39 per cent, of different *race*. An additional 9 and 10 per cent, respectively, would marry with some reservations and specifications. Some 35 and 46 per cent would not marry a person of different faith and of different race. Thus a considerable portion of our "good neighbors" show unwillingness to marry a person of different faith, and still greater unwillingness to marry a person of different race. For the majority of the unwilling, their preference to marry a person of a similar faith or race is not prejudice or discrimination against a different religion or race. Most of them would not marry a person of different religion or race simply because such a marriage is likely to be less happy and stable than a marriage with a person of similar racial, religious, and cultural background. Some "good neighbors" refer to statistical and sociological data showing that this sort of heterogeneous marriage shows a higher rate of divorce, desertion, and other difficulties, while, on the other hand, mutual understanding and happiness are more likely when the marriage parties have a similar, or the same, religious, racial, educational, and cultural background. This is applied by "good neighbors" not only to religion and race, but also to other biological and sociocultural characteristics of the parties: health, biological constitution, education, economic status, nationality, aesthetic tastes, intelligence, and all other important values. Too great differences in all these respects are not conducive to a happy marriage. This shows that even those of our group who would not marry a person of different faith or race do so, not because they are prejudiced against other religions or races, but simply because too great a difference in any of the important values of the marrying parties is regarded by them as a factor negative to the happiness and stability of a marriage.

This point deserves real attention. In many current views, any unwillingness either to marry or to live in the same apartment or to be a member of the same club as a person belonging to a minority or an "out" group is interpreted as prejudice and discrimination. As a matter of fact, such unwillingness often has little to do with prejudice or discrimination. Like our "good neighbors," a person may have the profoundest admiration, respect, and democratic feelings for persons of different religions, races, and nationalities, and to prefer at the same time a marriage, an intimate circle or club, with persons congenial to himself. Such a preference for congeniality is neither a prejudice nor a discrimination against all other groups and persons. In some form it is a universal and inevitable trait of practically all human beings including the most liberal, unprejudiced persons and groups. One may genuinely admire Hinduism, Taoism, Confucianism, Mohammedanism, Judaism, or any great religion different from one's own; at the same time one may prefer, for one's close friends or for one's religious activities, persons of one's own religion. One may admire blondes and brunettes equally; at the same time one may fall in love with a blonde. Such a preference in no way means discrimination or prejudice against brunettes. The same is true about race or nationality.

A preference for marrying a person of a similar religion, nationality, race, of color of eyes and hair, of stature or weight, of education, of aesthetic taste, or of other values does not mean in many cases any discrimination or prejudice against persons and groups of different characteristics or sets of values. The preferences of our "good neighbors" are of this unprejudicial and non-discriminatory nature.

9. SOCIAL, OCCUPATIONAL, AND ECONOMIC STATUS

Socially our samples of "good neighbors" are taken from the middle-class strata (84, 54, and 86 per cent of the whole in our three groups: "Letters," "Biographies," and "Questionnaires"), with 5, 11, and 10 per cent from the upper-class strata and 5, 34, and 3 per cent from the lower-class strata (the rest being unspecified).

Their economic status is somewhat similar: 75, 42, and 82 per cent belong to the middle economic strata, with an income from $3000 to $10,000; 9, 13, and 11 per cent to the upper economic strata; and 2, 45, and 7 per cent to the lower economic strata.

Occupationally the largest group is made up of housewives (46, 50, and 44 per cent in our three groups); these housewives in the majority are, however, wives of professional and business husbands. Apart from wives, other "good neighbors" who indicated their main occupation are professional (public service, private social service, education, teaching, medicine, and other professions): 18, 30, and 31 per cent; business: 13, 11, and 9 per cent; white-collar employees: 2, 8, and 5 per cent; farmers: 2, 5, and 3 per cent; industrial labor: 2, 3, and 3 per cent; the rest are either scattered among various occupations or unspecified.

The parents of "good neighbors" (usually their fathers) belonged in 16 per cent of the cases to professional groups, in 23 per cent to business groups, in 33 per cent to farming groups, in 24 per cent to industrial labor, the rest being scattered among white-collar employees, housewives (only 1 per cent), and so on. The parental group thus is made up in some 58 per cent of the farm and industrial labor classes; while among the "good neighbors" these occupational groups are in a decisive minority, the bulk being represented by the professional and business or middle-class persons.

These percentages cannot be taken as representative for the whole population; they do not indicate in which occupations or strata or classes "good neighbors" are more and less frequent, or which of these produces the highest or the lowest rate of "good neighbors." The data, however, may be significant in pointing out three things. First, that the middle-class strata are possibly more good-neighborly than the upper and lower, being free from the demoralizing luxury, power, and activities of the upper classes, and free from the brutalizing influences of the misery, need, and ignorance of the lower classes; the middle strata are likely to be more understanding and less selfish than the lower and the upper strata. Second, that good-neighborliness is no less diffused among the lower strata than the upper strata. Each of these upper and lower classes seems to have its own conditions favoring or hindering good-neighborliness. The above data and a considerable body of evidence outside of this study (in criminology, mental disease, taxation, in studies of the contributions of various classes for community and public purposes, etc.) seem to support these conclusions. Third, a small proportion of "good neighbors" manifest a strong dislike for the profession of law and especially for the judge. One "good neighbor," herself a servant and illiterate, was ashamed of her son's becoming a lawyer. Another "good neighbor" declined the remunerative position of a judgeship. A third disrespectfully calls lawyers and judges hypocrites, paid defenders of the vile and dishonest rich, politicians, criminals, and so on. The general reasons given for this critical attitude were God's command to forgive

—a commandment contrary to the vindictiveness of lawyers and judges; God's prohibition upon judging others; the wrongfulness of sending anyone to jail, since our jails make their inmates worse instead of better; the low moral standards of judges and lawyers, "cynical and hypocritical sellers of doubtful justice," "violators of Jesus' commandments." This attitude explains why notable altruists as well as "good neighbors" almost always come into collision with official law and justice and their enforcement agencies, why most of them have a very low opinion of the official law itself, and why they try to supplant it with higher moral standards and principles (see Section 22).

10. RURAL–URBAN AND NATIONALITY DISTRIBUTION

Seventy-four per cent of "good neighbors" were born in rural, 24 per cent in urban America, 2 per cent abroad. From 38 to 43 per cent of them live in rural districts, from 44 to 27 per cent in urban districts, and from 15 to 30 per cent in "rurban" United States (combination of urban and rural conditions). These figures cannot be taken as representative for the whole population. From the standpoint of nationality extraction, Scotch, Irish, English, Russian, Scandinavian, Dutch, Belgian, French, Italian, Jewish, German, Swiss, Czech, Romanian, Hungarian, Finnish, Canadian, Polish, Danish, Italian, and combinations of these are represented in our samples. The percentages of each nationality are not given here because they are not representative for the whole population of the United States; nor are they rough indicators of good-neighborliness of each nationality.

11. EDUCATION AND SCHOOL INTELLIGENCE

The educational status of our samples is typical for middle-class groups: it is somewhat above the average educational level of the total population of the United States. Among the "Biographies" and "Questionnaires" groups we have respectively 28 and 22 per cent with elementary education; 37 and 28 per cent with high-school education; 20 and 38 per cent with college education; 6 and 10 per cent with postgraduate education; then 8 and 2 per cent with vocational and business-school training; the rest not being specified.

Though the school training of the "good neighbors" in our sample is rather high, they were not necessarily brighter than the average student body of our schools. Forty and 3 per cent of "good neighbors" were poor students; 24 and 62 per cent were average; and 36 and 35 per cent were above the average in their school grades and marks. These results confirm the conclusion that *there is no close relationship between altruism or good-neighborliness and school intelligence as measured by mental tests, school grades, and similar devices* (whose testing adequacy is very questionable).[1]

More typical for "good neighbors" is their *attitude toward their teachers*. None reports an unfavorable attitude toward teachers. Ninety and 92 per cent report a favorable attitude, the remaining 10 and 8 per cent indifferent or mixed attitudes. Our "good neighbors" seem to have disliked their teachers

---
[1] See my *Reconstruction of Humanity*, pp. 73ff., and bibliography.

much less, and liked them much more, than the ordinary body of students. This kind, favorable, and trustful attitude toward their teachers is possibly one of the early manifestations of good-neighborly disposition on the part of our group. (Later on we shall see that the majority of "good neighbors" have a similar attitude toward the whole world and humanity.) *Perhaps an overwhelmingly favorable attitude of pupils toward their teachers may be taken as one of the real tests of pupils' good-neighborly disposition, especially when it is paralleled by their favorable attitude toward their family, playmates, and other persons.* The pupils with good-neighborly dispositions— potential "good neighbors"—are likely to have more favorable attitudes toward their teachers than the pupils more lacking in this potential good-neighborliness. The potential "good neighbors" are likely to have much less of a grudge against their teachers and find much less fault with them than the potential egoistic pupils; the latter tend to justify their own shortcomings by attributing the reasons for them to someone else—in the schools, to teachers and other students. From this standpoint a favorable or unfavorable attitude toward teachers is certainly a trait connected with good-neighborliness much more closely than so-called "general intelligence" or "school intelligence" or even intellectual brilliance.

12. ATTITUDES TOWARD THE WORLD AT LARGE

Loving their parents and favorably inclined toward their teachers, "good neighbors" entertain a most friendly attitude toward physical and social reality and the world at large. In two groups, 90 and 98 per cent of them report such an attitude. Only 1 per cent have a hostile attitude, while some 8 per cent in the first group are ambivalently friendly. In this respect our group is strikingly dissimilar to criminals, psychoneurotics, and other negativistic groups. Their prevalent attitude is hostility toward most of the people and the world at large. A friendly attitude implies a somewhat optimistic conviction that man and society are basically good. In this respect the majority of "good neighbors" do not share the Augustinian-Calvinistic dogma of the inherent sinfulness of man and of predestination.

An overwhelming majority (90 per cent) find the decisive factors of a person's goodness or badness in man's environment. Only 10 per cent stress the factor of heredity. Of the environmentalists, 25 per cent find the most important factor of man's personality in religion, 31 per cent in parental training, 4 per cent in special training in school or other special agencies. In a more detailed form somewhat similar factors are stressed concerning their own neighborliness.

Thus the American "good neighbor" appears to be an optimistic, friendly person who stresses the importance of environmental factors in distinction to a pessimistic, hostile person who stresses the importance of hereditary factors. Only a small minority—less than 1 per cent—are hostile toward the world, and only 10 per cent stress heredity.

13. RELIGIOUS ATTITUDES AND AFFILIATIONS

The "good neighbors" are scattered among many religious denominations. The majority in our sample are Protestants; then come the nonsectarians, then Roman Catholics, then Jews, with others scattered among various denominations. Two per cent declare themselves atheistic and have no religious affiliation at all. The denominational percentages of our sample are, of course, in no way representative for the whole country; therefore they are not given here.

Sixty-one per cent of the "good neighbors" attend church services now and then; 30 per cent attend frequently and regularly; 9 per cent do not attend at all.

Thus American "good neighbors" appear to be a predominantly religious group. However, a minority have no affiliation with any of the institutional religions; do not attend any church service; and some declare themselves explicitly atheistic, materialistic, or agnostic.

This raises an interesting question: How is this possible? Can one be a "good neighbor" without being religious? Can one be religious without being a "good neighbor"? Is the percentage of disbelievers among our "good neighbors" about the same as in the total population or in other groups? According to the Census of Religious Bodies, about 55 per cent of the population at the age of thirteen and above are church members.[1] In comparison with these data, our group is more "church-religious."

---

[1] See United States Bureau of the Census, *Census of Religious Bodies*, 1936.

A recent nationwide survey of religious beliefs and practices of the American nation by the *Ladies' Home Journal* (November, 1948) disclosed that 95 per cent of those sampled believed in God and that 76 per cent were church members. This is fairly close to the fact that approximately 97 per cent of "good neighbors" declare themselves religious in some sense, and that 90 per cent attend church services. Our "good neighbors" are either about the same as, or slightly more religious than, the average for the nation. In the nation at large there are about 5 per cent explicit disbelievers, as compared with approximately 2 per cent in our sample.

In recent studies of the religious attitude of Harvard and Radcliffe students, 19 per cent of the male students and 12 per cent of the female students declare that they do not need any religion, and an additional 13 per cent of Harvard and 6 per cent of Radcliffe students are "doubtful" whether they need any religion, except an ethical code of conduct.[2] Some 20 per cent of Harvard non-veteran and 34 per cent of Harvard veteran students do not attend any church service; 27, 24, and 40 per cent never pray; 22, 30, and 40 per cent never experience a sense of reverence. Somewhat similar are the results obtained at Princeton and other universities.[3]

Judged by these criteria the student body, especially the veteran student body, is less religious than the average for the nation and for our group. This is due partly to the lesser religiosity of the younger generation in comparison with that of the older generations,[4] and partly to other factors.

---

[2] G. W. Allport, J. M. Gillespie, and J. Young, "The Religion of the Post-War College Students," *Journal of Psychology*, 1948, Vol. XXV, pp. 3–33.

[3] See L. P. Crespi and G. S. Shapleigh, "The Veteran—a Myth," *Public Opinion Quarterly*, 1946, Vol. X, pp. 361–372.

[4] Fifty-one per cent of Harvard students state that their religion is less firm than that of their mother, while only 7 per cent state that their religion is firmer. Twenty-seven per cent state that their father's religion was firmer than their own, while only 16 per cent find their own religion firmer. Somewhat similar is the situation with Radcliffe students (Allport, Gillespie, Young, *op. cit.*, p. 15). Similar results were obtained in a few other studies. Students in

All in all, our group seems to be somewhat more religious (judged by the declarations of the "good neighbors," their church attendance, etc.) than intellectuals, students, and even the average American population. This would mean that religiosity, when it is earnest and influences overt action, is a factor facilitating good-neighborliness for an overwhelming majority of the population. However, not for all. The existence of from 2 up to 8 per cent explicit atheists and materialists among our "good neighbors" testifies that one may be irreligious in the usual sense or even atheistic; and yet be a "good neighbor" and have ethical overt conduct far more altruistic than that of many formally religious persons. This is reinforced by the fact that the overt behavior of "irreligious" Harvard-Radcliffe students seems in no way to be lower ethically than that of religious students. The overt behavior of intellectuals, particularly college professors and students—among whom the percentage of disbelievers in the divinity of Jesus, the immaculate conception, the immortality of the soul, and so on, was found to be about 40 to 50 per cent [5]—has not been more criminal or less honest and ethical than that of groups that declare themselves 100 per cent religious—for instance, ministers, the Knights of Columbus, and the American Legion.

Elsewhere in my work,[6] it is shown that among the great altruists of human history there have been atheistic altruists and minority currents. Gautama Buddha and early Buddhists (during the first five hundred years of Buddhism) were explicitly atheistic, denying belief in God, the soul, the ego, the personality, or any substance whatsoever. The only reality they believed in were about 75 *dharmas*, "point-flashes" that flash

---

theological seminaries are less dogmatically religious than seven hundred ministers (all Protestant) (G. Betts, *The Belief of 700 Ministers* [New York, 1929]). See also L. Fry and M. F. Jessup, "Changes in Religious Organizations," in W. Ogburn (ed.), *Recent Social Trends* (New York, 1933), Vol. II, pp. 1009–1060.

[5] See J. H. Leuba, *The Belief in God and Immortality* (Boston, 1916); repeated studies gave about the same results as the first study of Leuba.

[6] The forthcoming *Types, Techniques and Factors of Altruistic Experience*.

for the shortest imaginable moment and disappear. Everything is merely a stream of such "point-flashes." This potentially chaotic world of the "point-flashes" was united however by two laws: by strictly causal law and by the moral law of Karma. These moral-causal laws were the foundation of the high altruistic mentality and behavior of the early Buddhists: their sublime command of love for all living creatures and the whole world, and their prohibition against inflicting pain through thought, word, and deed upon any living creature (even poisonous snakes).

Our atheistic "good neighbors" are in this minority stream of so-called "irreligious altruists." This "atheistic good-neighborliness," and the coarse egoism often displayed in the overt behavior of many formally religious persons, find their explanation in related, though different kinds of, factors. "Good neighbors" and altruists who are atheistic or irreligious are defined as such only from a definite, institutionalized, formally religious standpoint. This standpoint does not mean that these persons are nihilists or cynics, or amoral persons having no supreme value and no unconditional moral authority. Buddha and the early Buddhists had, as their supreme value and categorical imperative, the causal-moral law of Karma, and the final liberation from an endless cycle of births and deaths in Nirvana. These values and imperatives were most deeply rooted not only in the mentality but also in the overt conduct of these Buddhists; hence their highly altruistic behavior and code of conduct. In so far as religion means a system of the ultimate and highest values, Buddhism is a genuine religion, in spite of its denial of God and the soul.

The situation with our atheistic "good neighbors" is somewhat similar. Explicitly or implicitly they all take the moral values of the Golden Rule, of the Sermon on the Mount, and so on, as the supreme values, regardless of their denial of God and other kinds of authority. Asked why she had been doing good deeds for others for many years, depriving herself of many conveniences and advantages, one of these atheistic "good neighbors" said: "Darned if I know! Perhaps it's my Yankee ancestors, who were a sort of domineering people; perhaps it's a manifestation of my own bossy temper; I don't know exactly what it is. There's only one thing I do know—namely, that when I see someone suffering, or some injustice, or something wrong, I can't stand it, and I try to straighten it out as much as I can. Maybe my own selfishness manifests itself in this way." When carefully analyzed, this "atheistic" phraseology reveals a person with a supreme set of moral values and deep ethical convictions of right and wrong—a person who practices what these convictions preach.

The ideological "atheism" or "materialism" of such people is partly a result of their rationalism, which wants to dispense with the superstitions and ignorance of an unscientific past; it is partly a result of their rational utilitarianism and hedonism; above all, it is a sort of ethical protest against the hypocrisy and low moral standards of many formally religious persons and groups. There always has been a discrepancy between the religious and ethical preachings of persons and groups and their practice: the overt behavior and relationships of religious Christians, Hindus, Jews, Mohammedans, etc., hardly ever conformed to what their ethics preached; more often their behavior was in direct contrast to their lofty preachings. At some periods, as during the present age, this discrepancy has grown enormously. For instance, the *Ladies' Home Journal* survey shows that, even in their own opinion, 82 per cent of religious believers enjoy life and happiness without any particular inner struggle due to the discrepancy between their lofty Christian preachings and their actual behavior. Even according to their own estimate (which is certainly biased), only 18 per cent believe that they succeed in living a life consistent with their religious beliefs; 28 per cent credit themselves with only 75 per cent success, and 32 per cent with 50 per cent success. Fifty-four per cent frankly state that their religious and moral ideas do not affect their political and business behavior. Eighty-two per cent state that the religious Christians whom they know personally practice Christian love for their fellow men only to a slight extent. In brief, the survey confirmed the well-known fact that—notably for the last four centuries and especially at the present time—most professed religious Christians have been negligibly Christian in their overt behavior and relationships. During these centuries it has been Western Christendom that has invaded, robbed, exploited, killed, exterminated, pillaged and enslaved all the other parts of the human race; and these same Christians have been perpetrators of the bloodiest wars among themselves. A series of other tests and studies have shown that during these past centuries, and especially at present, the overt behavior of Christians exhibits little if any application of the Sermon on the Mount or the other teachings of Christianity.[7]

This ineffectiveness of Christian and other religious ideology in the control of overt behavior, this discrepancy and resulting hypocrisy, together with many ritualistic and theologically dogmatic elements in established religions, have called forth a sort of ethical protest and revolt on the part of those whose moral conscience has been especially intense and pure, and who have wanted to practice consistently what their beliefs and convictions dictated. Some of these persons and groups merely withdrew from the institutionalized historical religions and established their own sects with high moral standards—such as the Friends. Others revolted against such religions in general, and in their moral indignation declared themselves "atheistic," "materialistic," "scientific," etc.

This motive plays a very considerable rôle in the alleged "atheism" of the great altruists of the past, as well as among our atheistic "good neighbors." Father Yelchaninov correctly remarks:

---

[7] See my *Reconstruction of Humanity*, pp. 76ff., 114ff.

There are men of a wonderful, paradisaic character—childlike, simple, unacquainted with anger and untruth. Curiously enough, these men very often stand outside the Church, and sometimes live entirely without religion. They are too simple, too much of one piece, to be able to live by principles drawn from theology; they are too modest and chaste to express their feelings in words or signs (rites). In religion the most important thing is not faith but the love of God; and they love God, because they love beauty, goodness, and truth; and all these are elements of divinity.[8]

This explains the paradox that in their personality structure, mentality, and conduct these "atheists" are unusually religious persons. Their moral standards are certainly higher than those of many who ardently profess themselves very religious persons but who practice little of what they preach. When such contemporary "pharisees" declare a "crusade" against atheists and disbelievers, the moral and religious value of their crusades is not worth a penny. Such crusades are, in fact, a misuse of religion for the doubtful and greedy politics of these "crusaders." Our atheistic "good neighbors" are incomparably more religious and moral than these misusers of religion and ethics.

Such, in brief, are the reasons for the existence of atheistic altruists and "good neighbors." Their existence means that one may be an unselfish person and have the highest moral standards without affiliation with any of the institutionalized religions, and without belief in a personal or impersonal God, the soul, immortality, or other religious dogmas.

However, such an "irreligious" altruism or purely ethical religion is possible for only a small minority (some 2 to 8 per cent in our sample). The majority of "good neighbors" (some 90 per cent) are *religious* altruists. Religion helped them to become "good neighbors"; for 21 per cent it was a decisive factor in their altruistic transmutation. This union of high religi-

---

[8] G. P. Fedotov, *A Treasury of Russian Spirituality* (New York, 1948), p. 436.

than of co-operation; of the lust for power rather than of self-denial or altruism. These functions are not conducive to good-neighborliness; and high-grade altruism is often incompatible with a deep involvement in a political party and the moral cynicism, the dishonesty, crookedness, underhanded operations —and sometimes even the downright criminality—connected with political parties. Only a very few saints can be politicians without being soiled by this political filth (Gandhi and the like). Most others either would terminate their political affiliations in order to preserve their integrity (like Sri Aurobindo in India) or would lose their saintliness in the morass of impure political activities.

15. AFFILIATIONS WITH OTHER ORGANIZATIONS

Besides being members of a family and kinship group, of a local community, of the state, of a religious or political group (with the exceptions cited), of an occupational group, and of a sex and age group,[1] the overwhelming majority of our "good neighbors" belonged to several additional groups: 21 per cent at least to one additional organization; 17 per cent to two; 18 per cent to three additional organizations; 11 per cent to four; some 20 per cent to five and more organizations. There is hardly any doubt that even this list of organizations does not include all the clubs, little cliques, and small associations to which "good neighbors" belong. As the data stand, they show that every "good neighbor" is a member of several—at least five—organizations; the overwhelming majority belong to more numerous associations or societies. Like those of almost every grown-up individual in the contemporary Western world, the memberships and loyalties of a "good neighbor" are multi-dimensional and multi-societal. One does not place all loyalties and interests in one group, be it the family or the state or any other group. Instead, "good neighbors" distribute their interests and loyalties among several societies or groups. Whether their group affiliations are more numerous than those of the rank and file of the population remains uncertain. We do not have reliable standards for comparison.

---

[1] For a systematic classification of social groups, see my *Society, Culture, and Personality*, chaps. ix–xiv.

AFFILIATIONS WITH OTHER ORGANIZATIONS

As to the character of the groups to which "good neighbors" belong (except the family, the community, the state, and other groups to which virtually all "good neighbors" belong), the majority (26 and 46 per cent in our two samples) are members of various community service groups such as the Red Cross and the Community Chest; next come various social organizations and women's clubs whose functions are entertainment, education, conviviality, and partly social service (some 11 and 43 per cent); then come various professional-occupational-business organizations (as satellites of professional or occupational or business activities); about 2 per cent belong to various honorary organizations; about 1 per cent to national and racial organizations; 1 per cent to veterans' organizations. In brief, the bulk of the group membership of our "good neighbors" is in various social-service organizations; then educational-service-entertainment groups; then various associations, as a result of occupational, business, or professional affiliations. The predominant position of social-service groups is simultaneously the result, the manifestation, and the cause of the good-neighborly character of our group. A "good neighbor" naturally tends to be affiliated first of all with persons and groups whose function is social service. Membership in such groups tends in its turn to re-enforce the good-neighborliness of its members. In groups other than altruists or "good neighbors," participation in social-service organizations probably would not be as pronounced as activities in recreational, occupational, educational or other organizations.

To sum up: "Good neighbors" tend to be affiliated mainly with organizations of the good-neighborly or social-service kind.

16. OTHER CHARACTERISTICS

The predominantly feminine composition of our group of "good neighbors" satisfactorily explains three main forms of its hobbies: almost equally frequent among our "good neighbors" are intellectual, aesthetic (including music), and homemakers' hobbies. Intellectual hobbies, such as reading, attendance at forums, and lectures, constitute 28 and 23 per cent among all the hobbies mentioned in our two samples. Aesthetic hobbies without music, such as attendance at theaters, cinemas, dances, and various shows, constitute 22 and 14 per cent; concerts, 12 and 8 per cent of hobbies. Taken together, aesthetic and musical hobbies make up some 34 and 23 per cent of all the hobbies mentioned. Homemakers' hobbies, such as knitting, sewing, cooking, and gardening, constitute 12 and 31 per cent. The predominantly feminine composition of our group explains the prominent place occupied by this sort of hobbies among "good neighbors." Nine and 5 per cent are the figures for technical hobbies: photography, building radios, shopwork, etc. Three and 8 per cent show passive sports (attendance at football, baseball, and other sports), and 9 and 1 per cent practice active sports: golf, tennis, etc. The large number of women among our "good neighbors" explains the comparatively low place that sports occupy in their hobbies. Three and 1 per cent have social activities as their hobbies: parties, meetings, etc. Some 5 per cent in one sample explicitly state that they have no hobbies. A larger percentage of all the answers do not list any hobby.

Looking more closely at the kind of books read as intellectual hobbies, at the kind of music listened to, and at the kind of sports participated in by "good neighbors," we obtain some interesting details. Asked to list the books from which they got their greatest inspiration, 55 per cent mentioned the Bible. Other authors, books, and magazines mentioned were John Milton, Charles Dickens, Louisa May Alcott, *War and Peace, Pilgrim's Progress, The Brothers Karamazov,* Mary Baker Eddy's *Science and Health,* Steinbeck's *Grapes of Wrath, The Life of Santa Monica, The Life of Lincoln,* my *Crisis of Our Age, The Reader's Digest,* and unspecified books on philosophy, history, sociology, and anthropology. The Bible thus still remains the most inspirational book, exceeding in this respect all the other books taken together.

As to the preferred sort of music, 39 per cent of our "good neighbors" prefer "classical" music; 37 per cent "religious," 18 per cent "popular," 1 per cent "choral"; the rest "mixed." These data show that our predominantly middle-class "good neighbors" are predominantly lovers of classical and religious music, only the minority preferring popular music, jazz, crooning, etc. Considering that popular music is only partly devoted to jazz, boogie-woogie, and crooning, and that old-fashioned popular music makes up some portion of it, and that only 18 per cent prefer popular music, the overwhelming majority of our "good neighbors" cannot be considered devotees of "hot" music. Advertisers sponsoring such "hot" music would find few listeners for it and for their advertised products among our group.

Asked about the reasons for their preference for certain types of music, 28 per cent mention "soothing and restful" effects; 21 per cent "appreciation developed through parental influence and training"; 13 per cent "inspiration," "soul-stirring"; 11 per cent "emotional release"; 9 per cent "easy understanding"; 8 per cent "feeling of joy, happiness"; 5 per cent "its sentimental character"; the rest several mixed reasons.

Finally, as to the kind of sports enjoyed, 38 per cent of the questionnaire group prefer active participation in athletics;

21 per cent, the passive rôle of an observer; 24 per cent enjoy most outdoor sports, such as hunting, fishing, and camping.

Such are the hobbies and recreations of our "good neighbors." Certain specific traits are due, as has been pointed out, to the good-neighborly character of our group, and to its predominantly middle-class and female composition.

17. FACTORS IN

GOOD-NEIGHBORLINESS

Asked to state to what factors they ascribed their good-neighborliness, 21 per cent indicated religion; 29 per cent, parental and family training; 8 per cent, school education; 3 per cent, unusual specific experience that served as a precipitant of neighborliness; 11 per cent, personal life experience; 28 per cent, universal life experience (the co-operative character of human nature, lessons of life and history that show human beings as social and good-neighborly persons, good-neighborliness as an absolute condition for the survival and progress of humanity, and so on); less than 1 per cent mentioned books.

If we rely on these data—and they seem to be in agreement with the bulk of the available evidence—then the family and parents still remain the most important single factor of moral socialization. Second comes general life experience—all the influences of all the sociocultural forces; other human beings, social institutions, and culture (minus the family, religion, and other specified factors) that incessantly and relentlessly shape our personality and conduct from the moment of conception to that of death; their total rôle is as great as that of the family factor. Next comes religion; as a single factor it is next to the family. Then comes general personal experience: the retroactive rôle of our own thoughts, feelings, emotions, and actions. Each of our thoughts, emotions, and actions does not disappear with its performance but continues to affect us

—our mind, body, and behavior. About 11 per cent consider that we are the product of our own actions and experiences. Such a weight of the personal-experience factor among all the factors is interesting in its definiteness. It ascribes to this personal-experience factor much less weight than do the Existentialists, or all the believers in complete freedom of the will— who in various forms claim that each person is what he has made himself through his own thought and actions. On the other hand, the 11 per cent weight given to this factor is much more than all the strict partisans of complete determinism claim; these deny the autonomous rôle of the personal-experience factor and interpret one as a passive result of cultural, social, biological, or cosmic forces. All in all, the result obtained from our material seems to be nearer the truth and agrees better with the existing body of evidence than extreme theories. Man's personal experience is, indeed, one of the tangible factors of man's personality, behavior and destiny; it is not zero, and man is not a zero factor, devoid of the freedom and initiative to shape himself. On the other hand, this personal-experience factor is only one among several shaping forces. The data show further that *the socializing rôle of school education is modest, and the rôle of books in shaping good neighbors is comparatively insignificant.*

All in all, in their essentials, these results agree with what we know about the factors in the sociality or anti-sociality of persons.[1]

---

[1] See my *Reconstruction of Humanity*, chaps. v, vi, xii.

18. TWO ROUTES TO

GOOD-NEIGHBORLINESS

Finally, some 3 per cent mention a specific unusual experience that was a turning point in their life and that started their moral conversion into "good neighbors." Studying the lives of notable altruists of history, saints, and "good neighbors," we cannot fail to note that these altruists, saints, and "good neighbors" fall into two main classes: One—the majority—had gradually and quietly grown into altruists or saints or "good neighbors" from early childhood, without any notable catastrophe or other event to mark a sharp turning point in their life. The other class—probably a minority, though hardly so small as our 3 per cent—experienced such a turning point marked with a definite "unusual" experience that divided their life into two different parts: sinful and selfish before the unusual experience, and saintly and unselfish after it. The first class seemed to start life with a proper set of values and a well-adjusted personality, steadily moving toward their goal in the course of their life. This class comprises the "fortunate" altruists and "good neighbors." They do not pass through the painful experience of a religious or moral conversion. The other class started life with an improper personality structure and set of values, moving up a wrong or false path until they reached an unusual experience. This is the experience that precipitates their conversion, and changes the direction of their life course.[1] Their road passes through some catastrophic or

---
[1] A detailed and precise analysis of this subject is given in my forthcoming *Types, Techniques, and Factors of Altruistic Experience.*

precipitating event that divides their life into the "preconversion" and "postconversion" periods.

Our data show that at least some 3 per cent of our "good neighbors" traveled this "catastrophic" way toward their neighborliness. It is probable that a larger percentage belongs to this "conversion" type of neighbors: the factors of "general personal and universal experience" also contain an element of this "unusual personal experience." A study of eminent altruists of history shows that many more than 3 per cent passed through this "conversion" event. Among Christian saints some 17 per cent were "catastrophic converts." [2]

Let us glance at the kind of experience that constitutes this "unusual personal experience" or serves as a precipitant that starts and accelerates the process of moral (and religious) conversion. Some 7 per cent of these experiences consist of religious conversion: when religious conversion occurs, the moral conversion into a "good neighbor" follows. Accidents involving a "good neighbor" himself represent 7 per cent of such precipitants. The deaths of loved ones constitute 22 per cent; 22 per cent are made up also of the illness of a "good neighbor"; 5 per cent result from the tragedy of war; 5 per cent constitute other kinds of personal tragedy; 3 per cent, an unexpected kindness toward a "good neighbor"; 6 per cent, general educational experience; and 4 per cent, a book, sermon, cinema, play, or similar experience.

Thus some 60 per cent of the unusual experiences precipitating moral conversion are made up of some sort of catastrophe; 3 per cent are caused by an event of unexpected kindness.

These results are highly significant in several ways. First, under some circumstances the factor of unexpected kindness is not only efficient but more efficient than the factor of punishment, chastisement, revenge, and intimidation. This precipitant transfigured not only Jean Valjean in Hugo's *Les Misérables* but a great many actual persons among the notable

---

[2] See Part Two.

altruists of history. Jesus' "Love your enemy" and similar prescriptions of practically all the great educators of humanity have changed many enemies and selfish persons into friends and "good neighbors" much more effectively than the prescription of an "eye for an eye" and hatred for hatred. "It is not possible that by dint of harshness and austerity a man shall lightly be recalled from his [selfish] intent; but by gentleness shalt thou call him back to thee," sums up the situation in the case of the Desert Fathers. This wisdom is particularly needed at the present time; the rulers and leaders of our hate-ridden world still seem to believe mainly in the effectiveness of hatred, coercion, and such forces, instead of those of "unexpected love and kindness." No wonder that they do not succeed in the organization of peace, but drift closer and closer to the precipice of war!

Second, our data on the catastrophic precipitating experiences confirm their rôle in the conversion of some of the famous altruists of history; they are confirmed in turn by these conversions, and suggest that some sort of painful traumatic experience may be sometimes prescribed to persons for their altruization. A careful study of the precipitants in the life history of great altruists of the past and present supports this result. Some sort of calamity, such as illness, death of loved ones, public calamity (war, plague, famine, or revolution) and so on, played, indeed, the rôle of the precipitating experience in their altruistic transfiguration. This is the case in the life history of most such altruists, beginning with Buddha, Chaytania, Al Gazzali, Saint Paul, Saint Augustine of Hippo, Saint Francis of Assisi, Saint Ignatius Loyola, and ending with the contemporary Sri Aurobindo, Gandhi (in part), and many others. Similar precipitants were responsible for an intensification of religiosity and altruism in Boccaccio, Beethoven, Alfred de Musset, Heine, Pascal, Paul Bourget, Van Gogh, Brother Lawrence, Saint Hildegard of Bingen, Santa Teresa, Cardinal Newman, Dostoievsky, Madame de la Vallière and many others. Generally calamity turns some from selfish libertines into saints, while some others are turned by it into still more selfish and reckless sinners.

Third, as to the catastrophic precipitants that make up the bulk of such unusual experiences, our data (reinforced by much other material) confirm the validity of the *law of polarization*,[3] according to which catastrophic and calamitous events tend to polarize the population—which in normal conditions is neither saintly nor criminal—into the two extremes. Our "good neighbors" represent an example of a positive polarization under the influence of catastrophe: the catastrophe helped them to be morally ennobled and improved.

Fourth, these data and the law of polarization mean further that the commonly accepted opinion that "*frustration invariably breeds aggression*" is utterly one-sided.[4] Catastrophe or calamity overtaking a person is an extreme form of frustration. Yet in the case of our "good neighbors"—and in all cases of Christian saints and many other persons—frustration did not make them more selfish and aggressive, but more altruistic and less aggressive. The statement of many religious, ethical, and other writers from ancient times up to now—including the recent statements of A. J. Toynbee and others—that suffering (catastrophe and calamity) invariably leads to a moral transfiguration, religiosity, and altruism is not completely true either. It is true only of some individuals and groups that pass through catastrophic sufferings: another segment of the world's population—and in some cases the larger part—becomes, on the contrary, less moral, more sensual, cynical, selfish, criminal, and irreligious. Both extreme views thus should be corrected and replaced by a more valid view of the law of polarization.

---

[3] For the law of polarization, see my *Man and Society in Calamity*, chaps. ix–xii; a detailed analysis of this is in my forthcoming *Types, Techniques, and Factors of Altruistic Experience*.

[4] See, for instance, S. Freud, *A General Introduction to Psychoanalysis* (New York, 1920); J. Dollard et alii, *Frustration and Aggression* (New Haven, 1939).

Finally, we note that the rôle of books, cinemas, sermons, theaters, and school education in the altruistic conversions is generally modest: it makes up only about 10 per cent of the precipitants. When we consider the prevailing character of current books (especially the best sellers), of papers and magazines, of movies and plays, of radio and television entertainments; when we analyze the predominant character of our school education—which hardly even tries to educate the character of the pupils—we should not be surprised at the modest rôle these elements play in the true socialization and altruization of human beings. Being in their bulk extremely sensate, they disintegrate, demoralize, and enervate rather than integrate, moralize, or socialize.[5]

On this point our data confirm other data given above concerning the factors of good-neighborliness; there, books gave us less than 1 per cent, and school education some 4 per cent, of all the factors in good-neighborliness.

---

[5] See my *Reconstruction of Humanity; Crisis of Our Age;* and *Social and Cultural Dynamics,* Vol. I et passim through 4 volumes.

19. RECIPIENTS OF HELP

Let us briefly touch upon some of the characteristics of the recipients of the help of the "good neighbors." The recipients were (1) individuals, (2) organized groups, (3) unorganized groups or "plurels." (A regiment is an organized group of soldiers; soldiers as individuals wandering in a city, each looking for his own amusement independently of the others, furnish an example of an unorganized group or plurel.[1]) More unorganized plurels than organized groups were helped. As to the kind of organized groups and plurels helped by the neighbors, we have the following chief categories:

Table 4

Military	39 per cent of all the groups
Invalid and sick	14 per cent of all the groups
Social	14 per cent of all the groups
Charitable	8 per cent of all the groups
Children	7 per cent of all the groups
Patriotic	6 per cent of all the groups
Educational	6 per cent of all the groups
Aged	6 per cent of all the groups
Religious	3 per cent of all the groups
Athletic	3 per cent of all the groups
Penal	2 per cent of all the groups

Others were scattered among various groups. Since the helping activities were studied in the time of war, it is natu-

---
[1] For organized, unorganized, and disorganized groups, see my *Society, Culture, and Personality*, chaps. iv, viii, and ix.

ral that military groups and plurels happened to be the main recipients of help. Then come the groups of invalids, the social groups, the charitable groups, the children, the educational, and other groups occupying a still more modest place. As mentioned before, the helping activities of our "good neighbors" in the case of these organized groups were supplementary to the institutionalized public help they received. "Good neighbors" rendered them services or help that was an "extra," something additional to official help, help that was individualized in accordance with the specific needs of a group. Most of the helped members of unorganized plurels were socially anonymous. Here our "good neighbors" come as a force mitigating anonymous isolation, lonesomeness, and confusion.

It is to be noted that our neighbors also helped penal groups, thus continuing a long historical tradition that charity, like sunshine, sheds its love on all. This truly charitable trait becomes still clearer in the kind of unorganized groups helped by our neighbors. A portion of such groups are disreputable from the standpoint of official relief: street urchins, hoboes, semi-criminals, prostitutes or unwed mothers, and the like. The warm heart of "good neighbors" seems to have followed the old maxim: it is not the saintly but the sinful who need a helping hand.

As to the individuals helped, their predominant characteristics are strikingly different from those of the "good neighbors" in several respects.

Among the recipients of help, males are from two to five times more numerous than the females, male and female percentages being 25 and 9 per cent in one sample, 10 and 2 per cent in another, and 4 and 1 per cent in the third sample (the rest of the percentage being represented by two or more persons of both sexes). Among "good neighbors" women were more numerous than men. The reasons for the larger percentage of helped males are the same as for the larger percentage of helping females among "good neighbors": First, the chief recipients of help were soldiers (in wartime), aided chiefly by women. Second, males contribute a greater share, as compared with women, to both positive and negative extremes of *Homo sapiens:* to the geniuses and the altruists, to criminals and the insane. The predominance of helped males in our case is partly explained by this general rule.

Among "good neighbors" an overwhelming majority were married; among the helped the situation was reversed: here the married make up only 23 per cent, whereas the single show 77 per cent of the total. This again is a partial case of the general rule that the single, as compared with the married, show a higher rate of suicide, criminality, and maladjustment. Such a situation is possibly due to two concurrent factors: (1) for some single persons, the very fact of their failure to marry is in itself a symptom of their maladjustment; in other words, their single status is a consequence of some sort of maladaptation they had before the marriageable age; (2) remaining single, persons are generally deprived of the protection which marriage gives, and are more exposed to various situations of a demoralizing and confusing nature than the married.

Among "good neighbors" the middle-age groups dominate. Among recipients, the proportion of the aged and of the young is considerably higher, as was indicated above. The reasons for this are evident and were also mentioned above.

From a sociocultural standpoint the main psychosocial classifications of the recipients of help are shown in Table 5.

Thus the bulk of the recipients of help indeed represent persons in need, either through the biological factor of sickness, the helplessness of infancy, childhood, old age, blindness or other organic handicaps, or through the sociocultural conditions of poverty, delinquency, unwed motherhood, grief, loneliness, and the like, and through the more specific conditions of being a somewhat lonely soldier or a needy student during the war years.

Table 5

Soldiers	22 per cent of all individual recipients
Infants and children	19 per cent of all individual recipients
The ill	15 per cent of all individual recipients
Everybody [2]	12 per cent of all individual recipients
Adolescents	7 per cent of all individual recipients
The poor	3 per cent of all individual recipients
The aged	2 per cent of all individual recipients
Students	1 per cent of all individual recipients
Criminals and delinquents	1 per cent of all individual recipients
The grieved	1 per cent of all individual recipients
Mothers	1 per cent of all individual recipients
The blind and handicapped	1 per cent of all individual recipients

The rest are scattered among various groups.

Thus the sex, age, health, and sociocultural characteristics of the recipients of help are considerably different from those that render this help.

---

[2] This indicates activity by a "good neighbor" on behalf of the public in general.

20. "GOOD NEIGHBORS" AND

THEIR DEAREST PERSONS

As a general rule of a perennial nature, human beings tend to help first and most those who are dearest and—socioculturally and psychologically—nearest to them. With an increase of sociocultural and psychological distance, the frequency and intensity of altruistic actions tend to decrease or subside. In our speech and in our preachments we talk of love toward all humanity, freedom from discrimination against this or that, fair-mindedness toward all, helping everyone according to his need, and so on. In our actual behavior, 99 per cent of us do not practice these Christian and universal ethical precepts, but rather violate them in favor of hating our enemies—often priding ourselves on such hate and on the number of enemies we have killed in war, in revolution, and in hunting criminals, subversive agents, etc. When we help, we help primarily only those who are dear and near to us. Strangers are rarely helped, if at all.[1]

With a view to testing this general rule on our material, we asked each "good neighbor" to indicate twelve of the dearest and nearest persons among all the persons he knows—those for whom he would be willing to make the greatest sacrifice. These twelve persons had to be mentioned in a descending order of dearness. The following are the chief deductions from their answers.

---

[1] For experimental evidence, see my "Experimental Study of Efficiency of Work" in *The American Journal of Sociology*, March, 1930; also "Experimente zur Soziologie," *Zeitschrift für Völkerpsychologie und Soziologie*, March, 1928.

1. The overwhelming majority indicated that the dearest and nearest persons to them are their kin or relatives, especially among the first six dearest persons. Thus kinship relationship is still most powerful among all the relationships binding individuals into one solidary "we"—into one loving union. This may be seen from the following percentages of the kinsfolk and the non-kinsfolk (or those very remotely related by kinship) among each of the twelve dearest persons.

Table 6

Twelve Dearest Persons

	I	II	III	IV	V	VI	VII	VIII	IX	X	XI	XII
Non-kinsfolk	12.9	12.7	19.3	9.7	36.0	37.3	52.8	60.9	62.5	72.5	84.9	90.7
Kinsfolk	87.1	87.3	80.7	91.3	64.0	62.7	47.2	39.1	37.5	27.5	15.1	9.3

The figures show clearly that among the first six dearest persons,[2] kinsfolk occupy the most prominent position. Among the first four they make up from 80 to 91 per cent of the dearest and nearest. Only beginning with the seventh dearest do the non-kinsfolk begin to become an increasing majority, which reaches some 90 per cent with the twelfth dearest person.

2. Moreover, it should be noted that about 9 to 12 per cent of our "good neighbors" have, even among the first four dearest and nearest persons, individuals not related (or very remotely related) to them. This result is highly significant. *It points to a considerable portion of our population for which the kinship relationship seems to have lost its dominance and is replaced by the friendship arising from other than kinship ties.* Since the human universe over which our neighbors'

---

[2] It should be noted that the first few dearest persons are comparatively easy to choose. As we continue the selection, the difficulty of clearly pointing out the dearest begins to increase progressively as we go from the first dearest to the fourth, fifth, sixth, and so on, especially as we go beyond the closest members of our family. Meanwhile, for many of our contemporaries in this country, the closest direct relatives are often exhausted by three, four, five, and especially six persons: spouse, children, and parents.

altruistic activities extend is probably somewhat larger and less narrow than that of the rank and file, this percentage of non-kinsfolk among the dearest and nearest is possibly higher than that for the rank and file of the American population. Nevertheless, it suggests that even among the ordinary population there is a portion which have some non-relatives among the dearest and nearest. Since the problem has hardly been adequately studied, there are virtually no data with which we can compare our percentages. In view of the importance of this subject, more information should be collected and studied. (The study on *Affiliative and Hostile Tendencies* confirms the present results.)

3. Among the dearest and nearest kinsfolk, the direct relatives—spouse, children, and parents—occupy the dominant position, especially among the four dearest. The more remote the kinship relationship, the smaller is the percentage of such

Table 7
Dearest and Nearest

	I	II	III	IV	V	VI	VII	VIII	IX	X	XI	XII
Percentage of the total kinsfolk among 100 per cent of the related and non-related dearest	87.1	87.3	80.7	91.3	64.0	62.7	47.2	39.1	37.5	27.5	15.1	9.3
Percentage of closest relatives (spouse, parents, children)	72.6	63.5	48.3	53.2	30.9	10.1	11.3	6.5	5.0	2.6	9.1	0.0
Percentage of remote kinsfolk	14.5	23.8	32.4	38.1	33.1	52.6	35.9	32.6	32.5	24.9	6.0	9.3

relatives among the first few dearest persons. Among the first two dearest it is insignificant. Only after the first four dearest do they become a majority among the blood relatives. This majority reaches its maximum at the sixth place, remains high (about one third of the dearest) up to the ninth place, and then declines, being driven out by the non-related dearest. These uniformities may be clearly seen from the figures of Table 7.

These figures suggest further that the closest relatives are the first four dearest persons; then come the less close relatives, who occupy the most prominent place among the *fifth and sixth dearest;* next come the non-related persons, who constitute a majority among the dearest and nearest, though the remoter relatives still occupy a notable place (about one third) in the seventh, eighth, and ninth places. In places ten to twelve the non-relatives form an overwhelming majority among the dearest and nearest.

4. As to the specific percentages of the closest relatives among all dearest and nearest relatives (taken as 100 per cent)[3] the following figures clearly depict the situation:

Table 8

Relationship	I	II	III	IV	V	VI	VII	VIII	IX	X	XI	XII
Child	11.4	39.7	38.7	35.5	9.8	8.4	9.4	2.2	2.5	2.6	0.0	0.0
Parent	20.9	17.5	6.4	16.2	11.5	1.7	1.9	4.3	2.5	0.0	9.1	0.0
Spouse	40.3	6.3	3.2	1.6	1.6	0.0	0.0	0.0	0.0	0.0	0.0	0.0

A spouse is the dearest for the overwhelming majority in the first place; then come the parents, then a child. From the second place up to the seventh place, a child is the dearest for the majority of our neighbors; while the spouse loses his preeminent place and dwindles below the parents and children,

---

[3] The remaining percentages are taken up by less close relatives and non-relatives.

beginning with the second place. After the fifth place the spouse disappears.

These results cannot be taken as a measure of the comparative dearness of child, parent, or spouse. They are an outcome of several other conditions besides the factor of comparative dearness. Not all the neighbors are married, and among even the married not all have children. Unmarried or childless persons, or both, naturally cannot indicate a spouse or child as the dearest. Moreover the parents of some of the neighbors were dead; as such they might either have been overlooked or else, owing to the lapse of some time after death, simply became less dear than some of the living persons. For these and similar reasons, the figures are not a measure of the comparative dearness of these direct relatives.

With this reservation we can, however, conjecture a few significant points respecting these figures. First, considering that all neighbors had parents, whereas only a portion of them were married (from 59 to 77 per cent), 40 per cent for a spouse, in contrast to 21 per cent for parents, as the dearest in the first place is symptomatic. These figures suggest that a spouse is dearer than a parent for most of the neighbors of our sample. Considering that the conjugal family limited to husband, wife, and children is the predominant type of family in our society, that further relatives are fairly remote, and that this conjugal family of husband and wife is ordinarily separated from the parental families by the act of marriage, such a preference for a spouse as compared with a parent is comprehensible and likely to be typical not only for our sample but for the entire population of the United States. Only a comparative minority of the married put a spouse in the second, third, fourth, or fifth place among the dearest (after which the spouse category is exhausted and becomes a zero percentage). This zero percentage for the dearest from the sixth to the twelfth place also means that a spouse is not a dear one of "low intensity." On the contrary, the spouse is a dear one of the highest intensity—higher than any other relative for the majority of the married; for the minority of the married, a spouse still remains a dear one of high intensity of the second to the fifth place.

After a spouse, parents occupy the first place among the dearest. This can easily be the result of the fact that not all neighbors are married and have children. However, beginning with the second place, a child becomes dearest for the majority of the neighbors and holds this highest percentage up to virtually the eighth place (among the relatives), after which parents take the upper hand. However, as was shown, after the sixth place all relatives give leadership to the non-related dearest. This confirms the closeness of the ties between husband, wife, and child in our conjugal family, and a somewhat looser relationship between husband and wife on the one hand, and their parents on the other. All this, up to the leadership among the dearest of the non-relatives after the sixth place, is in agreement with the character of our nuclear family. Owing to its limited size all its dearest relatives are approximately exhausted by the dearest of the first six places, and for this reason the non-relatives become a majority among the dearest from the seventh to the twelfth place.

5. Since, beginning with the seventh place, the non-related persons become a majority among the dearest, and this majority increases as we go from the seventh to the twelfth place, the question arises: Who are these dearest? By what traits do they become dear to a "good neighbor"? Through similarity in sex? age? a political party? an occupation? religion? nationality? race? economic status?

Unfortunately the material obtained does not allow a comprehensive answer to these questions.

(a) As to sex, both sexes varied inconclusively from the first to the twelfth dearest. Only for the first two places were males a majority (57 per cent as against 43 per cent for females); for the remaining positions, except the ninth and eleventh, females were a majority of 64 to 52 per cent among the dearest of these categories. Since the group was predominantly female, the prevalence of males in the first three places possibly means their sweethearts or other friends. Here we meet a well-known fact—namely, that in normal love relationships it is the opposite sex that attracts and unites its complement in love. For less warm categories of dearness (from the third to the twelfth place), the similarity in sex reasserts itself as a factor of dearness.[4]

(b) As to the nationality factor, our "good neighbors" listed their own stock clearly as Irish or Jewish or Scotch, etc.; but the nationality of their dearests they just styled "American." This makes it impossible to discover the rôle of national similarity or dissimilarity.

(c) A study of occupational similarity or dissimilarity yields the following results: The highest percentage of the dearest in all twelve places is occupied by housewives (from some 30 to 47 per cent). This result is probably due to two different factors: husbands among "good neighbors" listing their wives as the dearest, and the housewives (a majority in the sample) listing other housewives as their dearest friends. This second factor means that the similarity of the occupational (and social) status of housewives seems to be a tangible factor in their friendship. In other occupations, this occupational propinquity is not so conspicuous but it is tangible. Most of the dearest ones happened to be either of the same or related occupations (for example, education and other professions) or of a similar social status (when kinship is not a factor). A portion of the dearest, however, were of a different occupational and social status.

The tangible rôle of occupational similarity among the dear-

---

[4] Respecting the role of similarity and dissimilarity in friendly and unfriendly relationships, see my *Society, Culture, and Personality*, chap. vii. Compare the principal theories, literature, data, and conclusions on this subject.

est is again a result of two different factors. In a number of cases occupational similarity was a result of kinship relationship between the persons: the father and son were both farmers or professionals or businessmen. In other cases it was a result of similarity in occupations, social status, perhaps reenforced by other similarities and dissimilarities. Which of these two factors (kinship leading to occupational similarity and occupational similarity as such) is stronger and what comparative rôle each plays remain unknown exactly. The rôle of kinship and occupation appears, however, more efficient than that of a pure occupational propinquity.

(d) As to religious similarity or dissimilarity, its rôle shows itself in two forms: among the dearest of the first six places an overwhelming majority (more than 90 per cent) are of the same religion as a "good neighbor"; for less dear persons of the seventh to the twelfth place, there is an increasing tendency to select the dearest among persons of different religions. Thus on the average only 1.65 per cent of the dearest of the first six places belong to different religions, whereas 9.7 per cent are religiously different among the more remote dearest of the seventh to the twelfth places.

As in the preceding cases, these results are possibly due to two different factors: kinship and religion itself. An overwhelming majority of the nearest kinsfolk belong to the same religion (from 80 to 97 per cent). We have seen that up to the sixth place, inclusive, the kinsfolk constituted a majority among the dearest. Here we see that up to the sixth place, inclusive, the percentage of the dearest belonging to different religions is very low. Such a result may be due not so much to the religious factor as such as to the kinship relationship between the "good neighbors" and their dearest ones.

Beginning with the seventh place, kinsfolk become a minority among the dear ones. With a weakening of this factor the percentage of the dear ones of a similar or the same religion also declines. The percentage of the religiously dissimilar dearest ones tends to grow systematically as we pass from the seventh to the still more remote twelfth place.

The chief result of the foregoing may be put as follows: *As the intensity of love and friendship declines, religious dissimilarity tends to increase among less close friends. As the intensity increases, religious dissimilarity decreases.* How much all this is due to religion as such, and how much to kinship and other factors, remains unclear.

6. The totality of the foregoing data roughly confirms the generalization that real (ideological and behavioral) friendship or love is most intense among those nearest to one socially, culturally, or psychologically. It tends to decline in its intensity (purity and duration) as the sociocultural and psychological distance between the parties grows. Even our "good neighbors" in their overt actions love most intensely and help overwhelmingly those who are their closest kinsfolk, and, among the non-kinsfolk, those who either religiously or occupationally are the nearest. Thus even this somewhat more Christian and humanistic group is still "parishional" in its behavioral love and friendship. Its love of all humanity remains still mainly ideological and "speech-reactional preaching," borne out only in part by behavioral practice. This discrepancy is probably still greater among the rank and file. The circle of their dearest ones is probably still more parochial than that of our "good neighbors."

21. HAPPINESS

AND PEACE OF MIND

The data show that the majority of "good neighbors" have the sorrows and joys, pain and pleasures, hardships and comforts, typical of the American social groups to which they belong. Some of the "good neighbors" seem to have had even an unduly large share of sorrow and tragedy. Though the overwhelming majority have been happy in their family life, a small fraction encountered serious troubles in their families: a criminal, a psychotic, a profligate, an alcoholic, or some other pathological type. Thus Mrs. A.'s husband was insane and constantly threatening to shoot his family; Mrs. B.'s husband was an alcoholic and a criminal; Mrs. C.'s father chased his family around the house with a carving knife; Mrs. D.'s husband probably had had more illegitimate children than any other man in the town.

In spite of this extraordinary share of sorrows and hardships, the overwhelming majority of "good neighbors" feel themselves at peace with themselves, others, and the world at large. They find their life worth living, fruitful, and meaningful. They feel themselves happy. This happiness [1] is either of the sensate type, consisting of mainly enjoyable, pleasant experiences, good health, reasonable success, and *corresponding peace of mind;* or it is of the idealistic type—similar to the sensate but with sensate values occupying a lesser share, and

---
[1] There are many forms of happiness, and among these are the basic forms of ideational, idealistic, and sensate happiness. See my *Dynamics, passim.*

various idealistic values a larger share, in this eudaemonistic happiness. It is a richer, deeper, and more meaningful form of happiness than the sensate. It ordinarily contains a larger share of sorrows than hedonistic, sensate happiness. Finally, part of the happiness of "good neighbors" is ideational. Sensory pleasures occupy a very small place; so also do sensory joys. Sorrows and somber tragedy are conspicuous. Its values are mainly of the ideational, religious, ethical, or highly idealistic type. It is a somber form of happiness, but possibly less destructive and fragile than other forms. In some notable religious altruists of history it has been associated with meditation—the contemplation of death, the coffin, and the decay of sensory life and of the world.[2] In spite of the strange form of this ideational happiness for sensate man, it has for millenniums furnished millions with a happiness that is as real as—perhaps more real than—other forms of happiness.

All these three forms of happiness are experienced by our neighbors. All of them, especially those who are somewhat nearer to the ideational type, find life valuable and would be ready to live it through again if given a chance. The following statement of one of the neighbors is typical in these respects:

> And so ends the story of fifty-nine years of sorrows and happiness, and the knowledge that I have done my best and never gave up when the going got hard. And that I am happy and at peace with the world.

About all of them may be said what Saint Tychon's companion (Chebotarev) says of him:

> On the days when Saint Tychon had received the greatest number of poor and distributed the greatest amount of money and other alms, he appeared especially cheerful and

---

[2] In a prescription to a monk suffering from accidie (or mental depression and ennui), Saint Tychon, who prepared his own coffin five years before his death and daily contemplated it, advises that (among three other techniques for overcoming this melancholy) "the thought of death, which perchance may cross your mind, turns away dejection. Meditate on these things. Pray and sigh." G. P. Fedotov, A Treasury of Russian Spirituality, p. 229.

joyful. But on the days when he had been solicited by only a few or none at all, he would be sad and depressed. . . . He was like Job—the eye of the blind and the feet of the lame. His doors were always open to beggars and wanderers (and even criminals), who found food, drink, and rest under his roof.[3]

Thus this altruistic ego-transcendence turns out to be highly useful, beneficial, and eudaemonistic. Insofar it is the noblest form of utilitarianism. However, all this comes as a by-product or a mere consequence of unselfishness. He who would try to do these unselfish things just for their utilitarian value is likely to miss both unselfishness, and utilitarian or eudaemonistic results. A by-product elevated to an end value destroys or spoils both.

"Good neighbors" do not suffer from spleen, boredom, or the emptiness and meaninglessness of life. Even their tragedies they take as something that enhances the fullness of life and the urgency of love and kindness. As we have seen, for some of them their personal tragedy was a precipitating factor of their altruistic transmutation. Here again we see how altruism or unselfishness helps to make life meaningful and happy (in the deeper sense of the term); how it helps one to meet all sorrows and tragedies; how it leads to a transcendence of our little egos and enriches and ennobles our life.

This peace of mind expresses itself also in a sort of profound optimism which these people entertain in regard to the fruits of their good actions. Some of them stress the fact that now and then their kindness was reacted to with animosity, and immediately brought them bitter rather than sweet fruits. Nevertheless, in the long run they believe that any kindness engenders kindness, and that nothing is lost from any good deed. A good deed is imperishable and in due time brings its full fruition. Here is an example cited by one "good neighbor":

---

[3] C. P. Fedotov, A Treasury of Russian Spirituality, p. 199.

I'll give you an experience I had with one of my neighbors, showing how "bread cast out upon the waters" returns after many days. A mother, ill with pneumonia and hard-swollen breasts, came home with a baby boy. For some weeks I assumed the care and nursing of both mother and son. They regained perfect health. Years later the boy was chosen by Harvard for his fine scholastic achievements and ultimately his education was financed. He graduated from Harvard last year and is now engaged in United States personnel work in Japan. His parents have always been very grateful and have been helping others.

This testimony gives a good example of the reasons for the optimism and happiness of our "good neighbors."

22. "GOOD NEIGHBORS"

AS DEVIANTS

If criminals are deviants falling below the legally prescribed norms of moral conduct, "good neighbors" are also deviants, but above the level of moral conduct demanded by the official law.[1] As a rule "good neighbors" discharge not only the duties prescribed for and demanded from all, but something extra, above the minimum of social conduct required by official law. This extra something ordinarily does not conflict with the official law, but rather supplements it. In such cases "good neighbors" do not get into trouble with the official law or its enforcers.

In other cases this "superlegality" of altruistic deeds and of their commands does contradict the official law norms. It violates some of these norms—for instance, the refusal of conscientious objectors to be drafted; the refusal of some "good neighbors" to join a witch hunt for officially declared communists or other "subversives." In such cases, "good neighbors" undergo the same conflict with official law that has been the inevitable fate of almost all the great moral innovators and altruists: Buddha, Socrates, Plato, Aristotle, Jesus, the Apostles, Mohammed, Al Hallaj, up to M. Gandhi and Sri Aurobindo.[2] Since the ethical code and altruism of such un-

---

[1] For what is law, the official and intuitive law, the moral or ethical norms, and their difference from the legal norms, see my *Society, Culture, and Personality*, chap. iv.

[2] This has also been the fate of an extremely high percentage of men of genius in all fields of creativity. According to Havelock Ellis's study, of 975

selfish persons far transcends the often antiquated, always narrow, fairly low, local, group-selfish moral level of official law, they cannot help colliding with official law and its enforcers. And not only with its enforcers (government, judges, police, etc.), but also with many portions of the population who support the antiquated norms of official law; for whom, therefore, our altruists and "good neighbors" appear as suspicious or revolutionary "subversives," or as persons who through their high moral demands or conduct endanger the vested interests, privileges, and peace of mind of the supporters of the status quo.

This explains why virtually all altruists—even the greatest ones of history—have collided to a certain degree with official law and its agencies, and with many persons and groups. However paradoxical it may seem, the fact is that *all altruistic actions and persons have generated social antagonisms and conflicts.* They have brought not only peace but also war. "The Athenian Committee on un-Athenian Activities" and

---

British men of genius, 160, or over 16 per cent, were imprisoned, once or oftener, while many others escaped imprisonment by fleeing from the country or through other forms of voluntary exile. This was in a relatively enlightened and liberal nation. (Havelock Ellis, *A Study of British Genius*, p. 233.) "The man of genius is an abnormal being, and therefore arouses the instinctive hostility of society, which by every means seeks to put him out of the way."

Among the notable social, political, economic, ethical, and partly philosophical thinkers (whose works make up the history of social, sociological, political, economic, and ethical thought), a still larger proportion, some 70 to 80 per cent, have undergone a collision with the official law and government; have been imprisoned, exiled, banished, or penalized in other ways, or have fled for the sake of preserving their life and freedom. Among the founders and apostles of the foremost religions, almost 100 per cent collided with the official law, which protected the old existing religion. Thus from this standpoint, the collision of the great altruists and "good neighbors" with official norms is not just a coincidence but expressive of the same general law. It is necessary to distinguish between two kinds of so-called "social deviants": the subnormal types—criminals, psychotics, and other pathological types, and the "supra-normal"—or the positive, creative innovators in all fields of culture and social life. Though both classes are deviants and both collide with existing laws and values, they are, nevertheless, absolutely different kinds of deviants, much farther from each other than from "the bulk of law-abiding mediocrity." This distinction is often forgotten.

Socrates; "The Jewish Committee on un-Jewish Activities" and Jesus; some sectarian "Hindu Committee on un-Hindu Activities" and Gandhi; "The American Committee on un-American Activities" and several American "good neighbors" —they and their like are a perennial symbol of this conflict with members of even their own nation or group. Besides the members of their in-group, such altruists and "good neighbors" have invariably collided with many out-groups and their members. This is an eternal tragedy!

Since the bulk of our "good neighbors" are mostly law-abiding citizens, not deviating much from the level of official law; since their activities supplement rather than supplant the conduct demanded by official law, the bulk of our neighbors do not record any particular trouble with official law and its agencies. Only a small part have had collisions with them. And even these collisions have been comparatively mild. A somewhat greater proportion have had some conflicts with various individuals and groups upon whose toes they have somehow stepped. But even these collisions have been tempered and free from violence.

As a rule, the greater the altruism of a person, the sharper and more numerous are likely to be his collisions with official law and its enforcers, and with the persons and groups whose values are "depreciated" and challenged by such altruism. Christ would be likely to get into sharper and greater collisions than any of our ordinary "good neighbors" or Christian ministers and priests today.

Is there a way out of this tragic dilemma? Can there be a pure and lofty altruism, not generating collision and conflict? This problem is beyond the scope of the present study. It is analyzed elsewhere.[3] Tentatively, the answer is that there is such a way, but that it requires, among other conditions, an extension of our "in-group" feelings to all humanity; and this

---

[3] See my forthcoming *Types, Techniques, and Factors of Altruistic Experience*.

extension must be real, manifested not only in our speech reactions but in our entire behavior. Otherwise such conflicts and collisions are unavoidable. Jesus rightly said that he brought not only peace but the sword. So does any unselfish person or deed!

23. THE MEANING OF

GOOD-NEIGHBORLINESS

The foregoing reveals the essential traits of American "good neighbors." Most of these characteristics are typical of, and meaningfully-causally connected with, any American or any other plurel of relatively unselfish persons.[1] Some of these traits are purely local and temporary. All in all, we find that "good neighbors" are very different from pathological social groups and plurels (criminals, etc.) in almost all their essential characteristics. The contrast helps us to understand better both types of groups, especially which traits and relationships are inseparable from either criminal or "good neighbor" groups. The study has disclosed, further, several hows and whys of becoming a "good neighbor." The conclusions reached here are supported by other studies of altruistic persons, and, in turn, support the conclusions of these latter investigations.

Studying our "good neighbors," we have had to touch on several problems of a far more general nature than those dealing specifically with good-neighborliness: What factors are important in the formation of the character of a person? Who are the dearest and nearest for most of us? What are the rôles of various "precipitating" experiences and the nature of these experiences? What is the relationship between happiness or peace of mind, and self-transcendence in the form of good-neighborliness? Are "good neighbors" deviants, and, if so, of

---

[1] See *Types, Techniques, and Factors of Altruistic Experience*.

what kind? Do they collide with law and government, with individuals and groups, and, if so, how often and why?

There is no doubt that the factual material of this study is very limited; therefore most of the conclusions reached are purely tentative. Subsequent studies should show which of these results are valid and which are not. The work does show that greater concentration on the study of positive social, cultural, and personality problems is warranted—a study that would be at least as fruitful as those of pathological phenomena. Besides their cognitive value, such positive studies would have a practical moral value: they would tangibly stimulate good-neighborliness in the individuals and groups informed of such a study. The following observation of one of our investigators (Miss Catharine Woodson) is typical:

> If this case study [of ten "good neighbors" in a New Hampshire town] brings nothing to light on causes of goodness, it has still been of very great value in that it has served the community in which it was made. This is because it has defined unselfishness as good. It has served to make those not in the study stop to consider in what manner they have lived—that they are not qualified to be included in the study (a sort of *Who's Who among American "Good Neighbors"*). I have been amazed at the expressions of quiet sadness on the part of people who know they are not social (unselfish). The study has served to encourage those who are unselfish. Some of them were almost pathetically pleased at this recognition. After all, we live in a culture where greed and the acquisition of money and power are praised. It was a pleasant change for them to be rated as a success in living because they made others happy. I do not think that I imagined improvement in some of the people connected with the study. Having been informed about the study, a powerful local politician, generally considered a scoundrel, did not have the nerve to refuse to help someone in trouble, and mended his ways notably. For the people chosen it had real therapeutic value.

These observations are corroborated by the statements and remarks of hundreds of "good neighbors." The very fact of the study of "good neighbors," and of a sort of *Who's Who among "Good Neighbors,"* has exerted a quite tangible effect not only upon those chosen, but upon all who learned about the study. Perhaps for egoistic reasons, in order to qualify eventually for good-neighborliness, many unqualified persons began to do good-neighborly deeds that they had not hitherto performed.

These facts clarify the positive ethical effects of studies of this kind. Retroactively they suggest that too great a concentration on the study and publicity of pathological phenomena and persons is likely to exert a demoralizing effect. Studies of the effects of many detective stories, murder and crime movies, "comics," and "juicy" front-page descriptions of rape corroborate the negative influence of a one-sided concentration on the pathological side of our life, whether in social science and philosophy, the press or cinema, literature or the other fine arts.

A scientific study of positive types of social phenomena is a necessary antidote to that of negative types of our cultural, social, and personal world. The moral effect alone fully justifies a further investigation of persons and groups of good will and good deeds.

PART TWO

CHRISTIAN-CATHOLIC SAINTS

24. THE SOURCES OF THIS STUDY

In V. Solovyev's famous *Three Conversations* [1] several personages (a general, a diplomat, etc.), discuss, in the manner of Plato's *Dialogues*, fundamental ethical and religious problems. After a devastating criticism of Tolstoy's condemnation of resistance to evil by violence and his demonstration of the fruitlessness of resistance by arms and war, the general mentions the saints as additional evidence for his point:

> General: Have you ever glanced through the lives of the saints? And have you noticed what kinds of saints there are?
> Diplomat: Saints are of various kinds.
> General: But what is their social position?
> Diplomat: Diverse, I think.
> General: In fact, not so diverse as you think.
> Diplomat: How? Are they all military persons?
> General: Not all, but about one half of them.
> Diplomat: This is a great exaggeration.
> General: Of course I did not take an exact statistical census of the saints. I only contend that *all the saints of the Russian Church belong virtually to two social classes*: either they are monks of various ranks or else princes who are traditionally military leaders. There are no other male saints. Either a monk or a soldier.

A preliminary exploration discloses that up to now there has hardly been any statistical census of the saints. As a result, we

---
[1] V. Solovyev, "Tree razgovora," Works (*Sobrannyie Sotchinenii*, 2d ed., St. Petersburg, 1913), Vol. X, p. 96. (English translation by A. Bakshy, London, 1915.)

know little about the age, sex, nationality, race, occupational or economic composition of the saints considered as a group. Still less do we know about their other, less tangible, characteristics.

This study tries to fill the gap. It investigates from certain standpoints the Catholic saints as found in Butler's *Lives of the Saints*, revised by H. S. J. Thurston.[2]

In certain cases, however, nothing is known about a group of saints except that they were all martyred at the same place and under the same conditions. If these groups were composed of 26 or more persons, we have taken them in their totality as representing one unit. The final figures may be seen in the following table:

Table 9

Number of units	Number of persons represented by each unit
3,069	1
3	26
3	40
1	64
1	100
1	120
1	160
1	300
1	630
1	6,000
1	20,000
7	—(The actual number of persons in these martyred groups is unknown.)
3,090 Total Number of Units	

---

[2] Herbert S. J. Thurston, *The Lives of the Saints*, as originally compiled by the Reverend Alban Butler, Vols. I–XII (London, Burns, Oates and Washbourne Ltd., 1926). See Volume XII for a description of the complex procedure of the official sanctification of a person by the Catholic Church. See also

THE SOURCES OF THIS STUDY

Throughout the analysis, then, we shall be working with a base number of 3,090 units, which, for these purposes, may be taken to mean 3,090 persons or saints.

All the pertinent material was gathered from the biographies,[3] and then coded, punched and run through the I.B.M. Hollerith counter and sorter. All absolute numbers were then turned into percentages. The results are to be found on the following pages.

H. Delehaye, Sanctus (Brussels, 1927), ch. iv; H. Delehaye, Les Origines du Culte des Martyrs (Brussels, 1933).

The authors of Altruistic Love do not enter into a discussion as to what extent the official test of the saintliness of this or that person is infallible. We simply take the universe of the Catholic saints, sanctified by the Catholic Church, as a datum, and proceed to study some of the sociocultural traits of this universe, regardless of whether or not all these saints would be accepted as saintly by non-Catholics.

[3] Unfortunately, much of the history of the lives of the saints is unknown. Many of their biographies are brief and totally inadequate for relevant material. Hence we had to deal with whatever data we could manage to collect, and have simply left blanks where the information was lacking.

25. SEX DISTRIBUTION

Classification of the saints by sex is shown in the following table:

Table 10

Sex	Number of individuals	Percentage
Male	2,526	81.7
Female	519	16.8
Unknown	45	1.5
Total	3,090	100.0

The figures show that males are about five times more numerous among the saints than females. This glaring inequality of the sexes in regard to saintliness raises a number of interesting questions. Is this inequality due to the biological differences of the male and female organisms? Or is it due to environmental differences in which men and women are born and reared, live and act? Or is it a result of the biased selection of the Church which unduly favors males and disfavors females? Or is it a result of God's greater grace toward males?

Passing silently by the last hypothesis as being beyond the determination of science, we may say that this overwhelming preponderance of males among the saints is probably due to the other three conditions: (1) biological differences between male and female organisms; (2) environmental differences in their rearing, education, activities, and life; (3) a somewhat more favorable selection of males for saintliness than females. If we view saintliness as a high form of religious and moral creativity, as a specific form of genius,[1] then the prevalence

---

[1] "Saints belong to the élite. In the sphere of intelligence human beings bow before genius. In the sphere of energy and will, they venerate heroes. A person

of men in this field is an example of the prevalence of men among the highest forms of creative activity. Among the foremost leaders in science and philosophy, religion and the fine arts, economics and politics, men are consistently more numerous than women.

On the other hand, as has been mentioned elsewhere,[2] men show also a much higher rate of criminality, insanity, suicide, and other pathological types of human behavior. Such a preponderance of males at both extreme poles of human beings seems to be general for all great cultures or civilizations. It suggests that biological and psychological differences inherent in male and female organisms are partly responsible. At least, such a hypothesis fits the facts much better than a dismissal of this point as being unrelated to the causal factors of these phenomena. Among many evidences in favor of this biological, inherent factor, there is the continuation of the preponderance of males at both extreme poles in societies where women have been emancipated, where their educational and other opportunities have greatly increased and approached the standards of males.

That environmental factors also play an important rôle in this inequality of the sexes in saintliness is testified to by a large body of evidence. In practically all societies, including even those where women are essentially emancipated and considered the equals of men, the sociocultural conditions remain tangibly different for males and females. From the moment of birth, and increasingly in later years, male and female babies, boys and girls, young men and women, husbands and wives, are trained differently, educated differently, exposed to different stimuli and situations, subjected to different rights and

---

whom a Christian places at the very top of his respect and admiration, is one who, being in the service of God, lives the most superior life. A saint is a hero in the field of morals and religion: he is a perfect Christian," rightly says Delehaye. See his *Sanctus*, p. 235.

[2] See above in Part One.

duties, rôles and functions,³ engaged in different occupations and professions. In the whole of human history there has hardly been any large society in which the environment and its forces have been completely equal for men and women. This environmental difference is partly responsible for the preponderance of men at the extreme poles of human beings. With a decrease of this difference, the contrast between the sexes in this respect tends somewhat to decrease: males are still greatly preponderant at the positive and negative poles, but the chasm becomes somewhat narrower and less deep.

The Christian societies that furnished these saints had—for some eighteen out of the nineteen centuries studied—a great difference in the environmental conditions for men and women; the opportunities for women were much more limited than for men. It was only in the nineteenth century that the process of sociocultural emancipation of women began. In the Graeco-Roman world of the first four centuries of our era, a similar emancipation process was limited to a small portion of the women of the upper and, to a certain extent, of the middle strata. During these nineteen centuries in Asiatic and non-European countries such a process occurred on a scale hardly worth mentioning. Thus the environment of the centuries that produced our saints was much more unfavorable for the realization of genius in the female than in the male. Insofar it is one of three factors responsible for the marked difference in distribution of the saints between the sexes.

Finally, the Christian-Catholic Church, as an empirical institution, reflects in itself all the essential traits of the societies and cultures in which it has lived and functioned. Since these societies and cultures were man-dominated, the Church has also been predominantly a man's institution. Among hundreds of symptoms of such a domination, monopolization by men of all the highest positions and ranks of the Church, from

---

³ See my *Society, Culture, and Personality*, pp. 188ff.

bishop to patriarch and pope, is convincing evidence of this. As a man-dominated institution, operating in man-dominated societies, the Church could hardly escape a bias favoring males and disfavoring females in its selection of the saints. Corroboration of this is given in the fluctuation of the sex percentages of the saints by centuries. Tables 11 and 12 give the number and percentages by centuries.

The percentage table shows a notable increase of female saints in the eighteenth, nineteenth, and twentieth centuries. Whereas for all the preceding centuries (except the fourteenth and the fifteenth) the percentage of women fluctuated between 5 and 22 per cent, in the eighteenth century it rose to 46, in the nineteenth to 26, and in the twentieth to 100 per cent. We know that precisely these centuries have been those of the emancipation and equalization of women in the Western world.

Thus the data show how the Church, in its selection of the saints, reflects the basic processes (such as the emancipation of women) of the human society in which the Church lives and functions. Even the comparatively high percentage of women saints in the thirteenth (22 per cent), fourteenth (28 per cent), and in the fifteenth centuries (26 per cent) is hardly accidental: these were the centuries during which the medieval ideational culture of the West gave way to idealistic culture, with the emergence and growth of sensate culture. It was during this time that the feudal medieval world declined; urbanization and commercialization greatly progressed; urban revolutions enormously increased; and eventually the Renaissance took place, with a notable, though temporary, trend toward the emancipation of women, especially in Italy among the upper and, in part, the middle classes.[4]

---

[4] Even in such seemingly irrelevant cultural data as the proportion of male and female subjects in painting—the portraits of royalty, aristocracy, clergy, bourgeoisie, farmer, peasant, and laboring classes—even in such data there is a reflection of these basic processes in society. Thus in Europe the percentage

CHRISTIAN-CATHOLIC SAINTS

Table 11

Sex Distribution of Saints by Century

Century	1	2	3	4	5	6	7	8	9	10	11	12	13	14	15	16	17	18	19	20
Male	57	86	197	336	181	205	223	135	99	53	113	135	146	103	88	153	107	28	38	—
Female	16	12	37	64	26	22	41	36	20	13	7	17	42	41	31	25	14	24	14	1
Unknown	2	—	2	3	1	1	1	—	—	—	—	—	—	—	—	19	1	—	1	—
Total	75	98	236	403	208	228	265	171	119	66	120	152	188	144	119	197	122	52	53	1

Table 12

Percentual Sex Distribution of Saints by Century

Century	1	2	3	4	5	6	7	8	9	10	11	12	13	14	15	16	17	18	19	20
Male	76.0	87.8	83.5	83.4	87.0	90.0	84.1	78.9	83.2	80.3	94.2	88.8	77.7	71.5	73.9	77.7	87.7	53.8	71.7	—
Female	21.3	12.2	15.7	15.9	12.5	9.6	15.5	21.2	16.8	19.7	5.8	11.2	22.3	28.5	26.1	12.7	11.5	46.2	26.4	100.0
Unknown	2.7	—	.8	.7	.5	.4	.4	—	—	—	—	—	—	—	—	9.6	.8	—	1.9	—

Each vertical column totals 100 per cent.

It may be safely predicted that if, in the future, the process of sociocultural equalization of women progresses, their share among the Christian saints will continue to be great; the selection by the Church hierarchy and by influential groups and persons for the sainthood will tend to be less "biased" against women than before.

The moral of the foregoing data about women is that their opportunities still remain very unequal and inferior in the field of sainthood and the highest creative activities. The greatest and noblest steps in their real emancipation will be made when they notably increase their share of genius in all fields of creative activity, including sainthood.

The three foregoing factors explain to a great extent why the share of the sexes in the production of the saints has been so unequal.

---

of female portraits increased from 11 per cent in the tenth century to 38 per cent during the seventeenth to twentieth centuries; the percentage of the portraits of aristocracy decreased from between 74 and 100 per cent (during the tenth to thirteenth centuries) to 31 in the nineteenth, and 8 per cent in the twentieth century; the percentage of portraits of the bourgeoisie and laboring classes and intellectuals, on the contrary, increased. A less pronounced but notable increase of women saints in the later centuries of their emancipation was a phenomenon of the same kind. For details, see my *Social and Cultural Dynamics*, Vol. I, pp. 486–491.

26. AGE DISTRIBUTION

For 2,444, or 79.1 per cent of 3,090 saint units, life duration is unknown. Only for 646, or 20.9 per cent, is age at death known.

Table 13 gives the age distribution for the saints whose age at death is known.

Table 13

Age at death	Number of individuals	Percentage
3 days to 15 years	24	.8
16 through 25 years	39	1.3
26 through 40 years	60	1.9
41 through 60 years	171	5.5
61 through 80 years	242	7.8
81 through 100 years	93	3.0
Over 100 years	17	.6
Unknown	2,444	79.1
Total	3,090	100.0

The table deserves our attention for several reasons. First of all, it displays the extraordinary longevity of saints, far above that of the general population of not only the preceding centuries, but of the present time, when in this country especially, the average expectation of life at birth has notably increased. The figures of Table 14 roughly show the difference.

The comparison is not quite exact (the age groups being slightly different). The statistics about the saints are somewhat loaded against the saints. Here the first age group is taken at a younger age (16 to 40) than the first age group of the general population (20 to 39). Still the greater longevity of the saints, in comparison with the general population of the

Table 14

Frequency of distribution of ages in percentages among:

Age groups (years)	Those who died in the United States in 1920 at the age of 20 years and above	The saints' age groups (years)	Percentage
20–39	22.7	16–40	15.9
40–59	28.6	41–60	27.5
60–79	38.1	61–80	39.0
80 and above	10.6	81 and above	17.7
Total	100.0		100.0

United States in 1920, stands out clearly. When we consider that 99.9 per cent of the saints lived before the twentieth century and the bulk before the eighteenth century, in times when the average duration of life of general population was much lower than that of the American population in 1920; when we keep in mind that a large number of the saints died violent deaths as martyrs, without living their full life span—then the real longevity of the saints appears still greater than is shown by the above figures. Especially high is the percentage of the saints who lived 100 years and over.

These data also corroborate a general rule that the life duration of various leaders and of the higher social strata is longer, their mortality is lower and their vitality and health are better than that of the rank and file and of the lower classes.[1] This supernormal longevity of the saints is an example of this general rule. Leaders live longer than the common mass of those they lead. Thus the average longevity of monarchs and rulers (mainly for the centuries before the nineteenth) is 53.6 years; of eminent judges and lawyers, 68.9

---

[1] See my *Social Mobility* (New York, 1927), p. 275 and chaps. xi and xii. See the vast body of evidence showing the comparative life duration, mortality, and morbidity rates, and so on, of the leaders and upper classes of various societies and periods. With a few specified exceptions this rule seems to be universal and perennial.

years; of eminent statesmen, 67.4 years; of eminent army, navy and military men, 67.1 years; of eminent theologians and clergy, 68.7 years; of eminent scholars and scientists, 67.3 years; of the Roman Catholic popes, 69.8 years; of American millionaires (1850–1920 period), 69.2 years; of United States Presidents, 69.9 years; of eminent American inventors, 74.7 years; of the most eminent women of all countries and times, 60.8 years.[2]

When we take the leaders who lived mainly before the nineteenth, even before the eighteenth century, the Roman Catholic popes (many of whom became saints) lived somewhat longer than any other group of leaders of those centuries. Likewise the group of eminent theologians and clergymen lived about as long as any other group of leaders for the same centuries. The extraordinarily long duration of life of the saints is thus only an additional example of this rule. *Eminence, or leadership, is tangibly associated with vigorous vitality and longevity.*

If we cannot say that all centenarians and very healthy persons are eminent leaders or men and women of genius—as there are many such persons who do not display any sign of great creativity, genius, or real leadership—we may, nevertheless, say that long life and vigorous health are among the most important conditions of eminent leadership and of genius. With the exception of a small proportion of creators (in poetry, the fine arts, and a few other fields) who succeed in realizing their genius at an early age, the bulk of eminent leaders and creators have needed time, and sometimes a long time, for a realization of their potential genius or leadership. As a rule, almost any eminent creativity requires long training, experience, and an opportunity (sometimes occurring only late in life) to grow, to develop fully, and to realize itself. For this reason, many would-be creators who die early do not

---

[2] *Ibid.*, p. 259. Many other data are given there.

have the chance to realize their talent. The bulk of those who do realize their potentialities do so because they live long and have all the time necessary for turning their potential genius into actuality. Hence the supernormal longevity of men of genius and real leaders, including our saints.

The extraordinary longevity of the saints is probably a result of a healthy heredity, as well as of their own activity and environment. The reason for the factor of heredity in the case of our saints is this:

> The very severity of the monastic regulations was such that only the physically strong could stand it. The majority of the medieval monasteries, religious orders, and cloisters imposed such a physical régime as they did not dare to impose even upon the convicts in the galleys. The totality of the persons who submitted themselves to the severest ascetic life among the Christians or the Buddhists and the Brahmans had to be healthy for the same reason.[3]

Persons with a poor biological constitution and health could hardly withstand the hardships, the sometimes unbelievable self-mortification and deprivations, which most of the saints voluntarily endured.

The rôle of heredity is evidenced also by the fact that the longevity of the saints of the nineteenth and twentieth centuries does not show any notable increase in comparison with the longevity of the saints for the centuries from the ninth to the seventeenth inclusive. The figures of Table 15 depict the situation.

In spite of the improvement of environmental conditions in the nineteenth and twentieth centuries, which led to increased life expectancy for the general population (and possibly for the saints too), we do not note any appreciable increase of saints' longevity for these centuries as compared with the longevity figures for the ninth to the seventeenth centuries.

---

[3] *Ibid.*, p. 273.

Table 15

Age groups	Saints of ninth to seventeenth centuries		Saints of nineteenth and twentieth centuries	
	Number	Percentage	Number	Percentage
Up to 40 years	73	19.1	9	21.9
41 to 60	114	29.7	10	24.4
61 to 80	144	37.6	18	43.9
81 and above	52	13.6	4	9.8
Total	383	100.0	41	100.0

This suggests that the factor of environment has played a relatively unimportant rôle in the life span of the saints.

On the other hand, the very environment and régime of these "athletes of God" contained conditions which for a vigorous organism were healthy rather than harmful. The profound peace of mind which most of these saints acquired was one of the conditions which could easily counterbalance poor food, clothing, unhealthy environment, and self-mortification. Most of them knew well that peace of mind is one of the most important—sometimes the most important—of the conditions for health and longevity. Their unshakable belief in God and the values of the Kingdom of God, with freedom from most worldly worries, was another factor re-enforcing their health and vitality. When not excessive, their moderation in food, drink, and in other bodily appetites, together with vigorous physical exercise, their genuflections and various bodily movements in praying—sometimes such conditions as healthy desert or mountain or sea air in their eremitic or monastic habitats —and similar conditions contributed to the same result. To sum up: Their way of life, activity, and thought, and several of their environmental conditions, undoubtedly contributed a share to their longevity.

Longevity itself (like sex composition and other traits) stamps the saints with the same characteristics as those shared by most creative leaders of genius in all the main fields of activity. Our saints are creative geniuses in the fields of religion and ethics. As such they have several traits common to geniuses in all fields; they also have their own specific traits, different from those of eminent creators in science and the fine arts, in political and economic leadership, and in other fields.

27. MONTHS OF DEATH AND CANONIZATION

According to Catholic tradition, the death of a saint is actually his birthday—the day of the saint's entrance into the Kingdom of God. The saints are canonized on the anniversary of their death (fifty or more years after their death).

Table 16 gives the number and percentages for death and canonization by months.

Table 16

Month of death and of canonization	Number of saints	Percentage
January	278	9.0
February	256	8.3
March	267	8.6
April	293	9.5
May	293	9.5
June	273	8.8
July	331	10.8
August	241	7.8
September	226	7.3
October	226	7.3
November	214	6.9
December	192	6.2
Total	3,090	

These data show that the months of July, April, May, and January reveal the highest—and the autumn months from August to December, inclusive, the lowest—death percentages of the saints. For the general population, the months of the maximal and minimal death rates vary widely from country to country and even from period to period.[1] For most of the European countries, however, the months September through December show the lowest death rate, as in the case of our saints. For most European countries, January, February, and March are the months of highest mortality, and for European Russia, July has been the month with the highest death rate. July is also the highest mortality month for our saints.

Since the months of canonization are determined by the months of death, no specific factor is needed to explain the distribution of canonization by months.

---

[1] For data and analysis, see C. Mayr, *Statistik und Gesellschaftslehre* (Tübingen, 1917), Vol. II; C. Gini, M. Boldrini, L. de Berardinis, and G. Zingali, *Demographia* (Torino, 1930), pp. 226–229.

28. COUNTRIES OF
BIRTH AND DEATH

For 47.6 per cent of the saints, their country of birth, and for 74.3 per cent, their country of death, are not indicated in the sources used for this study. For the saints whose countries of birth and death are mentioned, Table 17 shows their distribution by the countries of birth. Large geographical divisions embrace the following countries:

1. British Isles: England, Ireland, Scotland
2. Western Europe (except Italy, as seat of the Papal See): Spain, Portugal, France, Germany, Belgium, Holland, Switzerland
3. Italy (including Sardinia and Sicily)
4. Central (and Eastern) Europe: Greece, Bulgaria, Yugoslavia, Austria, Hungary, Rumania, Armenia, Crete, Albania, Poland, Czechoslovakia, Lithuania, Latvia, Estonia, East Prussia
5. Scandinavia: Norway, Sweden, Denmark
6. Asia: Turkey, Persia, Arabia, Iraq, Syria, Assyria, Afghanistan, India, Trans-Jordan, Jerusalem, Mesopotamia, Phoenicia
7. Africa: Egypt and Northern Africa
8. Orient: China, Japan
9. North and South America

A few points in these tables are worth mentioning. First, out of all the single countries of the world, a comparatively small Italy (with Sardinia and Sicily) seems to have produced the largest number of saints. Italy alone produced almost as

COUNTRIES OF BIRTH AND DEATH

Table 17

Geographical Distribution of Saints at Birth

	Number of individuals	Percentage of total	Percentage of known
British Isles	352	11.4	21.8
Western Europe	437	14.1	27.0
Italy	429	13.9	26.5
Central Europe	132	4.3	8.2
Scandinavia and the Baltic lands	19	.6	1.1
Asia	161	5.2	10.0
Africa	82	2.7	5.1
Orient	2	.1	0.1
North and South America	4	.1	0.2
Unknown	1,472	47.6	
Total	3,090	100.0	100.0

Table 18

Geographical Distribution of Saints at Death

	Number of individuals	Percentage of total	Percentage of known
British Isles	125	4.0	15.7
Western Europe	188	6.1	23.7
Italy	215	7.0	27.2
Central Europe	55	1.8	7.0
Scandinavia and the Baltic lands	7	.2	0.9
Asia	114	3.7	14.3
Africa	63	2.0	8.0
Orient	24	.8	3.0
North and South America	2	.1	0.2
Unknown	2,297	74.3	
Total	3,090	100.0	100.0

CHRISTIAN-CATHOLIC SAINTS

many saints as the whole of Western Europe (Spain, Portugal, France, Germany, Belgium, Holland, and Switzerland), more than the British Isles, and more than Central Europe, Scandinavia, the Baltic countries, Asia, the Orient, Africa, and North and South America taken together. This record rate of production of saints by Italy is primarily due to the fact that Italy has been the seat of the Roman Catholic Papacy, and, through Rome, one of the two earliest centers of Christianity (the other being Palestine). Either because the highest authority of the Catholic Church granted sanctification more liberally to its Italian members, who were near to it and were its direct agents, than to those Christians who were remote from it; or because the seat of the highest authority of the Catholic Church attracted to it and to the near-by areas of Italy many potential saints—whichever of these reasons was operative (and in all probability both played important rôles), the fact of the unique productivity of saints on the part of Italy—greater in absolute number and per million of the population than in any other country—is clear.

This fact furnishes an example of a much more general sociological uniformity, namely: *almost any vast organized group—the state, academies of arts and sciences, occupational unions, business corporations, etc.—tends to grant its privileges and honors more liberally to those members who are near the seat of the highest authority of that group and are its direct and indirect agents.* A monarchical state grants its favors mainly to courtiers who are at the court and palaces of the sovereign. So also does a republican state: it grants its favors mainly to those who are near the seat of its power and are agents of its highest authority. The same is true of business firms, occupational unions, universities, academies of arts and sciences, and virtually any other large organized group. Members who live far from the seat of its highest authority, and who are not direct—or even indirect—agents, have little if any chance to receive a favor, honor, or privilege. The farther and more remote they are—spatially, socially, culturally, or politically—from the central authority of a group, the less their chances for promotion, honors, or even sanctification. Italy's leadership in the production of saints seems to conform to this general rule. In various parts of this planet there have probably been hundreds of the most saintly Catholics deserving official sanctification; yet because they were far from the seat of Catholicism, they remained unsanctified officially.

Next to Italy comes Western Europe. Its total share is slightly higher than that of Italy, but this is the combined share of seven countries, most of which are still predominantly Catholic.

The third place is accorded the British Isles: before the Reformation all three countries produced a large number of saints; after the Reformation, Ireland continued to produce a large number of Catholic saints, while the predominantly Protestant England and Scotland decreased their production—or produced Catholic saints mainly as martyrs who suffered from Protestant persecution and were sanctified for this suffering and for their faithfulness to the Catholic Church.

The fourth place is accorded to Asia, mainly because of Jerusalem and Palestine, where Christianity originated and produced a large number of great saints during its first few heroic centuries.

Only the fifth place belongs to Central Europe, though it is made up of some fourteen or fifteen countries, and though Poland, Austria, Hungary, and partly even Lithuania and Czechoslovakia remained mainly Catholic. It is interesting to note that the Slavic countries produced very few Catholic saints, and Russia did not produce any worthy of Catholic sanctification.

The sixth place belongs to Africa: during the first few centuries of Christianity a notable number of the Church Fathers, such as Saint Augustine, Origen, and Tertullian, were born and lived chiefly in Northern Africa. The African share of the saints was supplied mainly during these early centuries.

Only the seventh place belongs to Scandinavian and Baltic countries. Even before the Reformation only a few of their Christians were sanctified. After the Reformation, which made these countries overwhelmingly Protestant, their share of Catholic saints fell almost to the zero point.

Finally, only two saints were born in China and Japan, and only four in North and South America. If for non-Christian China and Japan this low figure is not strange, for the whole American continent, which produced only four saints, although most of its countries have been Catholic for at least five centuries, the record is exceptionally low. The remoteness of America from the Papal See; the secondary importance of American Catholics for the Catholic Church and the secular empire powers up to the nineteenth century; non-lobbying or less lobbying on the part of Americans before the Vatican for the sanctification of their Christians [1]—these and other factors are responsible for this illiberality of the Church in the sanctification of American Christians. Whatever the factors, the fact of the exceptionally small share of Catholic saints supplied by the Americas (before 1920) is clear.[2]

If we ask whether there have been notable changes in the

---

[1] In most cases, the initiative in sanctification of this or that worthy Christian comes not from the Church and its hierarchy, but from various local Christians who think that good deeds, martyrdom, and miracles on the part of such Christians deserve sanctification. The Vatican and other high authorities play in most cases a conservative, testing rôle: only after rigid investigation do they sanction the lobbying of the initiators of sanctification. For the procedure, tests, and investigation of beatification and sanctification, see Thurston-Butler's Lives of the Saints, Vol. XII, Appendix; H. Delehaye, Sanctus, ch. iv; and his Les Origines du Culte des Martyrs.

[2] At the present, when American Catholics are the principal financial source for support of the Catholic Church and the Vatican, when the rôle of the Americas, especially the United States, in the destinies of the Catholic Church, as well as for the whole of mankind, is paramount, the hierarchy of the Catholic Church is rapidly increasing the number of its high dignitaries in the Americas, and also the number of the saints among American Catholics. If this policy of a more liberal sanctification of American Catholics is continued —and such seems to be the trend—then the share of the Americas is bound to increase in the coming decades.

geographic distribution of the saints according to the country of birth during the twenty centuries of Christianity, the answer is given by Tables 19 and 20.

These tables, especially the percentual one, show that since the fifteenth century the Scandinavian and Baltic countries have not produced one single saint; that the same is true of the Americas and the Orient after the seventeenth and eighteenth centuries; that Asia, mainly Palestine, contributed its greatest share in the first century of our era, showing the highest percentage among all countries in that century (21.3) and rivaling Italy during the first five centuries of our era, after which period its rôle steadily fell until the tenth century, when a spurt in the production of saints occurred; that during the last ten centuries, the rôle of Asia, including Palestine, has fallen sharply to 1 per cent, more or less.

The curve of productivity of Africa is somewhat different. As has been pointed out, Africa contributed its greatest share of saints during the third, fourth, and fifth centuries of our era, when a notable proportion of the Church Fathers and Christian leaders came from Northern Africa (Saint Augustine, Origen, Tertullian, *et al.*). After the fifth century the African contribution fell sharply, fluctuating between zero and 2 per cent during the subsequent centuries from the sixth to the twentieth.

The contribution of Italy was significant from the first to the eleventh century, when it fluctuated between 3 and 14 per cent; after the tenth century it notably increased, fluctuating between 15 and 45 per cent, and reaching in the twentieth century (up to about 1910), 100 per cent. The exceptional liberality in the sanctification of Italian-born Catholics appeared not with the beginning of Christianity, but only after the tenth century; since that time it has increased, with minor fluctuations.

As for the British Isles, their production of saints shows two maximum periods: first, the sixth to eighth centuries

Table 19
Geographical Distribution of Saints at Birth by Century

Century	1	2	3	4	5	6	7	8	9	10	11	12	13	14	15	16	17	18	19	20
British Isles	2	2	1	5	15	54	54	45	12	8	12	19	9	2	2	73	26	1	3	—
Western Europe	—	2	14	17	15	44	42	29	24	12	19	36	38	18	22	21	38	8	22	—
Italy	6	14	26	27	18	14	15	5	17	2	18	19	47	60	54	33	20	20	10	1
Central Europe	4	4	10	23	8	4	3	5	7	4	11	5	12	11	6	4	6	2	4	—
Scandinavia and Baltic lands	—	1	—	—	—	—	—	—	—	1	3	7	—	2	1	—	—	—	—	—
Asia	16	5	14	45	18	11	2	2	7	7	3	2	2	2	1	—	1	1	1	—
Africa	1	2	13	35	14	4	8	4	—	—	3	—	—	1	2	1	—	—	1	—
Orient	—	—	—	—	—	—	3	2	—	—	—	—	—	—	—	—	2	—	—	—
North and South America	—	—	—	—	—	—	—	—	—	—	—	—	—	—	—	—	—	—	—	—
Unknown	46	68	158	251	120	97	138	79	52	32	51	64	80	48	31	65	3	1	—	—
																	26	19	12	1
Total by centuries	75	98	236	403	208	228	265	171	119	66	120	152	188	144	119	197	122	52	53	1

Table 20
Percentual Geographical Distribution of Saints at Birth by Century

Century	1	2	3	4	5	6	7	8	9	10	11	12	13	14	15	16	17	18	19	20
British Isles	2.7	2.0	0.4	1.2	7.2	23.7	20.4	26.3	10.1	12.1	10.0	12.5	4.8	1.4	1.7	37.2	21.3	1.9	5.7	—
Western Europe	—	2.0	5.9	4.2	7.2	19.3	15.8	17.0	20.2	18.2	15.8	23.7	20.2	12.5	18.5	10.7	31.2	15.4	41.5	—
Italy	8.0	14.3	11.0	6.7	8.7	6.1	5.7	2.9	14.3	3.0	15.0	12.5	25.0	41.7	45.4	16.6	16.4	40.5	18.9	100.0
Central Europe	5.3	4.1	4.2	5.7	3.8	1.8	1.1	2.9	5.9	6.1	9.2	3.3	6.4	6.9	5.0	2.0	4.9	3.8	7.5	—
Scandinavia and Baltic lands	—	1.0	—	—	—	—	0.8	1.2	—	1.5	2.5	4.6	—	1.4	0.8	—	—	—	—	—
Asia	21.3	5.1	5.9	11.2	8.7	4.8	3.0	2.3	5.9	10.6	2.5	1.3	1.1	1.4	0.8	—	0.8	1.9	1.9	—
Africa	1.3	2.0	5.5	8.7	6.7	1.8	1.1	1.2	—	—	2.5	—	—	0.7	1.7	0.5	1.6	—	1.9	—
Orient	—	—	—	—	—	—	—	—	—	—	—	—	—	—	—	—	—	—	—	—
North and South America	—	—	—	—	—	—	—	—	—	—	—	—	—	—	—	—	2.5	0.7	—	—
Unknown	61.4	69.5	67.1	62.3	57.7	42.5	52.1	46.2	43.6	48.5	42.5	42.1	42.5	32.6	26.1	33.0	21.3	37.2	22.6	—

Each vertical column totals 100 per cent.

inclusive, when their share became the greatest among all countries; their production again became the greatest in the sixteenth century and very high in the seventeenth. The history of the British Isles indicates that the first period was that of the blossoming of Christian culture in the British Isles, especially in Ireland, while the second was that of civil wars and religious conflicts between Catholics and Protestants: many a Catholic fell a victim in these conflicts, was martyred, and was then sanctified by the Catholic Church.

The religious wars and the conflicts of Catholics with Protestants are also largely responsible for the production in the seventeenth century of the second greatest number of saints in Western Europe. The highest percentage for the nineteenth century in this region is also due largely to the conflict between the Catholic forces and the forces of secularization of culture, school education, of separation of State from Church, and so on. In the conflict, many a Catholic was stimulated to exert himself for the protection of the Church's interests and of good deeds; a considerable number of them fell victim in the struggle, acquired a halo of martyrdom, and were eventually sanctified. Such, in brief, is the reason why the periods of religious wars and sharp social conflicts (in which an influential church always becomes involved) are marked by a sudden and sharp increase of saints. (See, below, the discussion of martyrdom.)

The contributions of Western Europe, though modest during the first five centuries of our era, notably increased beginning with the sixth century, and then fluctuated on a high level up to the seventeenth and nineteenth centuries, when their share reached its maximum.

The contributions of Central Europe fluctuated between 1 and 9 per cent throughout the nineteen centuries (9.2 per cent in the eleventh century).

These remarks show that our tables reflect the main processes and changes in the history of Christianity and Christian countries. Among other things the tables show the shifts of Christian centers of saintliness from region to region. If anything, these centers shift in time from Palestine to Africa and Italy; then to the British Isles and Western Europe; then from country to country, up to the aforesaid trend of increasing contributions of the Americas in recent years.[3]

The data concerning the *country of death* of the saints warrant the following conclusions:

Italy holds the first place among all the countries of the world for the number of saints who died there. Its percentage is even higher than in the case of the saints born in Italy (27.2 per cent by death and 26.5 per cent by birth among the saints whose places of birth and death are known). This increase in the percentage of saints who died in Italy is especially significant when one observes that practically all the other regions of Europe considerably decreased their percentage of saints by death in comparison with those of saints by birth. Thus the British Isles' percentage decreased from 21.8 per cent for births to 15.7 for deaths; that of Western Europe, from 27 per cent by birth to 23.7 by death. Similarly the percentages of Central Europe and the Scandinavian countries fell from 8.2 and 1.1, respectively, to 7.0 and 0.9 for deaths.

This means that a certain proportion of the saints born in Western Europe, Central Europe, the British Isles, and the Scandinavian countries migrated and died elsewhere. The countercurrent of the saints coming to these European regions from elsewhere was somewhat thinner than the current of emigration from these countries. The result is that a smaller number of saints died in these regions than were born there.

Italy occupies a different position. A number of the saints born there also migrated and died in other places. But this

---

[3] For the shift of cultural systems, the centers of creativity, and the center of history from region to region in the course of time, see my *Society, Culture, and Personality*, pp. 547ff., and chap. xxxvii; also my *Dynamics*, Vol. IV, chap. iv.

stream of emigration of Italian-born saints was amply counterbalanced by the stream of immigration into Italy of saints born elsewhere. The result is the prevalence of the number of saints dying in Italy over the number born there. The main reason for this attraction of the saints to Italy is, first of all, its being the seat of the highest Catholic authority, with its vast administrative machinery, requiring many faithful agents and members. Some of the saints born outside of Italy were bidden to come and work there; others came by themselves for various reasons, ranging from a petition to the pope to a pilgrimage to Rome and the Vatican as the cradle and center of Catholic Christianity. Other parts of Europe, having no seat of Catholicism, sent more saints beyond their borders than they attracted.

The data show where the saints died who were born in all parts of Europe (except Italy). These are the countries whose death percentage of saints exceeds their birth percentage.

Such a region of the immigration of saints is Asia, with its 10 per cent of native saints and 14.3 per cent of saints who died there; Africa, with its 5.1 per cent for the births and 8 per cent for the deaths of the saints; the Orient, with percentages of 0.1 and 3. These continents were the regions of the immigration and death of a portion of the saints born in Europe. They were the saints who did missionary work among the non-Christian populations of Asia, Africa, and the Orient.

As to significant changes in the course of the centuries, the answer is supplied by Tables 21 and 22. Here are some of the points revealed by these tables:

Asia—mainly Palestine, Egypt, and the Middle East—occupied the first place according to the percentage of deaths of saints during the first, second, and fourth centuries of our era. Then its percentage sharply declined, remaining at zero for several centuries. However, beginning with the sixteenth century, Asia and the Orient (China and Japan) began to increase this percentage, and in the nineteenth century these Asiatic regions together regained first place in the number of saints dying within their bounds. This means that the missionary activities of the Catholic Church in Asia were greatly increased during these centuries—an ever-increasing number of the saints being sent there from Europe and remaining until their death.

The largest percentage of the deaths of saints in Africa occurred during the third, fourth, and fifth centuries. After that the curve declines, often reaching zero. In the nineteenth century the percentage increases. This means that during that century the Catholic Church increased its missionary activity in Africa, though not to the same extent that it did in Asia and the Orient in general.

The Scandinavian countries, which stopped producing saints after the fifteenth century, ceased being their place of death after the twelfth century.

The maximal centuries for the British Isles in this respect were the sixteenth and the seventeenth centuries: almost all the British Catholic martyrs and possibly some of the Catholics from the Continent died in these isles.

For Western Europe the maximal century was the eighteenth; for Central Europe, the fourteenth and the third; for Italy the twentieth, the fifteenth, and the third.

As mentioned before, the central fact in this respect in the last two centuries has been the exodus of saints from Europe, chiefly for increased missionary work in Asia, Africa, and elsewhere. For many such missionaries their departure was permanent.

The events of recent years, with a notable revolution sweeping over Asia and other parts of the world, have led to the weakening of this missionary migration from Europe, if not to its complete cessation. Its future depends upon the basic processes of revolutionary and evolutionary changes throughout the world.

CHRISTIAN-CATHOLIC SAINTS

Table 21

Geographical Distribution of Saints at Death by Century

Century	1	2	3	4	5	6	7	8	9	10	11	12	13	14	15	16	17	18	19	20
British Isles	—	1	—	2	5	7	7	6	3	1	1	—	4	1	1	64	17	—	1	—
Western Europe	1	7	13	17	8	9	12	13	6	7	8	8	10	9	8	25	3	18	6	—
Italy	3	10	41	38	3	10	1	4	2	—	10	6	23	14	21	9	4	4	2	1
Central Europe	2	3	13	9	—	—	3	2	1	1	—	1	4	8	3	1	3	—	—	—
Scandinavia and Baltic lands	—	—	—	—	—	—	—	—	—	—	—	—	—	—	—	—	—	—	—	—
Asia	7	—	—	—	—	—	1	1	—	—	3	2	—	—	—	—	—	—	2	—
Africa	—	11	11	54	4	6	3	2	5	—	—	—	1	1	—	5	2	1	1	—
Orient	—	—	19	27	9	1	1	1	1	—	—	—	1	1	—	—	1	—	1	—
North and South America	—	—	1	—	—	—	—	—	1	—	—	—	—	—	—	1	9	1	11	—
Unknown	62	66	138	256	179	195	238	142	100	57	98	135	145	110	86	92	82	27	30	—
Total by centuries	75	98	236	403	208	228	265	171	119	66	120	152	188	144	119	197	122	52	53	1

Table 22
Percentual Geographical Distribution of Saints at Death by Century

Century	1	2	3	4	5	6	7	8	9	10	11	12	13	14	15	16	17	18	19	20
British Isles	—	1.0	—	0.5	2.4	3.1	2.6	3.5	2.5	1.5	0.8	—	2.1	0.7	0.8	32.5	13.9	—	1.9	—
Western Europe	1.3	7.1	5.5	4.2	3.8	3.9	4.5	7.6	5.0	10.6	6.7	5.3	5.3	6.2	6.7	12.7	2.5	34.6	11.3	—
Italy	4.0	10.2	17.4	9.4	1.4	4.4	0.4	2.3	1.7	—	8.3	3.9	12.2	9.7	17.6	4.6	3.3	7.7	3.8	100.0
Central Europe	2.7	3.1	5.5	2.2	—	—	0.8	1.2	0.8	1.5	—	0.7	2.1	5.6	2.5	0.5	2.5	—	—	—
Scandinavia and Baltic lands	—	—	—	—	—	2.6	0.4	0.6	—	—	2.5	1.3	—	—	—	—	—	—	—	—
Asia	9.3	11.2	4.7	13.4	1.9	—	1.1	1.2	4.2	—	—	—	0.5	0.7	—	2.5	1.6	1.9	3.8	—
Africa	—	—	8.1	6.7	4.3	0.4	0.4	0.6	0.8	—	—	—	0.5	0.7	—	—	0.8	—	1.9	—
Orient	—	—	0.4	—	—	—	—	—	0.8	—	—	—	—	—	—	0.5	7.4	1.9	20.8	—
North and South America	—	—	—	—	—	—	—	—	—	—	—	—	—	—	—	—	0.8	.8	—	—
Unknown	82.7	67.4	58.4	63.6	86.2	85.6	89.8	83.0	84.2	86.4	81.7	88.8	77.3	76.4	72.4	46.7	67.2	53.1	56.5	—

Each vertical column totals 100 per cent.

29. CLASS ORIGINS

It is interesting to inquire what has been the social, economic, and occupational background of the saints. From what kind of social groups, determined by the position of their parental family, did the saints come and in what proportion?

We have divided the social orders, classes, and occupational, economic, and political strata of the parental families of the saints into the following ten categories, each category embracing the specified detailed divisions:

1. Wealthy royalty: king, queen, prince, princess
2. Wealthy nobility (including the ruling class in the sense of leaders): knight, governor, senator, head of the state, court official, lord, earl, count, viscount, Mercian chief, praetor, prefect of Rome, prefect of Gaul, chief of Thormond, general, patrician
3. Indigent nobility: includes once wealthy nobles who lost their riches but retained their titles
4. Wealthy middle class: proconsul, physician, commissariat officer, tax-gatherer for the Romans, politician, cloth and wool merchant, silk-weaver, banker, silversmith, burgher, master mariner, master shoemaker, mayor, distinguished scholar, bourgeois, actress, Constantinople official, persecutor
5. Middle class: centurion, poet, notary, entertainer, musician, bishop, lector, parson, deacon, priest, saint, army officer, apothecary, bard, schoolmaster, public orator, soldier
6. Peasant class (primarily indigent, with some prosperous): peasant (owner of small farm), shepherd, gooseherd, olive-cultivator, herdsman, proprietor of small vineyards, cooper, cowherd
7. Working class: brass-worker, coppersmith, blacksmith,

locksmith, cobbler, wool-dyer, saddler, tailor, bookseller, stonemason, miller, cartwright, weaver, carpenter, laborer, watchmaker, shoemaker
8. Slaves, serfs: includes freedmen
9. Servant class: page, steward, eunuch, agricultural laborers on a large estate
10. Fishermen
11. Unknown

Nothing definite is known as to the social background of 1,810 saints, or 58.6 per cent.

Table 23

Class Status of Saints

	Number of individuals	Percentage of total	Percentage of known
Wealthy royalty	215	7.0	16.8
Wealthy nobility	566	18.3	44.2
Indigent nobility	13	.4	1.0
Wealthy middle class	177	5.7	13.8
Middle class	137	4.4	10.7
Peasant class	92	3.0	7.2
Working class	40	1.3	3.1
Slaves, serfs	16	.5	1.3
Servant class	19	.6	1.5
Fishermen	5	.2	0.4
Unknown	1,810	58.6	
Total	3,090	100.0	100.0

This table shows that some 62 per cent of the saints came from the ranks of royalty and the upper nobility strata; some 24.5 per cent were supplied by the middle strata; and only some 13 per cent emerged from the vast free, unfree, and semi-free lower strata: peasants, artisans, and craftsmen, slaves, and serfs. Only about 0.4 per cent came from fisherman families, showing a smaller result than one might guess by reading the Scriptures and the lives of the saints.

So far as the saints, on the whole, are men and women of

genius in the field of religious and ethical creativity, these data are in substantial agreement with the socio-economic background of the men and women of genius in all fields of creative activity—science, philosophy, the fine arts, economics, and politics. The overwhelming majority of all leaders come from the upper and then the middle social strata; only a small minority come from the lower classes. Thus, in England 63 per cent of men of genius were produced by the upper, the ecclesiastical and the professional strata, and only 2.5 per cent by artisans and unskilled labor, and 6.5 per cent by farmers and yeomen. The data are similar in respect to eminent persons, creative geniuses, and notable leaders in France, Germany, Russia, and in practically all studies of men of genius and leaders in general.[1]

In all these studies the share of the men and women of genius produced by royalty is extraordinarily high, practically the highest of all the social groups.[2] The contribution of royalty to Catholic sainthood is perhaps even higher than in most other fields of creative genius. Very high also is the share of nobility. A considerable but much more modest share is represented by the middle, commercial, and professional strata. Their contributions to sainthood seem to be somewhat smaller than to several other forms of creative genius (the arts, sciences, etc.).

The contribution of the peasant class to sainthood is about the same as that of the Russian peasants to the class of Russian eminent scientists and scholars (7.9 per cent). It is close to the peasants' share in the production of genius in various other fields. A widely accepted opinion that sainthood (and the clergy's occupation) has been a more accessible channel to peasants for social climbing than many others is not sup-

---

[1] For the actual figures and a discussion, see my *Social Mobility* (New York, 1927), chap. xii; and my *Contemporary Sociological Theories*, pp. 279ff.
[2] *Ibid.*; also my "Monarchs and Rulers," in *Social Forces*, September, 1925, and March, 1926.

ported by our data when all centuries are considered. It is correct, however, when the last two centuries, the nineteenth and the twentieth, are considered; as we shall see, the peasant and working-class shares of the saints in these centuries greatly increased and exceeded the contributions of these classes to genius in all other fields.[3]

Such an opinion is more accurate in regard to the slaves, servants, and serfs. Their share in Catholic sainthood (2.8 per cent) seems to be larger than in most other fields of creative genius. For instance, up to 1920 in such a democratic country as the United States, not a single leading man of science came from the groups of domestic servants or the class of day laborers.[4] Though occasionally in the past an emperor or other person of creative genius emerged from the slaves and serfs, yet such instances have been rare and in most of the fields less than 2.8 per cent. Considering that at its earliest period the Christian Church was open to slaves; that slaves made a notable part of its members and could climb to the positions of priests and even bishops; that after the legalization of the Church, a slave becoming a priest was by this very act a free person; considering these and similar conditions it is easily comprehensible why "climbing the ladder of the Church" was an easier way for the slaves and serfs to climb to sainthood than to many other forms of creative genius. The door of the Church stood open to slaves and serfs mainly in the first few

---

[3] As we shall see, the percentage of saints supplied by the peasant and working classes in the nineteenth and twentieth centuries increased to about 60 and 100 per cent of all the saints of these centuries. Meanwhile, in other fields of creative genius, the contributions of these classes during these centuries either has not increased at all (for instance, in England), or increased very little (in some categories of eminent men and women in France, Germany, Russia, and elsewhere). Even in the contemporary United States, only 21.2 per cent of eminent scientists came from the agricultural class. (For the actual figures see my *Social Mobility*, pp. 282ff.) Thus in recent times the field of sainthood has become more accessible than before to the lower classes and more accessible than other fields of creative genius and leadership. For the reasons and details, see below.

[4] See my *Social Mobility*, p. 288.

centuries of our era. Later on, it became nearly closed and finally shut altogether to slaves and serfs who wished to climb to higher positions in the Church hierarchy and to sainthood.

Such then is the socio-economic, occupational, and political background of the saints. Even in "climbing this ladder" the upper and middle classes have climbed it much more successfully than the lower strata. So far as a saint is empirically a variety of eminent person like an artist, writer, scientist, philosopher, educator or statesman, he is merely a concrete example of a general principle that the production of persons of genius increases as we go from the lower to the higher strata and decreases as we go from the higher to the lower strata.

If we ask whether there have been any changes in the social background of the saints in the course of time, the answer is given by Tables 24 and 25. The changes in the production of various strata are largely the result of the changes in the social structure of Western society—of the rise and decline of these classes in the course of twenty centuries. The following deductions may be drawn:

1. After the sixteenth century the *stratum of slaves and serfs* ceased to contribute any share, because this stratum largely disappeared in almost all Western societies except the Americas and Russia. Another point is that slaves and serfs showed the highest percentage of saints in the first three centuries of our era, in the heroic centuries of the Christian Church. After the third century the slaves' share declines to the zero point in several centuries and to somewhat below 1 per cent in other periods. Main reasons for this are: the strong disapproval of slavery and serfdom on the part of the Christian Church; a perfectly open door for the slaves and serfs into the Christian community of the first few centuries; the lack of discrimination against the slaves and serfs on the part of the Christians; and a considerable influx of slaves and serfs into the Christian Church during the first centuries A.D. As a

result, a considerable number of slaves became deacons, priests, leaders, or even bishops. These conditions, plus the lack of discrimination against enslaved Christians, permitted Christian slaves to elevate themselves to saintliness and eventually to become officially sanctified.

Later on, when the Church and its hierarchy became one of the most privileged, powerful, and wealthy groups, its attitude towards slavery and serfdom changed considerably. The hierarchy itself became one of the largest masters of a group of semi-dependent, semi-free people (virtually serfs). Under these circumstances the disapproval of serfdom was toned down, some Church authorities even justifying it as a God-sanctioned institution. The discrimination against serfs increased, and their climbing of the Church ladder became much more difficult. As a result, the rise of slaves and serfs to hierarchical positions of the Church and sainthood declined. Hence the decrease and complete dying out of the contribution of serfs in later centuries.

2. The share of royalty was largest during the sixth to the fifteenth centuries inclusive. After that its share rapidly declined, disappearing after the eighteenth century. This disappearance is due mainly to the increasing obsolescence of royalty and monarchy. For this reason contributions of royalty to all fields of genius have decreased in recent centuries. The decrease of royalty's share after the thirteenth and fifteenth centuries is due mainly to three mutually connected factors: (a) the increasing deviation from Catholicism of many Christian countries and of their royal dynasties. The separation of Eastern and Western Christianity in the eleventh century made heretical all the dynasties that did not recognize the supreme authority of the pontiff. The Carolingian Renaissance, increasing heresies, and finally the Reformation made several countries and their dynasties Protestant and therefore ineligible for sainthood in the Catholic Church. (b) After

CHRISTIAN-CATHOLIC SAINTS

Table 24
Socio-economic Distribution of Saints by Century

Century	1	2	3	4	5	6	7	8	9	10	11	12	13	14	15	16	17	18	19	20
Wealthy Royalty	5	—	5	2	8	32	42	27	11	14	11	10	20	6	9	6	2	2	—	—
Wealthy Nobility	7	19	32	31	27	33	60	30	25	20	35	51	51	43	37	26	30	6	3	—
Indigent Nobility	—	—	—	—	—	—	2	—	—	—	2	1	—	1	—	—	—	1	1	—
Wealthy Middle	2	3	11	21	17	11	8	5	6	5	4	9	14	18	14	9	9	5	3	—
Middle	1	1	11	19	11	9	11	4	5	2	4	5	9	4	6	13	13	4	3	—
Peasant	1	—	1	2	1	5	1	—	3	1	4	6	8	14	9	8	12	5	9	1
Working	—	—	—	2	2	1	2	—	—	—	—	2	1	3	5	7	2	3	8	—
Slave	2	3	4	2	—	1	1	—	1	—	1	—	—	—	—	1	—	—	—	—
Servant	—	1	1	2	2	1	—	1	—	—	—	—	3	—	1	5	1	1	1	—
Fisherman	2	—	—	—	—	—	—	—	—	—	—	—	—	—	—	—	—	—	—	—
Unknown	55	71	171	322	140	135	138	104	68	24	59	68	82	55	38	121	49	25	25	—
Total by centuries	75	98	236	403	208	228	265	171	119	66	120	152	188	144	119	197	122	52	53	1

Table 25
Percentual Socio-economic Distribution of Saints by Century

Century	1	2	3	4	5	6	7	8	9	10	11	12	13	14	15	16	17	18	19	20
Wealthy Royalty	6.7	—	2.1	0.5	3.8	14.0	15.8	15.8	9.2	21.2	9.2	6.6	10.6	4.2	7.6	3.0	1.6	3.8	—	
Wealthy Nobility	9.3	19.4	13.6	7.7	13.0	14.5	22.6	17.5	21.0	30.3	29.2	33.6	27.1	29.9	31.1	13.2	24.6	11.5	5.7	
Indigent Nobility	—	—	—	—	—	—	0.8	—	—	—	1.7	0.7	—	0.7	—	—	3.3	1.9	1.9	—
Wealthy Middle	2.7	3.1	4.7	5.2	8.2	4.8	3.0	2.9	5.0	7.6	3.3	5.9	7.4	12.5	11.8	4.6	7.4	9.6	5.7	
Middle	1.3	1.0	4.7	4.7	5.3	3.9	4.2	2.3	4.2	3.0	3.3	3.3	4.8	2.8	5.0	6.6	10.7	7.7	5.7	
Peasant	1.3	—	0.4	0.5	0.5	2.2	0.4	—	2.5	1.5	3.3	3.9	4.3	9.7	7.6	4.1	9.8	9.6	17.0	
Working	—	—	—	0.5	1.0	0.4	0.8	—	—	—	—	1.3	0.5	2.1	4.2	3.6	1.6	5.8	15.1	100.0
Slave	2.7	3.1	1.7	0.5	—	0.4	0.4	—	0.8	—	0.8	—	—	—	—	0.5	—	—	—	—
Servant	—	—	0.4	0.5	1.0	0.4	—	0.6	—	—	—	—	1.6	—	0.8	2.5	.8	1.9	1.9	—
Fisherman	2.7	1.0	—	—	—	0.4	—	—	—	—	—	—	—	—	—	0.5	—	—	—	—
Unknown	73.3	72.4	72.4	79.9	67.2	59.0	52.0	60.9	57.3	36.4	49.2	44.7	43.7	38.1	31.9	61.4	40.2	48.2	47.0	—

Each vertical column totals 100 per cent.

the thirteenth century we observe a decline of the supremacy of the spiritual power (the Papal See) over the secular power, and the growth of the power of monarchical dynasties. This led in many cases to conflicts between the Papal See and the monarchs. Royal families that were open or secret enemies of the pope could obviously not expect sanctification by the pope. (c) After the thirteenth, and especially after the fifteenth century, the whole Western world became increasingly secular, or sensate. Royal families were no exception to this general rule. They began to care less and less about sanctity as an ideal state, and more and more about worldly values, such as lust for power, wealth, fame, material comfort, sexual indulgence, and other pleasures. A smaller and smaller number of royalty led saintly lives. As a result a smaller number were sanctified. These three reasons explain the essentials of the decreasing trend of royalty in this respect. The increasing disappearance of royalty after the eighteenth century clinches the process and brings to zero royalty's contribution to the saints in the nineteenth and twentieth centuries.

3. The fluctuations in the curve of saints derived from the nobility are similar. The nobility's greatest contribution to sainthood was during the sixth to the fifteenth centuries inclusive. After that the percentage of saints from the nobility sharply declined, reaching 5.7 per cent in the nineteenth century and zero in the twentieth century. The reason for this decline is about the same as for that of royalty: the increasing disappearance of the nobility as a class after the eighteenth century; the secularization of values and ways of life of the nobility after the fifteenth century; the increase of the non-Catholic nobility in many countries, especially after the Reformation; and so on.

4. The curve of *indigent-nobility* saints is somewhat different: it tends to increase slightly in the later centuries rather than to decrease. Poverty, hardships, failure to obtain power,

honors, and a luxurious way of life, along with the memories of past grandeur, seem to have induced a *portion* of such impoverished nobility to look for the imperishable values of the Kingdom of God and of a saintly way of life. According to the law of polarization, becoming more religious, more altruistic, and more saintly is a regular occurrence with one portion of a population subjected to catastrophes, calamities, sorrow, grief, and frustration (while another portion becomes more sinful and selfish). An increasing devotion to the saintly life on the part of a declining or frustrate nobility (in the face of those becoming more sinful, less religious, and less moral) is a typical example of a much more general rule.[5]

5. As to the *wealthy middle and the middle classes*, in general their share in contributing to Catholic sainthood fluctuates throughout the nineteen centuries considered, without any clear trend as we pass from the first to the twentieth century. However, it is to be noted that the centuries of the maximal production of saints by the wealthy, more privileged middle strata are the fourteenth and the fifteenth, while those by the less elevated middle strata are the sixteenth, seventeenth, and eighteenth. In the nineteenth century both kinds of middle classes yield a much lower percentage of saints. These maximal centuries are comprehensible: the fourteenth and the fifteenth centuries were the age of the emergence of the bourgeoisie and the urban professional groups, intermixed with middle-class government officials; in the sixteenth and seventeenth centuries the West witnessed a rise of the middle-strata clergy and moderate bourgeoisie, and a further rise of the intelligentsia and professional groups.

During these centuries the bulk of these strata still remained essentially religious, with sanctity as the highest goal man could attain. This elevation of the middle strata, with the

---
[5] For the law of polarization, see my *Man and Society in Calamity* (New York, 1942), chaps. ix–xii.

preservation of religious ideals and values, explains why the highest percentage of saints from these middle strata were contributed during these centuries. The social power and prestige of the middle strata did not decline after the eighteenth century. If anything they rose still higher; but the system of values of these strata sharply changed: from the religious-ideational system of values of the medieval centuries it gave place to a system of predominantly secular, sensate, material values of wealth, power, pleasures, and fame. From the standpoint of this new sensate system of values, sanctity ceased to be a notable value; now and then saints were "debunked" by some of the spokesmen for the middle strata as "madmen," "superstitious fanatics," "insane," "sadists," and "masochists." This led to decreasing efforts to emulate saintliness in the achievements and conduct of the middle strata; and all this resulted in a decisive decrease of saints contributed by the middle classes in the eighteenth and nineteenth centuries, with zero for the twentieth century.

6. If the share of saints decreased after the thirteenth century for royalty, after the fifteenth and the seventeenth centuries for the nobility, and after the fifteenth and eighteenth for the middle classes, then evidently the contributions of the lower classes must have increased during the latest two centuries in order to make 100 per cent. This we find to be the case. The contributions of the peasant and working classes were comparatively very low during the first centuries of Christianity and remained low up to about the fourteenth century.[6] After that, with minor fluctuations, they began slowly to rise, until in the nineteenth century they reached an unprecedented height. *In the nineteenth century the lower classes contributed some 60 per cent of all the saints, and in*

---

[6] It took some 400 to 600 years for the conversion of the peasants to Christianity after the upper and middle urban strata had become Christian. The resistance of the peasants to Christianity was so great that their Latin name *pagani* became a synonym of "pagan," or "non-Christian."

the twentieth century, 100 per cent. Thus the rôles of the upper and lower classes became reversed: during the first centuries of Christianity royalty and nobility contributed some 60 to 70 per cent of the saints, whereas the peasants, the working classes, the fishermen, and the slave-servant strata contributed about 15 to 25 per cent. In the nineteenth century the contributions of the peasant and working classes reached 60 per cent, whereas that of royalty and the nobility fell to a mere 14 per cent. In the twentieth century (up to roughly 1910) the peasant class contributed 100 per cent of the saints. This is a rather significant reversal! *Whereas in the early and medieval centuries saints were recruited mainly from the highest strata, in the democratic centuries of the nineteenth and twentieth they were recruited mainly, if not exclusively, from the lower classes of peasants and urban workers.* Thus the changes in the socio-economic background of the saints reflect the basic changes in the rise and fall of various social strata, classes, and groups.

The preceding analysis and tables warrant the following generalizations:

First, each social stratum, class, estate or caste tends to contribute its share of the saints during the periods of its maximal power and prestige. When the power of a given social stratum or group begins to decline, its contribution of saints begins to decline also.

Second, in regard to the Catholic saints, we notice an interesting "law of lag" or "succession" of strata in the production of the saints. This "law" is a consequence of the preceding generalization. In an abbreviated form it may be seen in Table 26.

As we go from royalty at the top of the social pyramid to the lower peasant and working classes at the bottom, we see that royalty had its maximal period of production of saints earlier even than the nobility and other lower strata, and the period

Table 26

Strata	Period of maximal production of saints (by centuries)	Other short-lived periods (by centuries)	Period of decisive decline (by centuries)
			After:
Royalty	6th to 11th	13th to 15th	15th
Wealthy nobility	7th to 15th	17th	17th
Indigent nobility	17th	17th	17th
Middle class (wealthy)	14th to 15th	18th	18th
Middle class	16th to 17th	18th	18th
Peasant	17th to 20th	14th	None
Working class	18th to 19th	15th	19th

of a decisive decline of production on the part of royalty set in again earlier than that of the nobility and the still lower classes. The same rule holds in regard to each higher stratum in relation to the lower ones. The maximal period for the lowest peasant and working classes begins in the seventeenth and eighteenth centuries and reaches its climax in the nineteenth and twentieth centuries. For the peasant class there is no sign of a decisive decline in its comparative production of saints. *The higher the stratum, the earlier occurs its maximal production of saints and a decisive decline in production; the lower the stratum, the later it reaches its climax, and the later it begins a decisive decline.*

Thus, here we have a case of a more general rule—namely, that as a rule *the upper classes are the first innovators and importers of the new cultural values in a given society and its culture, and especially the first molders of its highest ideals and values. The lower classes ordinarily lag behind and follow or imitate when the values cease to live and function within the upper classes.* In other words, the stream of innovations in a given society flows from the top to the bottom (in our case from royalty to the peasant and working class). The new highest ideal of sanctity follows this rule.[7] The rule has some exceptions, but they do not annul its general character.

According to the rule, the production of Catholic saints has run its course and reached the very bottom, beyond which it can hardly go without a fundamental change in the whole character of Christian culture and Western civilization. This means that the production of Catholic saints is beginning to cease: the total number of saints from all classes and strata is tending to decrease.

---

[7] For a discussion of this general rule, see my *Dynamics*, Vol. IV, chap. iv; also my *Society, Culture, and Personality*, pp. 564ff.

30. PARENTAL INFLUENCES

The whole life history of any person is still a mystery: it is shaped by so many forces, working in so many diverse constellations, that we can hardly give a satisfactory account of exactly which forces, in what combination, and under what conditions are responsible for the behavior and for the ultimate destiny of that person.

The incompleteness of our knowledge in this field, however, does not mean total ignorance. In a spotty and approximate way we know some of the decisive factors that mold, from earliest childhood, the life and destiny of every human being. One of these forces is parental influence. It is one of the most important factors determining what we are, why we behave as we do, and why our life history is as it is.

In seeking to elucidate the forces that led our saints to sainthood, we naturally begin with parental influence. Did it play an important rôle in the formation of the personality and life destiny of our saints? If so, was this rôle positive or negative, so far as the sainthood of our saints is concerned?

In order to answer these questions, we have divided the attitude of the parents toward the religious and saintly aspirations of their children into four classes: (1) encouraging; (2) indifferent; (3) opposing, but later approving; (4) relentlessly opposing. Out of 3,090 biographies, 2,585 give no definite data on this point. The remaining 505 cases (16.3 per cent of all the cases) yield the data shown in Table 27.

If these 505 cases are representative for the whole group of the saints studied, then the overwhelming majority of the parents played a positive, encouraging rôle in starting their

Table 27

Parental Attitude

	Number of individuals	Percentage of total	Percentage of known
Encouraging	330	10.7	65.3
Indifferent	29	.8	5.7
Opposing; later approving	51	1.7	10.1
Opposing relentlessly	95	3.1	18.9
Unknown	2,585	83.7	
Total	3,090	100.0	100.0

children on the road toward sainthood. Only a minority, from 18 to 28 per cent, opposed the saintly aspirations of their children, and 5 per cent were indifferent. These data suggest that encouraging parental attitudes toward the saintly aspirations of children were a positive factor in the life history of some 65 per cent. On the other hand, the fact that some 35 per cent of the saints became saintly in spite of opposition or indifference on the part of their parents testifies that the parental influence is not decisive and can be overcome by other factors and influences. This conclusion is strongly supported by the fact that 18.9 per cent of the parents strenuously opposed the aspirations of their children to the end. Since this opposition was overcome, other forces evidently proved to be stronger than parental influences. What these forces were is partly answered in subsequent sections.

31. TYPES OF ENTRANCE ON THE ROAD TO SAINTHOOD

If some 35 per cent of the saints started their saintly activities in spite of opposition or indifference on the part of their parents, what were the agencies and forces that helped the saints to overcome parental opposition? If 65 per cent of the saints were encouraged and started by their parents on the road to sainthood, what were the main forms of this encouragement? More generally, what were the principal agencies through which the saints entered upon the road to sainthood? The tables given in this section and the next one partly answer these questions.

The various ways in which the saints entered the road to sainthood may be classified in six main categories:

1. Self-consecration: early consecration to God.
2. Self-consecration in solitude: consecration to God due to induced solitude.
3. Dedication: dedicated to God by parents or others.
4. Holy or religious relatives influencing the saint.
5. Specific personage: education by, influence of, or disciple of, some specific religious individual.
6. Institution: education in some religious institution, such as a monastery or convent.

The expression "self-consecration" refers to all those saints who, while still very young, vowed to serve God and God alone for the rest of their lives. These children were born pious, so to speak. (See the next section.) From the cradle onward, probably under the influence of their parents in some 65 per cent of the cases, they evinced outward signs of piety, such as refusing to indulge in rough games with their friends, being obedient, helping others, and praying ardently. We find youngsters of nine or ten consecrating their virginity to God.

"Self-consecration in solitude" also refers to consecration to God, but with a slightly different connotation. There are many cases of shepherds or cowherds who tended their parents' or neighbors' cattle. While so doing, they were forced to spend many hours and days in isolation with only the sky and the grass and the livestock for company. This situation appears only among the peasant class, of course. This enforced solitude led to a good deal of thought and self-contemplation. Combined with other influences it was a tangible force in their consecration.

"Dedication" also refers to consecration to God. But the consecration is not effected by the individual himself; it is rather performed by someone else, especially his parents. For example, biographies describe many cases where the parents were long childless and vowed that if they had a child they would dedicate him to God's service. Again, there are many cases where some immediate relative, or perhaps the child himself, met with an accident or became ill; and the parents vowed that, if he recovered, they would dedicate him to God.

The term "holy relatives" refers to those individuals who, as a result of having saints, priests, bishops, archbishops, or some other religious persons as parents, uncles, aunts, or other ancestors, were constantly surrounded by a religious environment. Under the influence of these relatives, they too entered upon a religious vocation.

The term "specific personage" is used to refer to the religious or altruistic influence of one special individual, not related, rather than a group of individuals. In some cases the child was deliberately sent to one special person in order to be trained and educated. Or the influence may have been unintentional, as in cases where the child turned to religion after hearing a priest or a bishop deliver a sermon. This brings us to another facet of this category. Occasionally the influencing factor was not the individual who gave the sermon but the sermon itself. Or sometimes the child was influenced by a particular passage or book which he had read. This category also includes those who became disciples of either their own teachers or of other religious leaders.

Finally, the last category, "institutions," includes all those who were sent, or who asked to be sent, to some religious institution, such as a cloister, for their education. The child's training was supervised by the authorities of that institution —by monks in the case of a monastery or by nuns in the case of a convent. The divisions and computations are to be found in Tables 28, 29, and 30.

Approximately 73 per cent of the possible data are lacking; therefore any conclusions drawn will have to be drawn on the basis of the available 27 per cent.

If we assume that the ways of entrance via self-consecration of both kinds, dedication by the parents and holy relatives, are the methods effected mainly by the parental family, then the family and kinship agencies determined largely some 43 per

Table 28

Types of Entrance on the Road to Sainthood

	Number of individuals	Percentage of total	Percentage of known
Self-consecration	185	6.0	22.2
Self-consecration in solitude	27	.9	3.2
Dedication	44	1.4	5.3
Holy relatives	102	3.3	12.2
Specific personages	232	7.5	27.9
Institution	243	7.9	29.2
Unknown	2,257	73.0	
Total	3,090	100.0	100.0

cent of the saints in their initial steps on the road to sainthood. In some 5 per cent of the cases, the parents determined sainthood decisively by their dedication of the child to God. The remaining 57 per cent were influenced principally by specific unrelated personages and by religious and monastic institutions. Family influences possibly played a certain rôle in a part of these 57 per cent, too, because in a number of cases a child was sent to an institution or a specific personage by the parents. However, the rôle of the family among these 57 per cent was secondary: the chief determining agency was a specific personage or an institution. These agencies were those forces that overcame the opposing influence of the parents or their indifference toward the saintly aspirations of their child.

It is quite possible that in many cases the entrance upon the road to sainthood was determined by several of these agencies working in various combinations. Such facts, however, do not "smother" the six clear-cut types of entrance, nor the main rôle of each of the specific agencies considered.

Among other things, these data indicate that though the parental family's influence was enormous, it was not all-decisive, even in past centuries. Even then the rôle of non-related persons and especially of religious institutions was at least as great as that of family kinship, if we measure their proportionate rôles as instigators of the saintly life.

As to the changes in these ways of entrance upon the road to sainthood during the last nineteen centuries, the essentials are given in Tables 29 and 30. The most important change, after the eighteenth century, is the cessation of three ways of entrance: self-consecration in solitude, dedication by parents, and dedication by religious relatives. The reason for this cessation is largely social—the actual and legal emancipation of children after the eighteenth century from the dictatorial authority of the parents. Parents were legally prohibited from deciding various matters for their children. Before this they had the prerogative of deciding for their children the choice

Table 29
Types of Entrance on the Road to Sainthood by Century

Century	1	2	3	4	5	6	7	8	9	10	11	12	13	14	15	16	17	18	19	20
Self-consecration	1	5	3	19	5	11	20	12	6	4	10	9	12	13	16	10	12	8	7	—
Self-consecration in solitude	—	—	—	—	—	—	—	—	—	—	—	—	—	—	—	—	—	—	—	—
Dedication	1	—	3	2	1	2	—	5	—	2	2	2	—	4	—	2	3	1	—	—
Holy relatives	4	1	2	2	1	4	6	3	1	1	2	4	4	5	1	1	2	2	—	—
Specific religious individual	—	—	—	21	9	12	15	14	3	1	—	5	3	5	—	2	1	1	—	—
Religious institution	6	5	7	17	17	27	34	11	9	9	11	11	18	12	8	10	8	1	6	—
Unknown	—	3	3	6	6	15	19	17	11	8	19	25	22	16	23	17	22	6	5	—
	63	84	218	336	169	157	171	109	89	41	76	96	129	89	71	155	74	33	35	1
Total	75	98	236	403	208	228	265	171	119	66	120	152	188	144	119	197	122	52	53	1

Table 30

Percentage Distribution of Types of Entrance on the Road to Sainthood by Century

Century	1	2	3	4	5	6	7	8	9	10	11	12	13	14	15	16	17	18	19	20
Self-consecration	1.3	5.1	1.3	4.7	2.4	4.8	7.5	7.0	5.0	6.1	8.3	5.9	6.4	9.0	13.4	5.1	9.8	15.4	13.2	—
Self-consecration in solitude	—	—	—	.5	.5	.9	—	2.9	—	3.0	—	1.3	—	2.8	—	1.0	2.5	1.9	—	—
Dedication	1.3	—	1.3	.5	.5	1.8	2.3	1.8	.8	1.5	1.7	2.6	2.1	3.5	.8	.5	1.6	3.8	—	—
Holy relatives	5.3	1.0	.8	5.2	4.3	5.3	5.7	8.2	2.5	1.5	1.7	3.3	1.6	3.5	—	1.0	.8	1.9	—	—
Specific religious individual	8.0	5.1	3.0	4.2	8.2	11.8	12.8	6.4	7.6	13.6	9.2	7.2	9.6	8.3	6.7	5.1	6.6	1.9	11.3	—
Religious institution	—	3.1	1.3	1.5	2.9	6.6	7.2	9.9	9.2	12.1	15.8	16.4	11.7	11.1	19.3	8.6	18.0	11.5	9.4	—
Unknown	84.1	85.7	92.3	83.4	81.2	68.8	64.5	63.8	74.9	62.2	63.3	63.3	68.6	61.8	59.8	78.7	60.7	63.6	66.1	100.0

Each vertical column totals 100 per cent.

of bride or bridegroom, their occupation or vocation, and so on. This sort of parental authority, curtailed or terminated in many fields, was also terminated in this particular field—that of dedication of a child to God, to monastic or clerical occupations and institutions. If some parents continued to attempt to wield this authority, the child, when grown up in the new atmosphere of emancipation, could annul it in most cases.

During the last two centuries the kinship family group greatly diminished in size, passing from a comparatively large kinship group, in which members were closely united with one another, to the conjugal family, consisting of husband, wife, and children. Ties with other relatives became looser and less binding. As a result, relatives ceased to exert their previous influence in many matters, including that of directing a child toward sainthood. In addition, during the later centuries, the transmission of the socio-economic and occupational status from the parents to the children, from kinsman to kinsman, increasingly declined.[1] This general decline manifested itself also in the religious, ecclesiastical, and clerical vocations. This explains why the rôle of religious relatives also declined.

Finally, solitary occupations like that of the shepherd and cowherd decreased quantitatively with the urbanization and industrialization of the Western world during the past two centuries. They also changed radically qualitatively: a solitary, contemplative shepherd was replaced by an active and scarcely contemplative cowboy, or by an agricultural farmhand. Medieval religious values were replaced for modern shepherds, peasants, farmers, and lumber jacks by secular and sensate values. In their camps and cabins pin-up girls replaced the holy icons and pictures of saints. In this secularized, publicity-crazy, sensate culture, the chances of shepherds and other "solitudinal" unskilled or semi-skilled and even skilled workers of becoming saints dwindled almost to the zero point. If they did become

---

[1] See my *Social Mobility*, chaps. xvii, xviii, xix, *et passim*.

saintly, they had the publicity essential to make their saintliness known to others. Without this publicity they could hardly be brought to the attention of the Church hierarchy.

These considerations are sufficient to explain why "consecration in solitude," "dedication by parents," and "dedication by relatives" disappeared after the onset of the eighteenth century.

Other changes fail to disclose any clear-cut trend during the nineteen centuries: the percentages fluctuate somewhat irregularly. There is a slight increasing trend toward sainthood due to self-consecration after the thirteenth century. But the increase is neither steady nor regular. So far as it is real, it may be the result of an increase of freedom, self-determination, and individualism on the part of Western persons after the Middle Ages, particularly in the last two centuries.

32. ROUTES TO SAINTHOOD

The preceding sections do not clearly indicate how early in life saints enter upon the road to sainthood; whether they travel it painfully or painlessly, with or without catastrophe, with or without a dangerous turn in their life course. The elucidation of these problems is the task of this section.

Studying the lives of the saints, one may easily discern four main types of saints and of their life course. These types may be called *fortunate, converted by catastrophe, intermediary* and *martyr*.[1]

By "fortunate" saints are meant those saints who evinced signs of religiosity and love and devotion toward God from the very beginning, both in their overt actions and in their speech. "These men of wonderful character, with souls born before Adam's fall, childlike, simple, direct, unacquainted with anger or untruth, are born that way—without sin. . . . Many so-called 'believers' say that 'we shall be on our way to God,' but they do not go that way; these simple and holy persons often *make no statement, but simply fulfill the Father's will.*"[2] Certain events may hasten an unfolding of potential saintliness; but for these saintly types, the process was begun at the earliest age, and continued with their maturation. There was no crisis or sudden conversion in their lives. We have met this type of person in the preceding section under the categories

---

[1] For these types, see my forthcoming *Types, Techniques, and Factors of Altruistic Experience*. See also the account of the "healthy-minded" type in William James's *Varieties of Religious Experience* (Modern Library Edition, New York), Lectures IV and V, pp. 77–224.

[2] Father Yelchaninov, in G. P. Fedotov, *A Treasury*, p. 436.

of "self-consecration" and "self-consecration in solitude." We find that some children and shepherds or cowherds consecrated themselves to God very early in their lives. In the case of the herders the process was hastened by their enforced solitude. In our time Mohandas K. Gandhi and Albert Schweitzer may be cited as examples of this type of person.[3]

The "intermediate" type includes those persons who changed their way of life to a more saintly one because of a series of events. Their entire personality was reorganized and reintegrated through a group of experiences that turned them toward a positive religious life from one of sin or scant piety. However, there is no one specific event that marks the change; it is the cumulative totality of events which leads to the transmutation. The transformation is complete, and takes place on both the ideological and the behavioral level. The change does not involve merely lip service with the old overt actions continuing. A genuine metamorphosis of overt actions, as well as speech reactions, occurs. The total transfiguration may take a comparatively short time or it may extend over a period of years. This type is the midpoint, so to speak, between the fortunate and the catastrophic types.

In the "catastrophic" type, one or a few specific events occurring in a brief period mark a sharp turn in the entire life of the person. Before that certain event the person was not saintly; he was often, in fact, a complete sinner. But that single incident or group of incidents precipitated a complete reorientation of values, a sudden religious conversion.[4] In accordance with the law of polarization, which operates during periods of crisis, the catastrophic event often played a positive

---

[3] See Mohandas Gandhi's *The Story of My Experiment with Truth* (Washington, 1948); and Albert Schweitzer's *Out of My Life and Thought* (New York, 1933).

[4] For a discussion of religious conversion, see William James, *Religious Experience*, Lectures IX and X, pp. 186–253; A. C. Underwood, *Conversion* (New York, 1925); S. de Sanctis, *Religious Conversions* (London, 1927); E. D. Starbuck, *Psychology of Religion* (London, 1899).

polarization rôle in the lives of our saints.[5] The precipitating factors may be of several kinds: painful shock or suffering, sickness, old age, a death, or unexpected extraordinary kindness or love shown toward the future saint, especially in those cases where he feels unworthy of it.[6] Here again, a complete metamorphosis occurs, in that the change takes place in both the individual's speech reactions and his overt actions.

Finally, "pure martyrdom" refers to those who became saints partly or purely through being martyrs. Martyrdom fell upon many unforeseen and unexpected. This road to sanctity is a very specific example of the "catastrophic" road. Its uniqueness makes it advisable to treat it as a separate type.

The biographies of 767 martyrs out of the total of 1,115 give little or no indication of any outstanding saintly or altruistic activity before their martyrdom. Both children and grown-ups among these 767 martyrs seem to have achieved saintliness through having been murdered either in a mass persecution of Christians, or during religious wars, or during the political struggles of the Catholic Church with its enemies—Protestants, heretics, and pagans. Otherwise these "pure martyrs" did not distinguish themselves before their martyrdom for their saintliness or altruism. Their sanctification is due almost entirely to their martyrdom, preceded in some cases by the courage they showed in not renouncing their faith—a renunciation which in most cases would have saved their lives; in other cases they were not given even this choice of renunciation and were merely massacred.[7]

The remaining 348 martyrs out of the 1,115 are included in one of three categories (fortunate, intermediary, and catastrophic) of Table 31. This table gives the numbers and

---

[5] For a discussion of the law of polarization (as applied to the religious and ethical life of society, as well as to its individuals), see my *Man and Society in Calamity* (E. P. Dutton, New York, 1942), chaps. ix–xii, pp. 161–193, 227–240.

[6] See my *Reconstruction*, pp. 239–241. Precipitating factors, effects of calamity, and polarization are treated there.

[7] Cf. H. Delehaye, *Les Origines du Culte des Martyrs* (Brussels, 1933).

percentages of each of these types of saints and their roads to sainthood.

Table 31

Routes to Sainthood

	Number of individuals	Percentage
Fortunate	902	43.5
Intermediary	177	8.5
Converted through catastrophes	230	11.0
Martyr	767	37.0
Total	2,076	100.0

Out of 3,090 cases, for 2,076, or 67.2 per cent, we have information about the type of road and the saint. Table 31 shows that the "fortunate" type is the most frequent. Forty-three per cent of the saints belong to this type and traveled this road. They were born potential saints, and gradually, harmoniously, without any catastrophe, their potential saintliness unfolded into actuality. By the phrase "they were born potential saints" is meant the fact that at a very early age they showed in their personality and behavior some of the characteristics of potential saintliness. Whether this is due to their biological constitution, to their prenatal and postnatal environmental influences, to both, or to something else entirely (the "grace of God," the incarnation of a saintly soul in their organism, etc.), it is impossible to decide definitely. We may only state that as early as they were observed, they appeared to be saintly types.

The catastrophic-converted type as well as the intermediary type is a minority in comparison with the fortunate type. It is interesting to note that among American "good neighbors" the fortunate type is also a majority, whereas the catastrophic-converted and the intermediary type are also minority types of "good neighbors" and of the roads to good-neighborliness. The widely accepted opinion that most of the saints or "good neighbors" or other notable altruists have passed through an acute catastrophe and conversion is thus unwarranted. Its acceptability is due more to the dramatic character of the catastrophic type than to its greater frequency. Just as the majority of creative geniuses in all fields showed at an early age some of the potential characteristics of their genius and then gradually unfolded their creativity as they matured —so did the majority of saints follow a similar fortunate road. A majority of creative geniuses are born such (in the above sense of this expression); only a minority experience a sudden catastrophic conversion or "explosion" of their genius during a later period in their life.

Finally, the martyr type of saint is the second most frequent type among saints. Its peculiarity and its tragedy have already been discussed. Until all the numerous "in-groups" of the present time, including the Catholic Church itself, are freed from their monopolistically privileged claims that only their group is the true, the just, and the beautiful one, and that all other in-groups are either inferior, or even "unholy, heretical, and destined to be eternally damned," to be fought against and eradicated—until this unification of humanity into one real in-group is achieved, the tragedy of martyrdom, of altruists and saints creating enmity, hatred, and even bloody conflicts where they fall themselves as victims, will continue.

Even Jesus brings not peace but a sword. Until unification is achieved any number of martyrs will unavoidably be saints and altruists, to say nothing of the less noble victims of political, social, and economic struggles.[8] Until unification is achieved martyrs will continue to be a perennial category of human history and social life. Until then, too, the Lamb of God will continue to be sacrificed for the sins of the world and the Son of God will be crucified and martyred.[9]

---

[8] A much more precise and detailed analysis of this cardinal problem is given in the forthcoming *Types, Techniques, and Factors of Altruistic Experience*. An abbreviated treatment may be found in my *Reconstruction of Humanity*.

[9] In another section of this work, data are given that show the fluctuation of the number and percentage of martyrs and confessors among the saints during the nineteen centuries of Christianity.

33. MARRIAGE STATUS

What was the marriage status of the saints both before and after their entrance upon the road to sainthood? The moral attitude of the Christian Church respecting sexual life was clearly established almost at the moment of its emergence: chastity or virginity, and a complete abstinence from sexual indulgence, were viewed as the highest virtue. Marriage was viewed as a socially sanctioned way of satisfying sexual impulses for those who could not reach a higher state of chastity; finally there was sinful sexual life outside of marriage. Thus marriage was a lawful and approved institution for Christians; but it was considered an inferior state compared to chastity or virginity.

The marriage status is unknown for 1,938 saints out of 3,090; only for 1,152 saints is it known. Table 32 gives data respecting the marriage status of the saints.

Table 32

Marriage Status of the Saints

	Number of individuals	Percentage of total	Percentage of known
Unmarried	858	27.8	74.5
Married involuntarily	58	1.9	5.0
Married voluntarily	236	7.6	20.5
Unknown	1,938	62.7	
Total	3,090	100.0	100.0

"Involuntary marriage" refers to all those who wished to devote themselves only to God and to good works, but who were forced to marry because of parental or other pressures.

After marriage, however, the spouse understanding the situation, both took vows of mutual continence. Many of these forced marriages took place on the upper socio-economic level. If a princess or a noble's daughter made known her desire to enter a convent, she was often dissuaded and forced to enter a marriage which had been contracted some months or years before. This situation may also be applied to involuntary male marriages, although they occurred less frequently. Voluntary marriage includes all those individuals who married of their own free will, but who, for certain reasons, later took a vow of continence and turned toward religion. Their reason may have been the death of the spouse; in certain situations, where a child died, a mutual vow of continence was taken by both parents. Oftentimes, by mutual consent, the husband would enter a monastery, and the wife a convent.

The figures show that 75 per cent of the saints remained unmarried, and a greater part of these supposedly preserved their chastity or virginity. A smaller number of the unmarried saints led a sinful sexual life before their conversion. (A few were even prostitutes.) An additional 5 per cent had involuntary marriages, some of which resulted in sexual continence. Only 20 per cent were voluntarily married. But a considerable part of these, when they began their saintly life, became sexually continent. The data thus suggest that Christian Catholic sanctity is tangibly connected with sexual continence.

In this respect the saints differ not only from the ordinary populations but even from American "good neighbors." Among these, some 75 per cent are married, and some 6 per cent in addition are widowed. Among the saints the situation is the reverse. In chastity and sexual continence our saints resemble many great altruistic and religious leaders of other countries and religions. They all stress the indispensability of strict control over the sexual impulse; some of them, including Gandhi and Sri Aurobindo, go further and categorically insist on complete sexual continence as an absolute necessary condition for attaining union with the divine, for sainthood, for the state of *samadhi*, and for truly altruistic conduct. Insisting upon this, they mean not only a mere sublimation of the sex libido to religious and altruistic purposes, but its complete eradication. Though difficult, such an elimination is possible, and, according to these saints, has to be achieved if a person wishes to become truly altruistic,[1] or to attain sainthood, or union with the Absolute. The Catholic saints strongly corroborate these claims, though the experience of a minority shows that one can become saintly even in the state of marriage and a lawful satisfaction of sex impulses.

---

[1] For a further discussion, see my forthcoming *Types, Techniques, and Variety of Altruistic Experience*.

34. SOCIO-OCCUPATIONAL

STATUS

Having learned the social background of the parental families of the saints, as well as their age, sex, marital status, the country of birth and death, the chief types of saints and the chief roads to sainthood, we may now inquire as to the socio-occupational status of the saints themselves. More specifically: through what kind of work or activities did they achieve sainthood and canonization? Is the statement of Solovyev, quoted in Section 24, accurate? Table 33 gives the answer to these questions.

The categories for most of the saints are socio-occupational. But a few categories such as martyr, penitent, and virgin indicate the specific activity that led to sanctification rather than the socio-occupational position. Such categories are introduced because in some cases only this sort of activity is indicated in the sources, which give no further information about the social status of these saints.

The figures, especially the percentages, show that about 30 per cent were high Church dignitaries, occupying the top strata of the Church hierarchy. An additional 30 per cent occupied lower positions in the Church hierarchy. If we add to that the martyrs (many of whom were members of the clergy or monks), almost 90 per cent of the saints prove to be directly or indirectly members of the Church hierarchy. If we exclude half of the martyrs from the clergy and also penitents and pilgrims, we still have some 75 per cent of the saints as members of the Church hierarchy.

Table 33

Socio-occupational Status of the Saints

		Number of the Saints		Percentage	
I	Apostle, evangelist	37		1.0	
	Pope	79		2.0	
	Patriarch	11		0.3	
	Cardinal	12	1,159	0.3	29.2
	Archbishop	75		1.9	
	Bishop	609		15.3	
	Doctor of the Church	13		0.3	
	Abbot, abbess	323		8.1	
II	Priest	8		0.2	
	Martyr	1,115		28.0	
	Confessor	1,018		25.2	
	Apologist	1			
	Inquisitor	1		0.1	
	Prophet	2	2,288		57.2
	Deacon, deaconess	7		0.2	
	Hermit, anchorite, recluse	108		2.7	
	Monk	7		0.2	
	Penitent	10		0.3	
	Pilgrim	8		0.2	
	Missionary, preacher	3		0.1	
III	Holy woman	2		0.1	
	Actor	1			
	Virgin	290	383	7.3	9.7
	Matron	30		0.8	
	Widow	60		1.5	
IV	Emperor, empress	7		0.2	
	King, queen	46		1.2	
	Prince, princess	4	64	0.1	1.7
	Duke, duchess	2		0.1	
	Patron, patroness	5		0.1	
	Unknown	87		2.2	
	Total	3,981 [1]		100.0	

[1] The total here is more than 3,090, because many saints had to be classified under two categories.

Only some 10 to 25 per cent of the saints have a secular social status. Of these, women—virgins, matrons, patronesses, widows, and holy women—constitute almost 10 per cent of the secular saints, who achieved sainthood through secular occupations. Finally 1.7 per cent of the saints came from royalty, and the highest aristocracy, or the merchant class (patrons and patronesses). Since sainthood is the highest Church honor, it is natural that the Church bestows it chiefly upon its best, most loyal, and most ideal members. Any social institution bestows its honors and privileges primarily upon its best, most useful, and most serviceable members: the State, upon its officials; a university, upon its members; a business firm, upon its directors, chairmen, and presidents. The prevalence of the clergy or hierarchy among the Church's saints is natural and represents a case in point.

It is natural also that the high dignitaries of the Church should be sanctified at a much higher rate (per unit of their population—say, per 1,000) than the lower members of the Church hierarchy (per 1,000 population) or, especially, ordinary Christian parishioners. Royalty and the highest nobility are sanctified more liberally than the rank and file of Christians; but even royalty seems to have been canonized less liberally than the high dignitaries of the Church. Especially high is the rate of sanctification of popes: out of 256 popes who lived from 42 A.D. to the present time, 79—or some 30 per cent—were sanctified. This sanctification of the highest authorities of the Church in comparison with the lower ones, and of clergy in comparison with secular Christians, is in harmony with the Church's teaching that the consecrated clergy has a higher sanctity or grace than secular Christians, and that the higher authorities also have greater grace than the lower authorities.

Considering that the selection of the pontiff is exceedingly rigorous (as a rule); and that, in this selection, the moral and saintly qualities play a most important rôle, it is comprehensible that so many popes should have been sanctified by the Church which they headed and ruled.[2]

It is interesting also that a much larger number of hermits, anchorites, anchoresses, and monks have been sanctified than priests (living supposedly in the secular world). Life in the ordinary world seems to be thought of by the Church as not so conducive to sainthood as the life of a monk or especially of a hermit and recluse.[3]

One notes, further, that only one inquisitor qua inquisitor was sanctified, and only two prophets qua prophets were canonized. Prophets are always unorthodox to some extent and are always transgressors of some of the formal rules of an established church. As such, prophets almost always get into conflict with the formal and official authorities of the institutionalized church. For these reasons, as a rule, prophets are not particularly favored by the official hierarchy for sanctification. (Only when a damned prophet establishes his own church does he achieve official status and an air of sanctity.) This explains why we have only two prophets among the saints.

The most numerous among the saints are the categories of martyrs and confessors. By "martyr" is meant a Christian who has suffered capital punishment because of his faith and his refusal to renounce it. By "confessor" is meant two different types: first, Christians who have made a profession of faith and suffered persecution in various forms, except capital punishment; second, a non-martyr saint, especially an ecclesiastical adviser and spiritual guide to some king or noble or group

---

[2] For an analysis of 256 popes from the standpoint of their ideational sanctity and sensate worldliness, see my *Dynamics*, Vol. III, pp. 522ff.

[3] It is significant that no member of the secular clergy has found a place among the saints of the Russian Church (in which the secular priests are married). In this respect the Russian Church goes even further than the Catholic Church in an unfavorable attitude toward the sanctification of the secular clergy. See G. P. Fedotov, *A Treasury of Russian Spirituality* (New York, 1948), p. 346.

of Christians.[4] The first type of confessor is similar to the martyrs. The second is similar to the Church authorities. Another difference between martyrs and the second type of confessors is that, among the martyrs, 21 were children of an age from 3 days to 15 years, and 16 were between the ages of 16 and 25. Among the confessors there were hardly any young children or adolescents. Unfortunately, in most cases we do not know the social, occupational, and economic status of adolescents and children. Their sanctification is due largely to their martyrdom. Of the known 11.7 per cent of the martyrs, their age distribution is given by the following figures:

Table 34

Age of Martyrs at Death

	Number of Martyrs	Percentage
Child: 3 days to 15 years	21	1.9
16–25 years	16	1.4
26–40 years	23	2.1
41–60 years	40	3.6
61–80 years	21	1.9
80–100 years	7	.6
Over 100 years	2	.2
Unknown	985	88.3
Total	1,115	100.0

Forty of the martyrs were between the ages of 41 and 60, whereas only 21 were children. These figures are necessarily based on a small group of the total number of martyrs, inasmuch as the bulk of their ages is unknown. Of the 21 child martyrs, 18 were children who either professed their Christian religion or else encountered mass persecution. We know, further, that 15 of the known martyrs were merchants; others were "housewives" or belonged to various occupations; the majority were clergymen.

---

[4] For a discussion of confessors, see H. Delehaye, *Sanctus*, pp. 74ff., 109ff., 122–125.

The sanctification of martyrs by their "in-groups" is a general social phenomenon, not limited to a religious group. Political parties, including even communists, sanctify their martyrs as "heroes" and consider them the incarnation of the highest virtues. So does any state in regard to its war heroes who have killed many enemies of the state and who have themselves been killed. So does any clan, tribe, local community, nationality, labor union, or other social group. They all sanctify and canonize their martyrs, who have suffered for the sake of their in-group. The martyrdom of the Lamb of God, who took upon himself the sins of the world, is a general symbol of this rule. The religious group's sanctification of its martyrs and confessors (first type) is thus only an example of this general rule. One of its additional reasons is well explained by Father Yelchaninov:

> Our Lord has infinite pity for us, and yet He sends us suffering; it is only when we are stricken by calamity that we are able to yield a certain sacred fire. This is the meaning of wars, revolutions, sickness; I think of the meaning of sweat, tears, and blood for our purification and sanctification—of work, penance, and martyrdom. Through them the body is freed of its psychic-animal elements, and the spiritual impulse pervades the whole man; this is why the Church elevates its martyrs, emphasizing the shedding of blood; and this is why people honor those killed in war.[5]

Though in this statement the real effects of suffering and calamity are interpreted one-sidedly, their effects upon the martyrs and confessors were indeed purifying and sanctifying.[6] Their suffering and blood were thus the cement that bound together and invigorated the growth of the Church. The very fact that even such a saintly institution as the Christian

---

[5] G. P. Fedotov, *op. cit.*, pp. 422–426.
[6] Calamities purify and ennoble some, whereas others are demoralized and brutalized. For this law of polarization, see my *Man and Society in Calamity*, chaps. ix–xii.

Church could not grow without martyrdom and bloodshed is tragic evidence of the inevitability of bloodshed and martyrdom in the building up of any important institution. Hitherto this tragedy has been a general rule. Practically every great saint or great altruist has had conflicts with many persons and groups and often has fallen victim to hostile forces. Jesus and Gandhi furnish classical examples of this universal rule. All such saints and altruists have been destined to be Lambs of God, who have taken upon themselves the sins of the world. The purest and most sublime altruism and love have always generated much conflict, hatred, and bloodshed. Whether such a tragedy is inevitable in the future, and, if not, under what conditions it can be avoided, are problems discussed elsewhere.[7]

The above considerations explain why about 53 per cent of all the saints were martyrs and confessors.

Secular persons are represented by canonized royalty and a group of women: virgins, matrons, widows, holy women, actors and patronesses. Although the canonization of some members of royalty who rendered most important services to the Church is comprehensible, that of the women is somewhat obscure in all those cases where the only data given are that a girl or woman was a virgin, widow, or matron. Since mere virginity (even when it is certain) or widowhood is not enough for sanctification, there must have been other reasons for the sanctification of these women. These reasons were probably lost, if the canonization was really justified.[8]

Among these sanctified women about 75 per cent were virgins. This well reflects the attitude of the Church toward sexual indulgence. Virginity or chastity is considered by Christianity to be the highest virtue; next comes lawful marriage;

---

[7] See my forthcoming *Types, Techniques, and Factors of Altruistic Experience*, where it is shown that this tragedy is not inevitable and under certain definite conditions is avoidable.

[8] For a discussion of saints that never existed, see H. Delehaye, *Sanctus*, ch. v.

finally, one of the lowest sins is sexual satisfaction outside of wedlock. Hence the prevalence of virgins in this group. This attitude did not, however, keep the Church from sanctifying a few women who before their conversion were either prostitutes (like St. Mary, St. Pelagia, and so on), or mistresses, etc. The same is true still more in regard to the male saints. Before conversion some of them lived what the Church regarded as a very sinful life.

Finally, scattered among our categories of patron, matron, martyr, confessor, pilgrim, and penitent, there are 82 merchants, some men and some women. They were sanctified not because they were merchants, but because they either gave themselves up to death as martyrs, or contributed considerable funds to the Church in time of need, or in some way protected the Church from its enemies. Whatever the reason was for their sanctification, *the total number of the merchants among the saints is comparatively modest*. It is larger, however, than the number of saints derived from the lowest social strata.

Such are the main socio-occupational categories of the saints. These data show that there was small chance, if any, for a common person—a farmer, laborer, clerk, professional, or businessman—honestly discharging his vocation, and being an unselfish "good neighbor," to be canonized, so long as he remained in the secular world and did not become a member of the clergy or of a monastic order, or their direct agent (in the capacity of a protector, patron, or benefactor, etc.). For such secular "good Christians," only the avenues of martyrdom and persecution were open as ways to sanctification. During its nineteen centuries of existence, the Church has been very parsimonious in granting sanctification to plain, good secular Christians—incomparably more parsimonious than toward the clergy, members of monastic orders, and the royal and aristocratic protectors and benefactors of the Church. The ethical and religious value of a quiet, good Christian life has been somewhat underestimated up to recent times. There is now some sign that it is again beginning to be appreciated.[9]

This leads us to inquire what changes in the socio-occupational status of the saints occurred in the course of time. Tables 35 and 36 give the answer to this question.[10]

Several changes in the course of the centuries are significant. First, several socio-occupational groups ceased to supply the saints after the sixteenth and seventeenth centuries—popes, royalty, widows, matrons, patrons and patronesses, abbots and abbesses, priests, deacons and deaconesses, missionaries, preachers, pilgrims, monks, hermits, prophets, penitents, apologists, inquisitors, actors, holy women, and recluses.

This cessation of the contribution of saints by these classes is the result of several factors. First, some of the above socio-occupational groups, such as inquisitor, prophet, penitent, hermit, recluse, and royalty either entirely disappeared from the social scene, or became exceedingly small or insignificant in the eyes of the Church and Christendom. Another factor was the secularization of the values of royalty and some of the other groups.

In contrast to these groups, the remaining groups of martyrs, confessors, "high ecclesiastical authorities," and virgins have continued to produce saints almost up to the present.

Second, the group of martyrs supplied its maximal percentage of saints in the first to fourth centuries and most especially in the sixteenth, seventeenth, and eighteenth centuries. The reason for this maximal percentage is rather clear: martyrs appear in abundance in the periods critical for the Church. The first supremely critical period was that of the emergence

---

[9] H. Delehaye states that the predominant types of saint in early christianity were ascetics and martyrs; in the Middle Ages, mystics; in recent times, charitable and good Christians. *Sanctus*, pp. 241ff.

[10] In these tables the category "High Ecclesiastical Authority" embraces archbishop, patriarch, cardinal, bishop, doctor of the Church. "Lower Clergy" means priest, deacon, deaconess, missionary, preacher, pilgrim. "Monk, Hermit, Prophet" embrace penitent, apologist, inquisitor, actor, holy woman, recluse.

and establishment of Christianity during the first centuries of our era; the pitiless persecutions of that period supplied a large crop of martyrs. With the legalization of Christianity, and its ultimate dominance as a religion after the fourth century, the percentage of martyrs sharply declines and, with the exception of the ninth century, stays low until the new critical period of the Reformation and the religious wars of the sixteenth and seventeenth centuries. These centuries give the highest percentage of Catholic martyrs in the history of the Christian Church.

With the cessation of the religious wars, the percentage of martyrs goes down somewhat but remains rather high in the eighteenth, and even the nineteenth, centuries. This high percentage is due to a somewhat milder continuation of the critical period for the Church: attacked and threatened by secularization, with its sensate values, the Church had to fight for its existence and its authority. This fight yielded victims and martyrs. After 1914 this fight between the Catholic Church and its enemies became still more intensive and desperate. On both sides it produced its victims and martyrs. Our sources do not cover this later period; therefore they do not list any martyr-saint of the twentieth century. There is however no doubt that the fight between the Catholic Church and the Vatican State, on the one hand, and the anti-Catholic forces, on the other, has already produced many martyrs some of whom, no doubt, will be sanctified in the years to come. As long as the critical period continues, it will be growing its crop of martyr-saints. When it is replaced by a peaceful and secure period, martyr-saints will give away to saints of other types.

The curve of the confessor-saints fluctuates mainly in contrast to the curve of the martyrs. The percentage of confessors is low in the first four centuries when the martyrs' percentage is high. The confessors' percentage is high from the fifth to the fifteenth centuries, when the martyrs' percentage is low;

Table 35
Socio-occupational Distribution of Saints by Century

Century	1	2	3	4	5	6	7	8	9	10	11	12	13	14	15	16	17	18	19	20
Martyr	31	71	206	288	43	15	43	25	34	8	16	14	25	13	7	131	65	22	16	—
Confessor	4	10	19	58	89	113	121	72	34	28	54	70	82	72	67	38	40	20	20	—
Pope	3	8	13	10	10	6	7	5	5	—	4	1	3	2	—	1	—	—	—	—
High Ecclesiastic Authority	—	—	—	—	—	—	—	—	—	—	—	—	—	—	—	—	—	—	—	—
Lower Clergy	11	17	32	79	97	97	113	58	29	21	34	52	26	10	12	7	8	4	7	—
Monk, Prophet, Hermit, etc.	16	2	4	2	5	2	2	2	8	—	2	1	3	1	—	5	1	—	—	—
Abbot, Abbess	5	2	—	14	18	12	11	9	8	4	4	12	14	13	6	1	—	—	1	—
Virgin	4	2	—	9	14	55	64	44	19	16	39	40	11	1	3	3	2	—	—	—
Matron, Patron	6	6	27	28	13	16	24	22	12	6	2	10	26	25	17	14	9	7	12	1
Widow	—	1	—	3	3	3	5	1	3	—	—	2	3	3	3	2	—	—	—	—
Royalty	5	1	—	6	3	3	4	4	1	3	1	1	8	8	2	4	5	—	—	—
Unknown	6	—	3	1	2	5	11	5	6	5	8	2	2	1	2	1	—	—	—	—
			3	4	5	4	2	1	2	—	—	1	17	5	6	5	1	3	4	—
Total by century	91	120	307	502	302	329	406	248	161	91	164	206	220	154	131	212	131	56	60	1

Table 36
Percentual Socio-occupational Distribution of Saints by Century

Century	1	2	3	4	5	6	7	8	9	10	11	12	13	14	15	16	17	18	19	20
Martyr	34.0	59.1	67.1	57.2	14.2	4.6	10.6	10.1	21.1	8.8	9.8	6.8	11.4	8.4	5.3	61.7	49.6	39.1	26.6	—
Confessor	4.4	8.3	6.2	11.6	29.4	34.4	29.9	29.1	21.1	30.7	33.0	33.9	37.2	47.1	51.1	17.9	30.5	35.7	33.3	—
Pope	3.3	6.7	4.2	2.0	3.3	1.8	1.7	2.0	3.1	—	2.4	.5	1.4	1.3	—	.5	—	—	—	—
High Ecclesiastic Authority	12.1	14.2	10.4	15.7	32.1	29.5	27.8	23.4	18.0	23.1	20.7	25.2	11.8	6.5	9.2	3.3	6.1	7.1	11.7	—
Lower Clergy	17.6	1.7	1.3	.4	1.7	.6	.5	.8	5.0	—	1.2	.5	1.4	.6	—	2.4	.8	—	—	—
Monk, Hermit, Prophet, etc.	5.5	1.7	—	2.9	6.0	3.6	2.7	3.6	5.0	4.4	2.4	5.8	6.4	8.4	4.6	.5	1.5	—	1.7	—
Abbot, Abbess	—	1.7	—	1.8	4.6	16.7	15.8	17.7	11.8	17.6	23.8	19.4	5.0	.6	2.3	1.4	6.9	12.5	20.0	100.0
Virgin	4.4	5.0	8.8	5.6	4.3	4.9	5.9	8.9	7.5	6.6	1.2	4.9	11.8	16.2	13.0	6.6	—	—	—	—
Matron, Patroness, etc.	6.6	.8	.8	.6	1.0	.3	1.2	.4	1.9	—	—	1.0	1.4	1.9	1.5	.9	—	—	—	—
Widow	—	.8	—	1.2	1.0	.9	.7	1.6	.6	3.3	.6	.5	3.6	5.2	6.9	1.9	3.8	—	—	—
Royalty	5.5	—	1.0	.2	.7	1.5	2.7	2.0	3.7	5.5	4.9	1.0	.9	.6	1.5	.5	—	—	—	—
Unknown	6.6	—	1.0	.8	1.7	1.2	.5	.4	1.2	—	—	.5	7.7	3.2	4.6	2.4	.8	5.6	6.7	—

Each vertical column totals 100 per cent.

the confessors' percentage sharply decreases in the sixteenth and the seventeenth centuries when the martyrs' percentage sharply flares up; finally, in the eighteenth and nineteenth centuries, the confessors' percentage tends to increase slightly (from the sixteenth and the seventeenth centuries) while the percentage of the martyrs declines.

The confessors were persecuted but non-martyred Christians. Their percentage increases in the non-critical periods when only a mild persecution of the Church exists here and there, and when spiritual advisers (*pater spiritualis*) among the church authorities rise in prestige and power and often become influential statesmen and politicians. In such non-critical periods the percentage of martyrs tends to decline and the percentage of confessors to increase. When the critical period comes, mild persecution is replaced by pitiless struggle, with no quarter given on either side. Persecution gives way to execution, confessor-saint to martyr-saint. Hence the decline of the percentage of confessors when the percentage of martyrs rises. On this basis it is reasonable to predict that the first part of the twentieth century will provide more martyr-saints than confessor-saints.

Another interesting point is the curve of the pope-saints. Its maximum period comes in the first five centuries of the Christian Church. After that, with some fluctuation, the curve tends to go down and falls to zero in the fifteenth century and then, after a brief renewal, falls to zero again after the sixteenth century. Such a movement of the curve is determined by several factors. The most important ones are probably: a) the Church's decreasing need for saintliness as it grew, and its increasing need for able executives; b) the decreasing saintliness of the popes themselves; c) the increasing conservatism of the Church and of the hierarchy in the sanctification of popes during the last few centuries. All these three factors are mutually connected.

At its initial, most heroic, and most saintly stage, the Church was a small organization, and needed for its head a real saint (who would also be capable of charismatic leadership). The whole membership of the Church at this stage was very ideational, other-worldly, and saintly; and it was dedicated to more truly religious values than have been the Christians of the last few centuries. The popes during these early centuries had to be, accordingly, more or less saintly. My investigation of 256 popes from this standpoint shows that among the popes from 42 A.D. to 844 A.D., many more were ideational or saintly in terms of their character, personality, and behavior—regardless of official sanctification—than in the later periods, especially in the periods from 1448 to 1644 and from 1847 to 1920.[11] The Catholic Church, grown into a great empire, now needed for its head a most capable and wise executive rather than an otherworldly saint. Western culture and society after the fifteenth century became predominantly sensate instead of predominantly ideational and idealistic as in the Middle Ages. The Catholic Church, forced now to live and to act amidst such a sensate universe, could not help becoming, in its adjustment to the new order, somewhat sensate also—at least in its hierarchy, strategy, policies, and techniques. This led to less saintly but more capable administrators, including the popes. Hence the trend. It has been facilitated by the wise conservatism of the hierarchy in the sanctification of the popes in these later centuries.

The high Church authorities, including abbots and abbesses, produce their maximal percentage of saints from the fifth to the twelfth centuries. These centuries are non-critical periods for the Church: In the fifth century it was safely established and legalized. It became dominant and remained so up through the twelfth century. Such safe ideational centuries seem to be conducive to the cultivation of saintliness among the higher church hierarchy, and this hierarchy may also be liberally in-

---

[11] See my *Dynamics*, Vol. III, p. 522.

clined towards its own canonization. Hence the high percentage of saints from these social strata in these centuries. After the thirteenth century the percentage of saints from this stratum decidedly decreases and stays low up to the present time. From the seventeenth to the nineteenth centuries the trend shows a slight but modest increase, indicating no decisive turn. Persecution of several high Church dignitaries in the twentieth century by the communists and their allies will eventually result in a notable increase of the saints from this stratum.

The most significant changes within the other categories have already been discussed, and therefore need not be examined now. The only additional trend to be mentioned is that of a *"democratization" of the saints during the last three centuries.* When we analyzed the socio-economic background of the parental families of the saints, we saw this trend in the increasing quota of saints from the lower classes in the last few centuries, and in a decreasing quota of saints from the upper social strata.

A trend closely related to this is also noticeable in the class of virgins. During the eighteenth, nineteenth, and twentieth centuries this category of saints has grown more steadily than any other. The virgin-saints of the last three centuries are women mainly from the middle and lower strata and few, if any, are from the higher strata.

Women as women were somewhat discriminated against during the medieval period. The emergence of a more democratic process is shown in their decisive increase among the saints during the last three centuries.

Such are the main changes among the saints in the course of nineteen centuries.

35. ADAPTATION TO ENVIRONMENT

In what sort of sociocultural environment did the saints become saintly? In what way did they overcome the obstacles of a sinful environment? Since they succeeded in becoming saints, they evidently solved the problem fairly successfully. The ways of the solution were diverse according to the specific circumstances of each saint's life. All this diversity, however, can be reduced to four main types: [1]

1. *Eremitic retirement* (physical or mental) from the world, or self-imposed isolation in a desert, forest, mountain, island, or other area (uninhabited except perhaps for a few similar hermits or disciples), away from human activities, material cultures, or civilizations. Such isolation dissociates one from practically all groups, terminates one's connections with the rest of the sociocultural world, and leaves one face to face with one's self and with God. No worldly distractions directly disturb hermits; their soul is alone, more easily able to find its creator. Some of the isolationists later return, at least for a time, to the social world; but the greater part of their life is spent alone, in complete solitude. The case of Saint Anthony—who thus spent eighty-five out of one hundred and five years of his life—and of Saint Paul of Thebes—who spent, in almost absolute isolation, some ninety years out of one hundred and thirteen years of his life—are classical examples of this

---
[1] A detailed analysis of each type, with its subdivisions, will be given in the forthcoming *Types, Techniques, and Factors.*

eremitic isolation. It does not include short-time retreats from the world. Short-time self-imposed isolation occurred in the lives of most of the saints, and it occurs with most of the creative geniuses in all fields of creativity. Such short-time solitude seems to be one of the most effective ways for developing or revitalizing the creative powers of a genius.

2. *The creation of a special environment* by a monastery, convent, abbey, religious school, training institution, and so on, is another method by which the problem of environment has been solved for saints. These special environments were planned institutions: their aim and function was to stimulate piety, love, saintliness, and other Christian virtues, and to inhibit every sinful impulse. Beginning with the regulation of material objects and ending with the most detailed regulation of all the activities of their members twenty-four hours a day, all was carefully and scientifically planned with the purpose of religious and moral transmutation.

3. The method of a *wanderer or pilgrim* who continues to stay in the empirical "city of man," although no longer a part of it, is the third method by which saints have solved the problem of environment and self-control. The saintly pilgrim or wanderer is not attached to any special environment; he does not have any specific place to rest; he is a stranger to any given spot, and he is at home in the whole world. As either a penitent, disciple, preacher, teacher, missionary, "God's fool," or pilgrim, he moves from place to place, incessantly discharging his religious and moral duties. God and God's will are his sole values. He aspires to them and performs his duties under all conditions.

4. Finally, the fourth method is *remaining in society and doing God's will there, in spite of all obstacles and temptations.* This worldly environment ranges from the best to the worst; from the luxurious palace of a pope or cardinal to the

poorest hut; from the mansion of a duke to the den of a prostitute. Exposed to both positive and negative stimuli, the saint rejects the negative and accepts the positive. Living in an ordinary environment, he remains untarnished by its sinfulness, and steadily carries on his duties. We find many religious officials whose duties require them to take part in certain secular activities, such as attending an international conference, or meeting philanthropists in order to allocate funds for the building of a cathedral or monastery. There were bishops at royal courts bound to carry out royal obligations amidst the pomp and luxury of royal social circles. Saintly merchants, laborers, kings, and scholars have remained in their worldly abodes, discharging their occupational and other duties and attaining sainthood in spite of an unfavorable unsaintly environment.

Let us now see how the saints—those on whom we have data in this regard—used these four types of solutions to the problem of environment. Table 37 gives the answer.

Table 37

Method of Environmental Adjustment

	Number of individuals	Percentage of total	Percentage of known
Self-imposed isolation	177	5.7	9.4
Special environment	585	18.9	31.1
Wanderer, pilgrim	247	8.0	13.1
Sociocultural world	871	28.2	46.4
Unknown	1,210	39.2	—
Total	3,090	100.0	100.0

Almost half of the saints about whom we have relevant information remained in the normal sociocultural world. Thirty-one per cent created a special environment for themselves. The rest alternated between the way of life of a wanderer and that of self-isolation, with the percentage of wanderers being slightly higher than that of the isolationists. The great majority of the saints solved their environmental problem by remaining in the sinful world of society. Only a minority chose the way of a hermit, breaking with human companionship, facing dangers, hardships, and loneliness, albeit in the spiritual company of God. In fact, about half preferred to continue their daily routine rather than enter monasteries or become pilgrims. Evidently one need not escape the world and its temptations in order to be saintly. If one devotes one's thoughts, words, and deeds to God and follows God's commandments, one can live amidst mundane secular enticements and yet not succumb to them—rather, one can overcome them.

What changes in these types occurred during the last nineteen centuries is shown by Tables 38 and 39. Table 38 indicates that the method of eremitic or semi-eremitic isolation began to decline after the fourteenth century, and fell to zero or 1 per cent during the subsequent centuries. The saintly hermit has thus practically disappeared from the social and religious life of recent times. The reasons for such a trend are clear: The increase of the world's population—especially in Christian countries—and of communication and transportation, urbanization and industrialization, together greatly decreased the areas suitable for isolation.

The decline of ideational and the rise of sensate values to dominance made the very ideal of eremitic isolation and its asceticism unpopular in the sensate Christian world. Many Christian thinkers of recent centuries have viewed hermits as insane, as pathological sadists and masochists. The very lonesomeness and ascetic hardships of hermitage appear to be unbearable to modern Christians. On the other hand, the attractions of large cities and crowded and densely populated centers of civilization and culture have been increasing during these recent centuries. So also has crowd-mindedness. An ever-increasing percentage of the Christian West has become incapable of living a solitary life, outside of crowds and groups.

ADAPTATION TO ENVIRONMENT

Finally, the heroic spirit of the hermitage enormously declined during the sensate centuries in even the Christian Church itself. As a result of these forces the decline of eremitic isolation is easily comprehensible.

In contrast to the eremitic way, the way of remaining in a worldly environment shows an increase after the fourteenth century. While before the fourteenth century it was mainly below 30 per cent, after the fourteenth century it stayed—with the exception of the sixteenth century—above 30 per cent, rising to 39, 47, and even 100 per cent in the twentieth century. This trend is partly the result of the decreasing trend of self-imposed isolation and (as the table shows) of the way of monastic and similar "special environments," and partly of the dominant sensate culture of these later centuries. The dominant system of Western culture becoming increasingly sensate and secular after the fourteenth century, the secular method of attaining sainthood (remaining in this sensate world) has increased also. Its increase is one of the thousand forms of basic transformation of the ideational and religious culture of the Middle Ages into the sensate and secular culture of the last five centuries.

Though the way of a special, mainly monastic, environment increased somewhat from the sixteenth to the nineteenth century (from 11.7 to 20.8 per cent), these percentages are tangibly lower than the 25 to 32 per cent for the sixth to the fifteenth century inclusive. With the general decline of monasticism after the fifteenth century, the monastic and related types of special environment seem to have declined. In the twentieth century this method of solving the problem of environment, as well as the eremitic and wanderer methods, disappeared completely. They have been replaced by the method of remaining in the social world and in secularized forms of special environment (secular schools, camps, and other educational and socializing institutions). We seem to look for saints less and less in monasteries and convents, among

Table 38
Distribution of Saints by Century According to Method of Adaptation to Environment

Century	1	2	3	4	5	6	7	8	9	10	11	12	13	14	15	16	17	18	19	20
Isolation	—	2	2	18	21	26	18	14	8	7	5	11	15	14	7	2	2	—	1	—
Special environment	—	8	7	20	32	59	75	47	35	20	37	50	51	47	33	23	18	9	11	—
Wanderer	10	3	13	17	12	19	20	20	7	7	19	14	13	16	16	9	14	6	6	—
Sociocultural world	20	13	44	95	63	58	87	41	38	24	37	45	59	40	45	55	58	17	21	1
Unknown	45	72	170	253	80	66	65	49	31	8	22	32	50	27	18	108	30	20	14	—
Total by Centuries	75	98	236	403	208	228	265	171	119	66	120	152	188	144	119	197	122	52	53	1

Table 39
Percentual Distribution of Saints by Century According to Method of Adaptation to Environment

Century	1	2	3	4	5	6	7	8	9	10	11	12	13	14	15	16	17	18	19	20
Isolation	—	2.0	0.8	4.5	10.1	11.4	6.8	8.2	6.7	10.6	4.2	7.2	8.0	9.7	5.9	1.0	1.6	—	1.9	—
Special environment	—	8.2	3.0	5.0	15.4	25.9	28.3	27.5	29.4	30.3	30.8	32.9	27.1	32.7	27.7	11.7	14.8	17.3	20.8	—
Wanderer	13.3	3.1	5.5	4.2	5.8	8.3	7.5	11.7	5.9	10.6	15.8	9.2	6.9	11.1	13.4	4.6	11.5	11.5	11.3	—
Sociocultural world	26.7	13.3	18.6	23.6	30.3	25.4	32.9	24.0	31.9	36.4	30.8	29.6	31.4	27.8	37.9	27.9	47.5	32.7	39.6	100.0
Unknown	60.0	73.4	72.1	62.7	38.4	29.0	24.5	28.6	26.1	12.1	18.4	21.1	26.6	18.7	15.1	54.8	24.6	38.5	26.4	—

Each vertical column totals 100 per cent.

the pilgrims and wandering penitents, and more and more in the sinful world of society where the prospective saints must live and act.[2] They have a most difficult task: to live in the world and to remain unsullied by its sordid sins. No wonder that such an environment is not conducive to an abundant crop of saints! Indeed, as we shall see in the following sections, saints have tended to dwindle to an ever-declining figure during the last three centuries. The place of saints is increasingly being taken by "good neighbors," or comparatively altruistic persons. The majority of these are religious, the minority declaring themselves atheist or materialist disbelievers. Whatever their formal religious stand, they all render service to their fellow men, and almost all belong to ordinary secular occupations—the professions and business, agriculture, labor, and housekeeping.[3] These "good neighbors," living in the secular world and being overwhelmingly secular in their occupations and activities, tend increasingly to replace the overwhelmingly clerical and royal or aristocratic saints who lived either in isolation or in monasteries and other religious environments. The decrease of hermits and monks or other religious persons living in monasteries and similar milieus would seem to have some connection with the increase of saints who chose to remain in the secular world, and the fact that saints tend to be more and more generally replaced by secular "good neighbors" (cf. Sections 37 and 38).

---

[2] See H. Delehaye, *Sanctus*, pp. 241ff.
[3] See Part One.

36. TECHNIQUES

OF SELF-CONTROL

The beginning of real saintliness requires the mastery by one's highest self of all biological drives and sociocultural desires, ambitions, and passions. Since saints have succeeded in becoming saintly, they have evidently discovered the effective techniques of such self-control. Indeed, many such techniques were discovered long ago by great masters of religious and altruistic self-transformation. A discussion and analysis of these techniques is outside the scope of this work.[1] Only one method of these complex, intricate, and ingenious techniques of self-transmutation need be touched on here—namely, the technique of self-mortification. This includes the most diverse varieties of torturing and inflicting hardships on one's body. Many saints have regarded the flesh as the chief source of perdition and have tried to acquire full control over it through self-mortification. The underlying rationale was: "I kill my body because it kills me." Complete and prolonged fasting; complete suppression of sexual impulses, and castration of the sex organs; denial to the body of the minimum of sleep and rest; denial of every pleasure, and the infliction of all sorts of pain, physical and mental—these are examples of this technique.

Have all the saints applied this technique in self-mastery? If not all, then how many or what percentage? Of some 655

---

[1] See my *Reconstruction*, chap. xiv et *passim*. In considerable detail these techniques will be analyzed in my forthcoming *Types, Techniques, and Factors*.

saints about whom information is given on this point, 248 saints (some 38 per cent) applied this technique, whereas 407 (62 per cent) employed moderation in this respect, keeping themselves free from excessive austerities or self-torture. Their moderation is fairly similar to the advice of contemporary doctors and educators to keep within reasonable limits in the satisfaction of the needs and the lusts of the body, and the aspirations, ambitions, and passions of one's sociocultural personality.

The moral of these statistics is that, among the saints, about two-thirds attained sainthood without self-mortification; that such a technique has been unnecessary even for saints; and that it is still less necessary for "good neighbors." Elsewhere (in *Types, Techniques, and Factors*) it will be shown that the technique of self-mortification has been one of the least effective for the overwhelming majority of saints. Only for a small minority, under specific conditions, was the technique somewhat fitting.

Although we have not made a detailed study of the percentages of saints employing the technique of self-mortification during the last nineteen centuries, it may be stated that this technique of self-mastery began to decrease after the fourteenth century and has virtually disappeared during the past three centuries. Unless there is a new ideational era (with a revival of certain forms of self-mortification) there is little chance of a resuscitation of this technique in its extreme forms.[2]

---

[2] Contrary to H. Delehaye, who sees a resemblance between the technique of Simeon Stylites and that of the Curé d'Ars. These techniques are very different from each other. See Delehaye, *Sanctus*, p. 241.

37. FLUCTUATION OF THE NUMBER OF SAINTS THROUGHOUT THE CENTURIES

Let us now glance at the number of saints who appeared in each of the centuries studied. Table 40 shows the distribution of the saints by centuries.

Table 40
Distribution of Saints by Centuries

Century	Number of saints	Percentage
1	75	2.4
2	98	3.2
3	236	7.6
4	403	13.0
5	208	6.7
6	228	7.4
7	265	8.6
8	171	5.5
9	119	3.9
10	66	2.1
11	120	3.9
12	152	4.9
13	188	6.1
14	144	4.7
15	119	3.9
16	197	6.4
17	122	3.9
18	52	1.7
19	53	1.7
20	1	—
Unknown	73	2.4
Total	3,090	100.0

The table makes several significant points:

1. The number of saints rapidly rises during the first centuries of Christianity, reaches a peak in the fourth century, and then declines though still remaining high during the fifth, sixth, and seventh centuries.

2. After the seventh century the number definitely drops to a lower level for all the subsequent centuries, giving the first really low number in the tenth century.

3. During the eleventh to the seventeenth centuries inclusive the number rises considerably above that of the tenth, but remains below the first high level.

4. Beginning with the seventeenth century, the number of saints per century tends to decline sharply in the eighteenth, nineteenth, and twentieth centuries. In the twentieth century we have only one saint (up to the publication of the source of our study). Several persons have been sanctified subsequently, but the total number sanctified for the first half of this century remains definitely lower than in any of the preceding nineteen centuries. The stream of saints tends to dry up. This trend was noted above, when we analyzed the social strata from which the saints were recruited. We have seen that for the last few centuries they have been supplied principally or exclusively from the lower strata of the Christian population, and that even these strata tended to supply an ever-decreasing number. We have met this trend in other sections of this study. Now we meet it clearly in the very number of saints produced during the last three centuries. Unless a renaissance of ideational or idealistic culture recurs as the dominant supersystem, the stream of saints may actually dry up, and the Christian-Catholic saint may become extinct.

Before undertaking an analysis of other significant points in Table 40 and certain additional data, let us seek the main reasons or factors for the highly varied distribution of the saints over the centuries. The main factors lie partly within the

Catholic Church itself, partly outside of it in the character of the dominant supersystem of Western culture.[1]

The rapid growth of Christian saints during the first seven centuries of Christianity is due to the intensely and heroically ideational character of Christianity. *Saints as saints can appear only in an ideational and idealistic culture and society. The sensate culture and society has no place for a saint.* The very nature of the sensate cultural and social system denies supersensory and superrational reality, values, or saintliness. The sensate system admits and fosters empirical "good neighbors," utilitarian altruists, rational and scientific "good-doers," useful co-operation and mutual aid, and even unselfish persons who sacrifice their lives for others.[2] But a saint in the Catholic sense —a servant of God who later becomes a sacred figure in the eyes of an organized religious group—is for a sensate society and culture either a semantically inaccurate description of a person with altruistic tendencies or an idealization of certain abnormal types: mystics, psychoneurotics, sadists, masochists, or simply superstitious persons, often aesthetically disgusting or unhygienic. Since a sensate culture does not recognize any supersensory or superrational realities and values, such as God and his Kingdom, a saint is not admitted and still less respected, idealized, or sanctified.

Because Christianity emerged as an intensely ideational system, it looked upon saints as the highest ideal of human achievement. Because Christianity grew rapidly, the number of its saints also grew rapidly during the first seven centuries of its heroic struggle for survival in the inimical sensate culture

---

[1] I do not wish to give here even a brief outline of cultural congeries and systems of sensate, idealistic and ideational types of cultural supersystems and their domination in Graeco-Roman and Western culture. For this the reader is referred to my *Social and Cultural Dynamics* (4 Volumes), where it is demonstrated in great detail; to my *Crisis of Our Age* and *Society, Culture and Personality*, where an abbreviated outline of the theories of *Dynamics* is given.

[2] Cf. the various meanings the term saint (*sanctus*) had in the pre-Christian, pagan world and how its meaning grew in Christianity, in H. Delehaye, *Sanctus*, chaps. i, vi.

and society where it had been born. Whereas the intense ideationalism of Christianity during these centuries was highly favorable for the production of truly saintly non-martyr Christians, the persecution of Christians by the dominant Graeco-Roman sensate society and culture increased the number of Christian martyrs and confessors. As a result of this constellation of a successfully growing ideational Christianity amid an inimical sensate world, Christianity produced during these centuries its highest number of saints, although the total Christian population was comparatively small, especially in comparison with that of subsequent centuries.

After the seventh century, Christianity became firmly established as the dominant and privileged religion, as a cultural and social system, as a way of life. The transformation of the Christian Church from a persecuted to a dominant religion, and now and then a persecutor of other religions; from poverty to the richest institution in the West; from a minority current to the majority stream—all these changes notably lowered its ideationalism and otherworldliness.

The Church became more practical, less otherworldly, more "the city of man" and less "the city of God." Its hierarchy now became the most powerful rulers in the West, possessing factual and ideological superiority and control over all the secular powers of the West. Its leaders now became experienced and practical executives rather than saints. As an *empirical* institution the Church needed this type of eminent executive more than otherworldly and "impractical" saints.

This internal change in the Church itself was now less favorable for an abundance of saints than the earlier state of the Church. For this reason the number of saints during these centuries was bound to decline.

On the other hand, Christianity now spread much more widely than before. In comparison with the preceding period, the Christian population increased enormously. Christianity now rooted itself much more deeply in social institutions. Its ideational culture was now the dominant supersystem of Western culture. This spread of Christianity, the numerical increase of its members, and the establishment of a Christian ideational culture as dominant, favored the increased production of saints. As such, it somewhat counterbalanced the slackened production of saints due to the internal changes in the Church itself. The actual number of saints for these centuries is thus the result of these two main factors: the lowered intensity and purity of ideationalism in the Church, and the spread and growth of Christian ideational culture and society outside of the Church in Europe and elsewhere.

These two factors continued to work together even later, from the thirteenth to the seventeenth century inclusive. The internal state of the Church continued to shift in the direction of idealistic and less ideational "this-worldliness," increasingly unfavorable for the production of saints. The dominant cultural supersystem of the West likewise began to shift from the ideational to the idealistic type after the twelfth century. An idealistic culture admits saints and has a definite place for them, especially for the idealistic type of saint. However, an idealistic culture is not so favorable as an ideational culture.

These changes in the culture of the Church itself and in the total culture of Europe operated unfavorably for the production of saints.

On the other hand, Christianity continued to spread. The Christian population increased rapidly; so also did Christian culture and social institutions. This growth of Christianity operated favorably for the production of saints and somewhat counterbalanced the negative influence of the preceding factor. This negative influence was counterbalanced also by a conspicuous increase of Catholic martyrs after the appearance of various heresies and schisms in the Church itself, and especially after the Reformation and the religious wars of the sixteenth and seventeenth centuries. As we have seen, the proportion of martyrs among the saints during these centuries increased notably. Otherwise, one would have expected a downward trend after the fourteenth century; as it is, the trend did not actually set in until after the seventeenth.

In the West, the sensate supersystem of culture and society became dominant after the fifteenth century and continued to grow up to the twentieth. It infected also, to some extent, the Church itself. In its empirical, day-to-day existence it became even less ideational and more sensate. The religious wars ended in the seventeenth century. Thus the production of martyrs also ended. This enormous growth of sensate forms of culture and society, partly within the Church itself and especially in the external Western world, was bound enormously to decrease the production of saints during the eighteenth, nineteenth, and twentieth centuries. As has already been indicated, a sensate culture does not admit saints. The data indicate that after the seventeenth century the number of saints sharply decreased and during the twentieth century dwindled to an unprecedentedly low level.

The two main factors are the internal factor of the Church and the external factor of the succession of ideational, idealistic, and sensate dominant supersystems. These factors satisfactorily explain the main fluctuations in the number of saints throughout the nineteen centuries of Christian history.

If the number of the saints in a religion is taken as a measure of its spiritual creativity and of its religious and moral vigor— and to a certain extent it may be taken as such a measure —then the creativity and ethical and religious vigor of the Christian-Catholic Church were at their highest point during the first seven centuries of our era; they were lower, but still on a high plane, from the eighth to the seventeenth century; and they have decidedly dwindled during the last three centuries. The grace of saintliness seems to have decreased in the Church during this period.

38. THE SAINT IN SENSATE, IDEALISTIC, AND IDEATIONAL CULTURES

The predominant character of the internal culture of the Church and that of the external society around it explain not only the fluctuations in the number of saints throughout the nineteen centuries studied, but also the dominant type of saint in each type of culture. Tables 41, 42, and 43 give the relevant data.

A glance at the percentages of Table 42 shows several things that are still more clearly brought out in Table 43. From Table 42 we see the following: First, the percentage of martyrs is highest in these centuries: first to fifth, then in the ninth, then in the sixteenth, seventeenth, and nineteenth. Second, the "catastrophic" type has its highest rates in these centuries: first, tenth, twelfth to fourteenth, and the twentieth. Third, the "fortunate" type was very scarce in the first centuries of Christianity, then increased fairly steadily from the fourth to the fifteenth centuries, when it reached its highest percentage; after that it began to decline somewhat, with minor fluctuations.

Table 43 makes these data somewhat clearer. In this table the centuries are roughly grouped into four periods according to the nature of the dominant cultural supersystem.[1]

---

[1] "Dominant" means the leading but not the *sole* type of culture that existed in each of these periods. As a matter of fact, the total culture of any period is made up of eclectic (unintegrated and disintegrated) sensate, idealistic and ideational components. But in each period only one of these is the main stream, while the others are but minor rivulets flowing in the same area of the

Table 41
Distribution of Saints by Century According to Type of Saint

Century	Fortunate	Intermediate	Catastrophic	Pure martyr	Unknown
1	5	4	16	21	29
2	17	5	4	33	39
3	10	—	14	154	58
4	54	6	32	216	95
5	42	17	10	26	113
6	84	11	15	13	105
7	97	14	15	18	121
8	60	5	9	16	81
9	37	7	5	37	33
10	22	10	7	5	22
11	47	7	7	8	51
12	69	14	16	5	48
13	77	16	20	18	57
14	65	15	19	6	39
15	61	9	9	5	35
16	48	11	11	108	19
17	50	15	9	36	12
18	24	4	2	4	18
19	23	6	2	13	9
20	—	—	1	—	—

Thus, from the first to the fourth centuries the non-Christian, Graeco-Roman culture was still predominantly sensate (though its sensate character rapidly decreases as we move towards the fourth century). The medieval culture of the West (outside of the Church itself) was predominantly ideational from the fifth to the twelfth centuries. From the end of the twelfth to the fifteenth centuries it witnessed a domination of an idealistic supersystem. Finally, from the fifteenth

---

total culture. Some of the writers dealing with my theories often misunderstand "dominant" to mean "sole." The interpretation of "dominant culture" in this fashion as equivalent to 100 per cent of the total culture of a given period or area is quite wrong.

Table 42
Percentual Distribution of Saints by Century According to Type of Saint

Century	Fortunate	Intermediate	Catastrophic	Pure martyr	Unknown
1	6.7	5.3	21.3	28.0	38.7
2	17.3	5.1	4.1	33.7	39.8
3	4.2	—	5.9	65.3	24.6
4	13.4	1.5	7.9	53.6	23.6
5	20.2	8.2	4.8	12.5	4.8
6	36.8	4.8	6.6	5.7	46.1
7	36.6	5.3	5.7	6.8	45.6
8	35.1	2.9	5.3	9.4	47.3
9	31.1	5.9	4.2	31.1	27.7
10	33.3	15.2	10.6	7.6	33.3
11	39.2	5.8	5.8	6.7	42.5
12	45.4	9.2	10.5	3.3	31.6
13	41.0	8.5	10.6	9.6	30.3
14	45.1	10.4	13.2	4.2	27.1
15	51.2	7.6	7.6	4.2	29.4
16	24.4	5.6	5.6	54.8	9.6
17	41.0	12.3	7.4	29.5	9.8
18	46.2	7.7	3.8	7.7	34.6
19	43.4	11.3	3.8	24.5	17.0
20	—	—	100.0	—	—

Each horizontal column totals 100 per cent.

century up to the present time Western culture has been predominantly sensate.[3]

Looking at the percentual data, we observe the following: 1) *Martyrs are the most frequent type of saint in the sensate periods:* among the known types of saints, martyrs constitute 71.8 per cent of all the saints in the first sensate period (from the first to the fourth centuries) and 43.9 per cent of the

---

[3] For a fuller discussion of these fluctuations of the dominant cultural supersystems, see my *Dynamics, Crisis of Our Age,* and *Society, Culture, and Personality.*

CHRISTIAN-CATHOLIC SAINTS

Table 43
Distribution of Saints by Supersystem According to Type of Saint

Supersystem (by centuries)	Sensate (1–4)	Ideational (5–11)	Idealistic (12–15)	Sensate (16–20)
Fortunate	86 (14.5%)	389 (59.8%)	272 (64.2%)	145 (39.5%)
Intermediate	15 (2.5%)	71 (10.9%)	54 (12.7%)	36 (9.8%)
Catastrophic	66 (11.2%)	68 (10.4%)	64 (15.1%)	25 (6.8%)
Pure martyrdom	424 (71.8%)	123 (18.9%)	34 (8.0%)	161 (43.9%)
Total	591 (100%)	651 (100%)	424 (100%)	367 (100%)

second sensate period (from the sixteenth to the twentieth centuries). 2) Martyrs become the least frequent type of saint (only 8 per cent) in the idealistic period (from the twelfth to the fifteenth centuries). 3) The percentage of martyrs is also low (18.9 per cent) in the ideational period (from the fifth to the eleventh centuries). The percentage of martyrs would be still lower in the ideational centuries if the fifth and ninth centuries were excluded, the fifth because it was still the century of transition from sensate to ideational; the ninth because its martyrdom was largely the result of the invasion of Europe by the Normans, of the conflict with the Mohammedans, etc. 4) The "fortunate" type of saint blossoms most in the idealistic (64.2 per cent) and the ideational period (59.8 per cent), and the least in the sensate periods. This is especially true when a given ideational religion emerges for the first time amidst a predominantly sensate culture: the "fortunate" saints give only 14.5 per cent in the first to the fourth centuries when Christianity emerged and began to grow; and they give 39.5 per cent in the sixteenth to the twentieth centuries, when sensate culture re-emerged and became dominant among Christians and Christianity. 5) "Catastrophic" (converted) saints give the highest percentages in the idealistic and then in the first sensate periods (15.1 and 11.2 per cent respectively).

Why do martyr-saints predominate in the sensate periods? The answer is that sensate culture is agnostic, irreligious, and now and then militantly anti-religious. There is an almost irreconcilable conflict between the main values of a sensate society (wealth, material and physical comfort, power, pleasure, sensory utility) and of an ideational society with its Kingdom of God as the guiding ideal. When both the ideational and sensate groups are not intense and fanatic, the struggle between them goes on in the form of a "cold war." When one or both of these groups become intense and turn into militant crusaders against other systems of values, the struggle turns into a "hot war," with the consequent persecutions, imprisonments, tortures, and executions. The partisans of a sensate way of life become, for the ideational partisans, "heretics," "schismatics," and "atheists" (witness the Inquisition and the burning and torturing of heretics). For the partisans of a sensate culture, the ideationalists become "subversive and dangerous sects" destroying the state and the existing culture. Since the early Christians were considered "subversive" by the dominant sensate powers, they were severely persecuted, yielding thereby a great number of martyrs and confessors to the ranks of saints.

In the second sensate period many a Catholic saint became a martyr for similar reasons: some of them were persecuted for the flagrant way their values contradicted sensate values; other Catholics became martyr-saints in the "civil war" of a now divided Church. The very split of the Church into Catholic and Protestant denominations, not to mention many other factions, was already a sign and a consequence of the rising sensate culture. It was manifested in this ever-increasing schism and in the consequent inhuman and un-Christian coercive measures taken by one group of Christians against another.

Hence an increase of Catholic as well as Protestant martyrs in this second sensate period.

During the last three decades the irreconcilability of Catholic and Communist values (the latter being sensate to the extreme) has become enormous. Hence there has been an increase of mutual persecutions by both parties, and a notable increase of martyrs among both groups. There is hardly any doubt that there will be a notable increase of Catholic saint-martyrs in the present disintegrating phase of sensate culture. Instead of 43.9 per cent, it may easily reach the 71.8 per cent of the martyrs of the first centuries of our era; the largest share of Christian martyrs was harvested in the disintegrating phase of Graeco-Roman sensate culture, especially in the third and fourth centuries.

Since the ideational and idealistic values of a Christian-Catholic saint and the values of ideational and idealistic cultures are the same and do not contradict each other, there is no war between the saints and ideational or idealistic societies. There is no persecution of the saints by the society; therefore there is no martyrdom. If a few martyrs occur in these periods, it is for relatively inconsequential reasons—haphazard murder by criminals, pagans or other non-Christian persons or agencies who always exist as a minor stream in a predominantly ideational or idealistic culture.

Now why do the "fortunate" saints show their highest percentage in the predominantly idealistic and ideational periods and the lowest percentage in the first and the second sensate periods? Being born in an idealistic or ideational culture they "imbibe" their values and norms, standards and patterns, their mentality and their forms of conduct, from earliest childhood. They can and do grow without any tension or conflict between their "interiorized" values and the values of their sociocultural milieu. This milieu urges them to unfold these values and to make them more perfect and pure. Under these conditions, the saints grow in their sainthood quietly, steadily, without any catastrophe, any abrupt and tragic reassessment of their values —without any crisis or sudden conversion. Idealistic and ideational cultures are, by their nature, the cultures inspiring and extolling sainthood. The prospective saints born in these periods do not need any catastrophe or conversion to become saints. Specifically, idealistic culture is by its very nature the culture reconciling and synthesizing sensory, rational, superrational, and supersensory values, norms, and patterns. It is the most well-balanced, the least one-sided, and the most harmonious of all three forms of culture. No wonder, therefore, that it produces the highest quota of balanced, harmonious, "fortunate" saints.

On the other hand, a predominantly idealistic period means a period of transition from one of the extreme forms of culture to the other (from sensate to ideational or vice versa). A considerable part of its total culture remains unintegrated and disintegrated. A part of its population lives and acts in this transitional stream, with its unintegrated elements of the opposing cultural systems. Floating in this transitional stream, some of the "swimmers" start with ideational values, meet sensate values, and become sensate "converts"; others start with sensate values, meet catastrophe, and suddenly convert into ideational or idealistic Christians, and a few into "catastrophic" saints. By its transitional nature, the culture which is dominated by an idealistic supersystem is favorable ground for the emergence of "catastrophic" saints.

Since sensate culture is, by its very nature, inimical to ideational religion and its saints, and since its values conflict with those of the saints, it is unfavorable for an abundant crop of "fortunate" saints. In the growing and integrated phase of sensate culture, saints may be and often are tolerated, sometimes even cared for as either moral leaders or museum curios. In that phase, a considerable number of potential saints can grow into actual sainthood "fortunately," without great shocks or catastrophic conversions. In its later, disintegrating phase, sensate culture and its agencies lose this tolerance; they cynically declare a cold or hot war against ideationalism and its corresponding religion and saints; they begin to ridicule, criticize, and persecute ideationalists. In that phase, sensate society becomes utterly unfavorable for the production of a large crop of "fortunate" saints, and begins to yield mainly martyr-saints and "catastrophic" saints. This explains the second highest percentage of "catastrophic" saints in the first sensate period (in which sensate culture passed fully through its late, disintegrating phase) and, so far, a comparatively low percentage of "catastrophic" saints (and a comparatively high percentage of "fortunate" saints) in the second sensate period. Up to the beginning of the twentieth century this sensate period had not yet fully entered its disintegrating phase; it was still fairly tolerant toward saints and the Christian religion. Still paying them lip service, it was not, therefore, too unfavorable for the emergence and growth of "fortunate" saints.

If our study could have been continued from 1914 to 1950—when our sensate order definitely enters its phase of disintegration and suicide—the picture would have been different: we would have had a large crop of Christian martyrs and "catastrophic" converts to be eventually canonized as saints. During the last thirty years, our disintegrating sensate order has become quite unfavorable for the abundant growth of "fortunate" saints and quite favorable for that of martyred and "catastrophic" saints. Only for the last decade or so have a large number of spectacular conversions to Catholicism or Protestantism taken place in this and other countries. Large-scale mass conversions to Christianity occurred in the army and among civilians during the First and Second World Wars, and during the civil wars in Russia, Spain, and elsewhere. They all are examples of the general law of religious and moral polarization in times of calamity and *dies irae, dies illa*. Some of these "catastrophic" converts eventually will be sanctified.

In this way they will show a high rate of "catastrophic" saints similar to that of the first sensate period.

Finally the figures show that ideational periods also yield a considerable proportion of "catastrophic" saints (but much less than of "fortunate" saints). The reason for this is also clear. Not the whole population in such ideational periods becomes ideational in its mentality and conduct. A large proportion still remains essentially sensate and lives a sinful life. Under the impact of some catastrophic precipitating event, some of these may, now and then, undergo a real conversion from sinful to saintly ways. After conversion some of these converts live such a pious and truly Christian life that eventually they are sanctified. For instance, a prostitute was once sent by the enemies of a saintly desert hermit to his hermitage to seduce him. During the night in his cell, while the woman tried to accomplish her purpose, the hermit, to resist temptation, burned one finger after another in the fire of a candle. The woman was so deeply impressed that she confessed her sin, was converted, turned herself into a hermit and eventually was sanctified.

In different forms, similar catastrophic conversions eventually resulting in sainthood frequently occur in ideational periods: hence the comparatively high percentage of "catastrophic" saints in this period.

The preceding analysis explains the percentages of the different types of saints in the various periods dominated by our main cultural supersystems.

The explanation is so well grounded that one can make this prediction: If the Christian-Catholic Church continues to exist in the future, and if its rules for the canonization of saints remain essentially the same, we can expect that among the saints who lived in the first half of the twentieth century and who will be canonized in the future, the proportion of martyred and "catastrophic" saints will be much higher than they hitherto have been, and the proportion of "fortunate" saints will be much lower than it was for the second sensate period up to roughly 1910. The spectrum of saints from the standpoint of our four types will be fairly close to that of the first sensate period in our table.

The next generation can check whether this prediction will turn out to be correct. Such is the meaning of Table 43.

PART THREE

ALTRUISM AND THE PERSONALITY

39. GOOD-NEIGHBORLINESS

AND SAINTLINESS: SUMMARY

The activities of the American "good neighbors" supplement the inadequacy, bureaucracy, formalism, coldness, and other shortcomings of the relief activities of institutionalized service agencies. The largest percentage of the good deeds of our "good neighbors" comprise deeds that alleviate boredom, lonesomeness, grief, and various other troubles. Contemporary American life is full of boredom and loneliness for millions, and the official agencies fail to remedy this "vacuum" in our lives. If we consider all the good deeds of all the "good neighbors," their vitalizing, moralizing, beautifying and encouraging effects are likely to be more important than all the official relief of the institutionalized agencies. Real sympathy, a warm heart, unquestioning friendship, and generous love are the free gifts of the "good neighbors."

The social function of the saints, aside from the above rôle of the good neighbors, consists of being a living incarnation of the highest goodness, love, and spirituality of a given society. The saints are creative heroes in the field of moral values and they set a visible example for imitation. In the field of altruistic love the bulk of the saints are masters and creators of "love-energy," which they generate in large quantities of the purest quality. Without these masters of "love-production," society is bound to suffer greatly from a catastrophic scarcity of friendship and harmony among its members, and from an overabundance of deadly hatred and strife. Whatever the form in which these masters of "love-production" appear, be it religious or non-religious, a minimum of such apostles of unselfishness is as necessary for any creative and happy society as is a minimum of experts in the production of vital material goods. The concrete forms of love of these saintly apostles change, but their substance remains perennial and immortal: no society can live a long, happy, and creative life without the heroes of love and spirituality.

Some of the saints discharged these functions in a non-institutionalized, and some in an institutionalized, form.

Women comprise about 75 per cent of the American "good neighbors," and the remaining percentage consists of men and couples.

Among the Christian-Catholic saints *men provide 82 per cent, and women 17 per cent;* among the Russian-Orthodox saints *96 per cent are men and only 4 per cent are women.* The proportion of women among the Christian-Catholic saints tends to increase rapidly after the seventeenth century, and in the twentieth century women account for 100 per cent of the saints. This trend is not noticeable in the case of the Russian-Orthodox saints. The predominantly female composition of the American good neighbors and the overwhelming male composition of the saints is tentatively accounted for in the text by an analysis of the factors which were instrumental in bringing about such phenomena.

Since good-neighborliness is a creativity in the field of goodness, and since it takes time to become socially visible in such a creativity, we find that *about 70 per cent of all good neighbors range from 30 to 59 years of age.* This age composition and the age of social recognition is similar to that of eminent scientists, artists, money-makers, business leaders, political leaders, and other creative persons. The age composition of these constructive and leading groups is quite different from that of criminals, prostitutes, and other subsocial groups.

GOOD-NEIGHBORLINESS AND SAINTLINESS: SUMMARY

The duration of life of the Christian-Catholic and the Russian-Orthodox saints is extraordinarily long, and far exceeds not only that of their contemporaries, but also that of the present American population. Despite the fact that the majority of the saints lived between the first and seventeenth centuries when the average life duration was short, and that 15 to 37 per cent of them were executed as martyrs and thus their life was terminated violently before its natural end; and in spite of the saints' asceticism, hardships, self-mortification, and other conditions unfavorable to a long life, the saints as a group lived far longer than, for instance, those who died in the United States in 1920 at the age of 20 and above. Of the Christian-Catholic saints, 57 per cent died at the age of 61 and above, and 17.7 per cent died at the age of 81 and above. Again, we find that 57 per cent of the Russian-Orthodox saints died at the age of 71 and above. This extraordinary longevity strongly suggests that not only is there a causal bond between sainthood and long life, but that probably the saintly way of life is a very important factor in longevity. Through the highest kind of self-control, through the deep peace of mind and complete integration of personality, altruistic love and saintliness become truly life-giving and life-invigorating powers. Any individual or group desirous of living a long and harmonious life should take note of the fact that the therapy of unselfish love and saintliness is possibly a means to that end.

In spite of the sorrows and joys, pains and pleasures, hardships and comforts that fall to our "good neighbors" in the same degree as to the social stratum of the American population to which they belong, the overwhelming majority of the "good neighbors" have a serene peace of mind; they feel at peace with themselves, mankind, and the world at large. They are happy and feel that their life is worth living.

The saints, notwithstanding extraordinary hardships, "dark nights" of despair, persecution, martyrdom, self-mortification, and all sorts of sorrows, achieved for the most part "the peace of God which passeth all understanding," imperturbable and ineffable bliss of the *summum bonum*.

Viewed from this standpoint, unselfish love is not only a life-giving force, but is also the best therapeutic method for securing real peace of mind, meaningful happiness, real freedom, and creative power. The almost unfathomable possibilities of unselfish love remain practically untapped by contemporary science. The experience of the saints and of the good neighbors would make it advisable to study and develop this therapy of love as the most fruitful and efficacious means to the attainment of a worthwhile life.

The parental families of the "good neighbors" are larger than the average American family. More than 80 per cent of their parental families are well integrated. Seventy per cent of the "good neighbors" state they had a very happy childhood and were blessed by the love of their parents and other members of the family; an additional 18 per cent had a fairly happy childhood and the grace of love in their family; only 11 per cent had an unhappy childhood, although some of them were loved by at least one member of the family.

Almost 90 per cent of the saints were loved by their parents. At least 65 per cent were encouraged in their saintly aspirations by their parents, and an additional 5 per cent were neither encouraged nor hindered. Only 18 per cent of the parental families opposed saintly aspirations. *Thus an overwhelming majority of "good neighbors" and saints came from well-integrated families and were blessed by the grace of love in childhood and youth.* The progress these "fortunate" altruists and saints made in love and good-neighborliness throughout their lives was harmonious, free from any catastrophe and late conversion. Contrastingly, a minority had an unhappy childhood and youth, and consequently the course to good-neighborliness or sainthood was less smooth for them. Many of them suffered tragedies which resulted in conversion at a later period in life.

In their relationship to their parents the "good neighbors" and saints show no evidence of Freudian "complexes" and aberrations. These "complexes," "fixations," and "repressions," observed by Freud in the case of "pathological" clients, do not apply at all to the parent-child relationships among our "good neighbors" and saints. On the other hand, Freud's stress on the importance of "acceptance" or "rejection" of a child by his parents is corroborated by our findings in a more generalized manner, since it is not confined to the first few years of the child's life, nor to the love of his parents only. The love or hate of siblings, playmates, neighbors, relatives, and teachers is also important to the child and youth. Sometimes the love of these unrelated persons substitutes for the absence of love in parents or siblings.

These data confirm *the extreme importance of the parental family and of love in early childhood and youth.* The bliss of being loved and of loving appears to be a most decisive factor in achieving good-neighborliness, altruism, and sainthood. Even some of the "good neighbors" and saints who were deprived of this blessing in childhood, and suffered accordingly, had the blessing of love at a later period in life. Eventually it led to their conversion to sainthood and human kindness.

Different results are pointed out by the increasing number of studies of criminals and juvenile delinquents. A disintegrated parental family, in which the child is unloved and "rejected," is cited as possibly the decisive factor in creating criminal, delinquent, and generally selfish, un-social, or subsocial behavior. Cursed by hate and an unfriendly world during their early years, deprived of the life-giving "vitamin of love," they grow into sickly, disfigured, and hate-laden persons.

In a number of forthcoming research projects of the Harvard Research Center in Altruistic Integration and Creativity, it will be shown that a generally friendly approach of one person to another calls forth a friendly response in 65 to 90 per cent of the cases, whereas an aggressive approach is responded to aggressively, and an indifferent approach indifferently in about the same percentages. Thus the age-old observation that love generates love and hate generates hate is essentially correct.

These results speak for themselves. They indicate the paramount importance of love and friendship, especially in childhood and youth, in determining the future of a person. *Love appears to be the most important educational and therapeutic factor in achieving the physical, biological, mental, moral, and social well-being of a person.* On the other hand, hate and all its derivatives, including extreme selfishness, are the poisons that tend to harm a child for the rest of his life, causing him to grow into an ugly, poisonous, and sub-normal human plant.

Of the "good neighbors," 70 per cent are married, 7 per cent widowed, 15 per cent single, and 1 per cent divorced. Thus among the "good neighbors" there is a higher percentage of marriage and a much lower percentage of divorces than among the rank and file of the population.

The size of the family of the good neighbor is slightly larger than that of the average American family. Childless families are less frequent, and families with five and more children are more often found among the "good neighbors" than among the average American family. Similarly, the families of the "good neighbors" themselves are, for the majority, harmonious and well integrated. Only one family reports delinquency trouble among its offspring, and 5 to 11 per cent report incompatibility of the spouses. Some 50 per cent of the "good neighbors" would marry persons of a different faith, and 39 per cent of a different race. The rest prefer to marry persons of similar religion and race because they believe that such a marriage would be more stable, stronger and happier than marriage with a person of a different faith or race.

Some 74.5 per cent of the Christian-Catholic saints were unmarried, 5 per cent married involuntarily, and 20.5 per cent married voluntarily. On the whole, Christian-Catholic sanctity seems to be linked considerably with sexual continence. In this respect, the Christian-Catholic and the Russian-Orthodox saints resemble many great altruists and spiritual leaders of other religions and cultures. Many of these, right up to Gandhi and Sri Aurobindo, contend that complete sexual continence is necessary for attaining real sainthood and union with the divine.

On the other hand, 20 per cent of the saints were married. The pre-conversion sexual life of a portion of the unmarried saints among the Christians, Hindus, Sufis, Buddhists, Taoists, and other great spiritual and moral leaders, as well as the large percentage of marriages among the "good neighbors," suggest that sanctity and an orderly sex life are not necessarily mutually exclusive.

Socially and economically the bulk of the "good neighbors" belong to the middle strata or classes, and the minority is almost equally divided between the lower and upper socio-economic strata. Occupationally, almost one half of the group are housewives, married to middle-class husbands, and the rest are professional people: businessmen, white-collar employees, laborers, and farmers. Approximately 58 per cent of the parents of the "good neighbors" belonged to the farmer and labor classes, whereas among the "good neighbors" themselves, only 6 to 8 per cent belong to these classes. Under American conditions the middle classes appear more "good neighborly" than the upper and lower classes, and the lower classes are no less unselfish than the upper classes. As a detail it can be mentioned that a tangible portion of our "good neighbors" dislike lawyers and judges and accuse them of being vindictive hypocrites who transgress God's command to forgive and not judge others.

Some 62 per cent of the Christian-Catholic saints and 41 per cent of the Russian-Orthodox saints had royal and upper aristocratic origins, 13 and 17 per cent came from the peasant and lower classes respectively, and the rest hailed from a middle-class background comprised of government workers, the clergy, and merchants. Thus, in the last nineteen centuries, the saints have come mainly from the upper classes. In this respect, the saints, who are persons of genius in the field of spiritual and moral creativity, resemble the men and women of genius in the arts, sciences, technology, and social organizations, who also came largely from the upper strata of their respective societies.

The main trend we observe is that *as we move from the first to the twentieth century, the quota of saints contributed by the upper and, later, the middle strata tends to decrease while the quota of the lower classes tends to increase.*

Each social stratum contributes its maximum share of saints at the period of its maximal power and prestige. When these decrease, its share of saints likewise decreases. Consequently, an interesting law of lag or of successive strata in the production of saints appears.

Royalty produced the greatest number of saints between the sixth and eleventh centuries, but after the fifteenth century there is a decidedly smaller contribution which finally reaches the zero point.

Upper nobility provides the maximum number of saints from the seventh to the fifteenth centuries, but after the seventeenth century its share becomes negligible and eventually also arrives at zero.

The middle class contributed the greatest share of saints from the sixteenth to the seventeenth centuries, but after the eighteenth century its share declined to zero.

The peasant and labor strata contributed a very insignificant number of saints up to the fourteenth century. After that, their share increased until they contributed 60 per cent of all the saints in the nineteenth century, and 100 per cent in the twentieth century.

Thus the Christian-Catholic and the Russian-Orthodox Churches have ceased to receive their supply of saints from the upper and middle strata and are now scratching the very bottom of the social pyramid for their saints. Even here the supply is dwindling steadily so that the traditional Christian-Catholic and Russian-Orthodox saints may become an extinct social type. Saints are becoming synonymous with "good neighbors" and altruistic persons in general, persons who have diverse religious affiliations and in a minority of cases are not even affiliated with any institutionalized religion (free thinkers or atheists).

The social position and the activities of the saints that led to their sainthood are as follows: *75 to 90 per cent were directly or indirectly members of the Christian clergy; of these, 15 to 40 per cent were high dignitaries.* Only 2 per cent of the Christian-Catholic, and 12 per cent of the Russian-Orthodox saints belonged to the royal or princely stratum. The rest were merchants, patrons, pious virgins, and so forth. Some 7 per cent of the Russian saints were "God's Fools." *We can observe a historical trend here which increasingly democratized the social position and the activities of the saints.* As we approach the twentieth century the royal and aristocratic saints, and even the high Church dignitary saints disappear and are replaced to an ever-increasing extent by saints from the lower and middle social strata, and by saints who hold a lower position in the Church hierarchy. This trend resembles that of the parental families of the saints.

The saints are, first and foremost, ideal heroes of the clergy, and clerical activities led to sainthood much more frequently than any other social activities. Along with the decline in prestige and power of the Christian clergy, the saints have declined as a social type and have tended to assume increasingly different forms, one of which is that of an altruistic, secular "good neighbor."

Approximately 20 to 25 per cent of the "good neighbors" had an elementary education, 28 to 37 per cent a high-school education, and 25 to 38 per cent a college education. Their school intelligence (measured by grades and mental tests) did not deviate from that of the average student body. This confirms the observation that *there is no close relationship between altruism and school intelligence.*

Their attitude toward teachers and the world at large may be of some significance. Some 92 per cent report a very favorable attitude towards their teachers; the rest were indifferent. As many as 98 per cent report the friendliest attitude toward the world at large, in its physical, biological, and sociocultural aspects, whereas only 1 per cent report a hostile reaction.

Those who believe that man's environment is responsible for his goodness or badness constitute 90 per cent, whereas 10 per cent stress the factor of heredity. Thus, *the American "good neighbor" is an optimistic, friendly environmentalist with average school intelligence.*

The average saint received the education of his class in his respective century. Intellectually, the saints can be classed as average, with a minority deviating above and below this. An overwhelming majority was kindly and friendly from an early age onward; a minority underwent conversion at a later age, becoming subsequently friendly and altruistic.

The *religious affiliations* of the "good neighbors" are scattered among many Christian and non-Christian denominations. On the whole our "good neighbors" are slightly more religious than the average for the nation. *Two per cent declare themselves to be atheistic.* This should not surprise us, for even among the outstanding altruists of human history there have been "atheists." Gautama Buddha and the early Buddhists during the first five hundred years of their history serve as an example. They, too, denied the existence of God, soul, ego, person and substance, but believed in the existence of the causal moral law of karma and love.

About 40 per cent of the "good neighbors" belong to no political party, 35 per cent are Republicans, about 25 per cent are Democrats, and less than 1 per cent are Socialists. These data show that good-neighborliness is disassociated from membership in any political party. One can be a "good neighbor" without belonging to any political faction. "Good neighbors" are affiliated more closely with organizations that have particularly strong characteristics of good-neighborliness and social service, such as the Red Cross, the Community Chest, etc.

Of the "good neighbors," 62 to 91 per cent mentioned their relatives among the first six persons dearest to them. Beginning with the seventh person, the non-kinsfolk become an increasing majority and comprise 90 per cent in the case of the twelfth dearest person. This signifies that an overwhelming majority of neighbors consider the ties of kinship to be the most important and valuable ties, over and above other social ties and relationships. It is only with the seventh dearest person that the other ties—religious, occupational, national, economic, political, etc.—become more important (partly because many do not have more than six close relatives). A small minority of 12 to 36 per cent named non-kinsfolk as the first six dearest persons. This means that such a minority considers family and kinship ties to be of less importance than non-kinship ties of friendship.

Among the first dearest relatives, the spouse is the dearest for the majority of the neighbors, followed by parents, and then a child. From the second to the seventh place among the dearest, a child is the dearest in the majority of cases.

In order to adjust to their environment the saints used four different methods: 46 per cent lived and acted in the ordinary sociocultural world and achieved sanctity in this environment; 9 per cent solved the problem of adjustment to their environment by eremitically isolating themselves in the desert or other uninhabited place; 31 per cent lived in monasteries, cloisters, or environments especially designed and built for spiritual and moral ennoblement; 13 per cent were pilgrims and wanderers who were not attached permanently to any place or abode. In the course of time, between the first and the twentieth centuries, the saints became less and less eremitic and monastic, and an ever-increasing number solved the problem of environmental adjustment by remaining in the ordinary sociocultural world. Most of the contemporary saints, if there are any, live in the everyday world and do their altruistic and spiritual work as ordinary, mostly secular, good neighbors. Gandhi and Albert Schweitzer are conspicuous examples.

About 62 per cent of the saints achieved self-mastery and control of their passions, ambitions, and biological drives through a *technique of moderate self-discipline*, free from excessive austerities and self-torture. A minority, 15 to 38 per cent, used exceeding self-mortification and self-torture. From the first to the twentieth century, history shows a decline in the self-mortification method in favor of a more moderate technique of self-control and self-mastery.

The number of saints that emerged in each century increased greatly during the first four centuries of our era. Subsequently the number decreased but remained fairly high from the fifth to the sixteenth centuries. During the last three centuries, because of a rising sensate culture, *the number of saints declined catastrophically*, until there were no saints left in the Russian-Orthodox Church in the nineteenth century and only a very few in the Christian-Catholic Church in the twentieth century. The stream of saints seems to have dried up. Unless new springs appear, it may become totally dry.

In contrast to the criminal deviants who fall below legally prescribed norms, *the "good neighbors" and saints are deviants who rise above the level of moral conduct demanded by official law. Their actions are "superlegal."* Some of these superlegal actions do not conflict with the official law; others result in conflict between the "good neighbors" and saints on one hand, and the official law and government on the other. In such conflicts the "good neighbors" and saints become "subversives," "heretics," "criminal," "dangerous revolutionaries," and as such they are persecuted, punished, and even executed.

This tragedy repeats itself from Socrates and Christ on to Gandhi and Sri Aurobindo (also imprisoned twice). This explains the fact that a considerable number of our "good neighbors" have had some collisions with the powers that be. It also explains why 15 to 37 per cent of the saints consist of martyrs, not to mention a much larger percentage of saints who received milder forms of punishment. The tragedy of "superlegal" deviants continues to our very day.

Christian-Catholic martyrs are especially numerous in the centuries when sensate culture gained dominance; they accounted for 72 per cent of all the saints of the first four (predominantly sensate) centuries of our era, and for 44 per cent of the saints in the second sensate period from the sixteenth to the twentieth centuries. Martyrs become the least frequent (only 8 per cent) in the centuries of idealistic culture (twelfth and thirteenth centuries) and they comprise 19 per cent of all the saints in the centuries of ideational culture (the fifth to eleventh centuries). Generally, the number of martyrs increases notably in periods of profound crisis in the Church. Likewise, the collision of all superlegal altruists with official law and government tends to increase in periods of moral crisis. The moral values of a given society, of its official law on the one hand, and the moral values of the "good neighbors," altruists, and saints on the other, are often in conflict.

Among the "good neighbors" as well as among the saints, we meet *two fundamental types: the "fortunate" and "catastrophic"* (converted). The "good neighbors" and the saints who have well-adjusted personalities from earliest childhood, and who without any catastrophe or even conversion quietly grow into altruists or saints, make up the "fortunate" type. The "good neighbors" and saints who were neither altruistic nor saintly in the first part of their life but who, under the influence of increasing inner conflicts and various "precipitating factors" became altruistic or saintly, make up the "converted" or "catastrophic" type. *The "fortunate" type is in an overwhelming majority among both groups studied;* it accounts for 68 per cent of the Christian-Catholic saints and 69 per cent of the Russian-Orthodox saints, and together with an "intermediary" type it comprises 97 per cent of the "good neighbors." The "converted" (catastrophic) type makes up 3 per cent of the "good neighbors," 18 per cent of the Christian-Catholic saints, and about 30 per cent of the Russian saints.

Thus the majority of altruists and saints show their saintly-altruistic proclivities at an early age. Contrary to a widespread opinion they do not pass through any catastrophe and do not have any spectacular conversion. They quietly grow into their sainthood or goodness as grass or flowers grow, gradually and silently. The bulk of these "fortunate" persons had a happy childhood and youth and were loved by their families, playmates, neighbors, and others with whom they came into contact in their early years.

There are many kinds of experience involved in *the precipitating factors* that start the real moral or religious transformation of converted "good neighbors" or saints. Among our "good neighbors" these factors are: death of a loved one in 22 per cent of the cases; grave illness of a good neighbor in 22 per cent of the cases; the tragedy of war in 5 per cent; another 5 per cent is made up of personal tragedies; accident involving a "good neighbor" make up 7 per cent of these precipitating factors; religious conversion (preceding the moral-behavioral transformation) in 7 per cent of the cases; an unexpected kindness towards a "good neighbor" in 3 per cent; 6 per cent are produced by general educational experience; 4 per cent by a book, sermon, movie, play, and like experiences. Similar in kind were the precipitating factors of the "converted-catastrophic" type of saint. These data show that *some 60 per cent of the precipitating factors are catastrophic events involving a saint or a good neighbor.*

These facts sharply contradict a prevalent opinion that "*frustration invariably breeds aggression.*" In the case of our "good neighbors" and saints, their catastrophic frustration did not breed aggression, but rather kindness, love, and religious transfiguration. A study of other frustrated altruists and men of genius shows similar effects of frustrations. A study of the mass behavior of thousands and millions living under catastrophic conditions clearly displays at least two opposite effects: a part of such a population becomes more aggressive, more cynical, more selfish, materialistic and hedonistic; another part becomes more spiritual, more ethical, more altruistic, and more religious. In brief, the popular formula of the Freudians and of many other psychologists needs a radical correction: it contains only a part of the truth and a great deal of error.

The factors of good-neighborliness and sainthood in the opinion of the "good neighbors" themselves (in essentials corroborated by the lives of the saints) are as follows: 29 per cent of the "good neighbors" ascribe their good-neighborliness to their *parental family* (its love, harmony, discipline, and training); 28 per cent ascribe it to their *"general life-experience"* (altruistic human nature, lessons of history, mutual aid as a condition of survival, etc.) and to their social and cultural environment (aside from family and religion, specially mentioned); 21 per cent regard *religion* as the main factor of their neighborliness; 11 per cent indicate a specific *personal experience;* 8 per cent indicate *school education;* 3 per cent ascribe it to an unusual, mainly *catastrophic,* personal precipitant; less than 1 per cent mention *books.* Thus a good, integrated, and loving family; then the learned universal experience reinforced by the total sociocultural environment; then religion; then personal experience, the retroactive rôle of our own actions and thoughts, are the main factors of altruism. Our "good neighbors" ascribe less weight than the Existentialists do to man's ability to control his destiny, but they grant it more weight than do the complete determinists. According to the "good neighbors" in 11 to 14 *per cent of his goodness or badness, man is what he has made of himself through all his thoughts, emo-*

tions, words, and deeds. This is a fairly sound pragmatic solution of the eternal problem of man's determinism or indeterminism: to a certain extent, all of us are what we have made of ourselves by our own behavior and thoughts. Finally, the "good neighbors" give a very modest rôle to school education and a negligible one to books in the shaping of "good neighbors." These results agree with the existing bulk of evidence concerning altruism or egoism. Even the rough percentages ascribed to each factor seem roughly valid for contemporary America and generally for Western sensate culture and society.

Finally, the martyr type among the saints achieves its highest percentage in the sensate periods; the "catastrophic" type among saints is the most frequent in idealistic and then sensate cultures; the "fortunate" type of saint blossoms most successfully in predominantly idealistic and ideational periods. In accordance with this we should expect that the twentieth century, being the century of disintegration of an overripe sensate culture, will produce a high rate of martyr and "catastrophic" saints.

40. THE MEANING OF ALTRUISTIC LOVE

Such are the main results of the study. Some of these results concern the characteristics of the "good neighbors" and of the saints; other results throw light on much more general problems. Both together partly elucidate the mystery of the factors and processes of becoming a "good neighbor" or a saint. What is still more important, the results show some of the beneficial effects of unselfish love and sanctity, such as a remarkable vitality, a long duration of life, an unperturbable peace of mind, and an ineffably rich happiness. In the terms of a sensate utilitarianist or hedonist it could be said that "it pays to be unselfish, loving, and saintly." Love's dividends are infinitely greater and more lasting than those of any selfish enterprise. Even more: the study suggests that the potentials or "the fission-forces" of altruistic love are so gigantic and so sublimely rich that a better knowledge of these potentials is the noblest and the most powerful force humanity can have for its self-control and for a gigantic renaissance of its creative forces in the field of truth, beauty, and goodness. The time has come when an infinitely intensified study of the sublime "energy of love" should be on the agenda of history. If we acquire a deeper knowledge of its "fission-forces" and put them into operation, all will be well with mankind. If we fail, hate with its satellites—death, destruction, misery, and anarchy—will continue to blot human history and perhaps end it in mad destruction.

APPENDIX A

SAMPLE AMERICAN "GOOD NEIGHBORS"

1. Letters Received by the "Breakfast in Hollywood" Program

Dear Tom:
    We, the undersigned representative group of this village of Eldridge, Alabama, which has a population of around four hundred, do hereby, and for reasons we trust you will find obvious, nominate Miss Frances B. as our "Good Neighbor." Miss B. keeps house for her father and two brothers. Every summer she cans an oversupply of fruits and vegetables and gives it away. She teaches the third grade in the local grammar school. This summer she is serving as acting postmaster. Besides the performance of those regular duties, she extends to the entire village and adjacent community the following free and wholly unrewarded services:
    She acts as community nurse. Driving her own car, she carries the sick to the doctor or to the hospital and brings convalescents from the hospital. During schooltime she often takes underprivileged children home with her on bad days for warm, nourishing lunches. She regularly delivers fresh milk from her fine Jersey cow to persons who otherwise might not have the milk they need. She has delivered this milk for months at a time to several families. She has supervised the making of many gifts and given and collected many benefits for a nearby Veterans' Hospital. She serves as nurses' aid in hospitals on Saturdays during schooltime. She maintains a surgical-dressing room in her home at which around one thousand surgical dressings are made for the Red Cross each week. She goes for and then carries workers back to their homes.
    Tom, these are only a few of the many reasons why we think Miss B. is a "Good Neighbor." What do you think?
                                      Very truly yours,
                                      And the letter is signed individually by a list which represents what must be almost every merchant and official of the town of Eldridge.

APPENDIX A

Dear Tom Breneman:

I want to suggest a dearly loved couple for your "Good Neighbor" orchid—Mr. and Mrs. Archie C., National City, California. We cannot begin to tell the many splendid things these good folks do. Perhaps the thing they are best known for is their unselfish, untiring efforts in doing kind deeds for the physically handicapped. Archie, as a boy, encountered a lame child. From then on he dedicated his life to doing everything within his power to see that every effort was put forth to make those so afflicted comfortable and able to walk. They have personally delivered over three hundred wheel chairs to homes where they were needed; also an unknown number of crutches, walkers, braces, etc.

On Archie's day off he and Mary spend their entire time visiting shut-ins and doing errands or fixing gadgets for their comfort and convenience. If they cannot fix one, they find someone who can. One day each week, every week during the two years of 1935 and 1936 of the San Diego Exposition, they took a physically handicapped person to see the Fair. The Southern California Telephone Company, where Archie is employed, recognizing the philanthropic good he does, has made it possible for him to take time off any day, any time he is needed. Mr. and Mrs. C. collect radios, have them repaired, and distribute them where there is the greatest need.

Tom, I could go on and on and never do their deeds justice; so I will just ask a few of their friends to sign this with me, so that you will realize they are "Good Good Neighbors" and deserving of a whole basket of orchids—but one to them will make us deeply grateful.

Sincerely,
Ora W. C.
(and 140 additional signatures)

Dear Tom Breneman:

I should like to nominate as your "Good Neighbor" a fine woman who is mother to more than two thousand three hundred boys who are delivering the goods to our troops on the world's battlefronts. This "Good Neighbor" is Captain Mary C., 195 High Street, Denver, Colorado—the only lady captain in the United States Merchant Marine. When the United States entered the war, Captain Mary opened her home to all men who wanted to train in navigation and other maritime subjects, and from 1941

to this day has held classes daily to instruct men who sail our merchant ships.
Now get this, Tom. She is seventy-three years old; but, despite her age, she has been as much a part of our war effort as any soldier fighting overseas. The two thousand three hundred boys who have received her training in her own home are manning merchant ships to win this war. She receives an average of six hundred letters per month from boys she has trained, who sail to every port in the world. And at seventy-three Captain Mary is still working to train our young men so that they may deliver the goods to assure victory. I think that Captain Mary deserves your "Good Neighbor" orchid, and I feel sure that her two thousand three hundred boys join me in this sentiment.

      Cordially yours,
      JAMES B. C.
      Lieutenant,
      United States Maritime Service

Dear Tom Breneman:
Mr. and Mrs. Edward H., of 417 Market Avenue, East St. Louis, Illinois, are my nominees for your "Good Neighbor" orchid. They have been married thirty-seven years; and although childless, they have taken care of and helped to educate six children. Dozens of couples, too, have started "housekeeping" in the small two-room house in their back yard; or perhaps it's been an older couple who had no place to live, who moved in, and who stayed as long as they wanted to, rent-free.
Mr. H. is a railroad switchman, and he has brought home to his wife over a hundred runaway boys. These youngsters were always given clean clothing, good food, and a place to sleep. Sometimes, in the first few hours, the boys would confide their parents' names and their home addresses; again the H's would have to keep them several days before the boys would give them the necessary information. Then a long-distance call would be put through, and soon the boys would be put on a train for home. Many are the letters Mrs. H. receives from parents all over the United States for the kindness she and her husband have shown to their runaway boys. They haven't done anything spectacular; but don't you think they are "Good Neighbors"?

      Sincerely yours,
      MRS. K. H. McN.

APPENDIX A

2. Sketches of "Good Neighbors"

Miss H.

Sex: Female.

Age: Sixty-five.

Race: White.

National extraction: English.

Religion: Unitarian. Attends church regularly. Is superintendent of Sunday school. Says she gets emotional satisfaction from the service.

Occupation: Former schoolteacher. Now takes in boarders.

Intelligence: Above average.

Political affiliation: Republican. Joined Republican Party so as to work towards defeat of M. in primary. Republican primary was the election in this state. Has inclinations toward theoretical Marxism. Believes in "From each according to his ability, to each according to his needs."

Education: Graduate of Wellesley College.

Economic status: From a formerly wealthy family. Now has small pension from school system and takes in some slight money from boarders. Actually is living in poverty, because she shares whatever she has with poverty-stricken people, so that she has no more than they have.

Social status: Miss H. is from an old English colonial family, long established in this community. Both her parents were community leaders. She has nothing whatever to do with the recreational social life of the town, as she is too busy helping other people. Her upper-class position is definitely recognized by the older people in the community; but it is doubtful whether new people coming here, or young people not acquainted with the unwritten list of who's who, would ever guess that she is supposed to be in the upper social brackets, as she lives under such poor conditions.

Family: Miss H. never married. Her parents are dead, and she is out of contact with her brother's children. She thus has practically no family of blood relatives. However, she has a large circle of people who consider her house their home, always return there for vacations, and are close enough so that they really constitute a family group. They are all attached not only to her but to one another.

Personal appearance: Miss H. was probably born with about average attractiveness, but is so totally uninterested in her looks that she dresses and generally fixes herself up far below the average.

Evidences of sociality: So far as is known, Miss H. is the only one in this community who really puts the teachings of Jesus into practice. She has completely given up all thought of herself and devotes herself to the welfare of others. No human being, no matter how repulsive, sick, poor, dishonest, or what not, is turned away from her home. Those who can do so pay board; those who cannot don't.

Since the war, one of the local persecuted groups has been the wives and children of prisoners in the naval prison here. Prisoners' dependents do not receive allotments—the Red Cross has orders from regional headquarters not to help them, and the local state welfare office cannot help them in most cases because of residence requirements. This is a relatively new problem, because formerly to be in prison was considered a disgrace, and the families of the prisoners did not live near the prison. During the war, prison sentences have been given in a careless and unjust manner to enlisted men, so that many boys are here who are not of a criminal type. But many others are. Their wives often insist upon coming here to be near them. The only place these women are welcome is in the houses of prostitution and in Miss H's home. Miss H. has taken in many of them and their children. They live rent-free until they get a job, if they ever do get one. When they go out to work, Miss H. takes care of their children. Miss H. mentioned one girl who left owing her fifty dollars. She gradually sent the whole amount back. Miss H. tells this as a success story for the girl. "I thought she did awfully well." She did not seem to expect her to pay back the loan, nor did she even particularly want her to. She never mentions the cases of people who do not pay back.

Occasionally the state department of welfare has a child to

place in a foster home who has such difficult behavior problems that no foster home will take him. Various abnormal sexual practices and stealing are mostly looked down on by foster mothers, and for a child with both these habits it is most difficult to find a home. Every time a child comes along that no other home in town will take, he can always go to live with Miss H. In some mysterious manner, she usually manages to improve these children greatly.

Miss H. has done particularly good work with adolescent boys. Two of these, to all appearances headed straight for prison, are now ministers, very much reformed. The brother of one boy living with Miss H. was in prison at the time Miss H. heard about him. She started writing to him, assuring him that he had a home with her when he got out, if he wanted it. He had served several sentences, starting in early childhood. Stealing seemed to be a deeply rooted symptom. Miss H. said that she fully expected him to steal everything from her, and prepared herself to accept this before he came. She thought of the story of the bishop's candlesticks, and decided that was the way she would feel about anything of hers that might be stolen. The day he got out of jail, he was arrested again in another state for the same crime for which he had just finished serving time. He was involved in two states simultaneously. It seems this is legally impossible, but it can happen if no one of influence becomes interested. Miss H. got all the members of her "family" by adoption to rally round this cause, and thus obtained his release. He then came to live with her. All the people in the house knew of his past, but they told no one else. He has never been involved in any trouble since; he has gone into the army and has served his country well, even receiving a good-conduct medal.

Examples could go on to the length of a book, but this is enough to give the general idea of Miss H. She has spent all her inherited money on unfortunate people; and though nothing has been said about it, some valuable family antiques are no longer in her home. Perhaps she has sold them. I refer to objects too large to be stolen. Although her standards of integrity are high, her house is untidy.

She spends nothing on herself. She got to the point of looking really terrible, wearing extremely old clothes. One of her reformed boys, who got a good job, bought her a complete outfit of clothing last Christmas; now she looks better.

Length of time person has been characterized by sociality: In childhood Miss H. used to try to prevent her playmates from making remarks to Catholic nuns who passed by. This would indicate early emergence of sociality. But Miss H. herself thinks it developed chiefly around the college age. In college she was noted as a liberal. She thinks there was some influence from one of the teachers there, but it was not very important. She cannot think of any person or event which influenced her strongly. In college she refused to join the Christian Association because the girl who asked her to join said she should do so on the ground that it was good for one's college career.

Emotional security in childhood: Miss H. felt close to both parents and felt loved and safe.

Sociality of other members of family:

Father: Miss H. reports that her father was a social person, though perhaps not as much so as her mother. He was as nice to all the neighborhood children as he was to his own. He was a political liberal, against the Spanish-American War, against the Boer War, and against the protective tariff. He favored woman suffrage even before her mother did. He was not sure, however, that it was a good idea to take people into your own home.

Mother: Miss H's mother was a teacher before her marriage. She was the first woman in this town to be on the school board. She did not want her daughter to be a teacher; but when her daughter determined to be one anyway, she helped her in every way she could. It almost looks as if both Miss H's parents thought she might go to extremes of self-sacrifice; and they were not sure they wanted this—for the sake of her own survival. Miss H. reports that her mother taught her that the worst thing you could do was to make fun of anyone's infirmities. Her mother also taught her religious tolerance. At that time the conflict between Catholics and Protestants was very strong. Her mother told her that nuns were very good Catholic women who were giving up their personal lives for the sake of serving others and should be respected and treated with every consideration.

At that time there were two sources of servants: the Catholic immigrants and the Protestants from Nova Scotia. Many people preferred the Nova Scotians, because they were Protestants. But Mrs. H. would not have any of the Nova Scotians, because she could not stand their prejudice against Catholics.

APPENDIX A

In-group and out-group ethics: Miss H. dislikes Protestant fundamentalism. By "fundamentalism" she means the following beliefs: We all sinned with Adam, God was sorry he made man and condemned everybody to Hell, then came to earth and died on the Cross; it is all right to sin as long as you believe this.

Miss H. believes the organization of the fundamentalist churches is fascistic. She is rabidly opposed to the Youth for Christ Movement. She believes it is financed by capitalists who want children to work off their energies in religious emotionalism, so that they will be too tired to do anything about combating social evils.

She herself describes her feeling about fundamentalists as a prejudice.

She devotes her Sunday-school teaching to combating this fundamentalism. This is bad teaching, because she assumes that she is talking to people who already know the Bible and the fundamentalist doctrine, and are now ready to take the next step in working out their own philosophy. This, no doubt, was the case when the Unitarian Church was started. Now, however, she has a group of children, grown up, knowing refutations but having no positive beliefs. When I asked a group of high school students what Jesus taught, they did not know. They did not know that he taught love. This is mentioned not as criticism of Miss H., but to point out that, while she is wonderful in working with individuals by setting an example, she is not able to teach abstract concepts of goodness to groups.

Attitude towards property: One of her boys stole clothing from Andover Academy. She said, "If anybody is stealing, it is the boys of Andover Academy."

Attitude towards animals: Miss H. extends her social feelings to animals as much as to people.

Solidarity in home: The collection of people in the H. household offers a study in solidarity. None of them is related by blood to Miss H. Some of them are related to each other. But the blood tie is not particularly significant. They all take family attitudes toward one another. At present the group consists of one old woman, formerly wealthy, living there for the winter because she can no longer afford to heat her house; one middle-aged man and his wife; a prisoner's wife and baby; two adolescent boys; and three grammar-school boys. The group tends to have a shifting population, and a large number of people now away consider that her home is their residence and return on vacations, furloughs, etc. As seen in the case of the boy who was arrested, if any one of them gets in trouble, all the others go to his aid. There seem never to be any fights or misunderstandings, in spite of the fact that they are of widely different ages, classes, and generally different in every imaginable way. Without considerably more research into this case, it could not be said whether social people are attracted to this household or whether Miss H. socializes them after they get there. She must socialize them at least in part, as she has greatly helped the unadjusted people sent to her by the local department of welfare.

Attitude of community towards her: A few people in town have a very high regard for this woman and will co-operate with her in every way. Another small group dislike her and consider her absolutely crazy. The fact that she has taken so many strange people into her home has been interpreted as eccentricity on her part. It is even said that she has sexual relations with some of the boys. This is included in the report only as an example of how easily misunderstood such a person is. I am sure that such is very far from the case, knowing both her and the boys. The large majority of the population does not even know she exists.

When she was teaching in the local schools, some members of the school board were very eager to fire her, as she did not conform to the policies of the school (most of which were sadistic). Whether she was fired or retired at the usual age, I don't know. But in any case she feels no resentment towards her enemies and refers to their enmity very calmly, as if she were saying that they hated someone else. She has no resentment at all.

Miss H. says that she helps people because she enjoys it. "I guess it's compensation, really, because I never had any children."

Mr. P.

Mr. P., of Irish extraction, has devoted nearly two decades of his life to making life easier for other people. He made up his mind a long time ago: "I want to be the friend of the least, the last, and the lost."

APPENDIX A

The place he chose for his good work was a street in Joliet, Illinois, called "Whisky Row" because of its numerous saloons. In 1908 he founded his famous Morning Star Mission; and since that time he has supplied food to more than 265,000 men, women and children, and beds to 95,000, and has converted 13,000 people. In addition he has made thousands of visits to police courts and jails.

In his younger days Mr. P. was a boxer, street fighter, bartender, and barber. Through meeting and helping to carry in furniture for a new neighbor of his, a young minister, in 1901, he became attracted to religion and eventually decided to establish the above-mentioned mission on Whisky Row—a street occupied by twenty-seven nationalities—where 63 per cent of the crimes of Joliet were perpetrated.

He sold his own house and two other pieces of property and rented for his mission a two-story brick building. The first night, by the light of a kerosene lamp on the floor, he knelt and promised God that he would never take up a collection in the mission, that he would feed the hungry, clothe the naked, and visit those who were sick or in prison. This pledge he has never broken.

At the beginning he met with many rebuffs, and some dissenters abused him by throwing bricks through his windows. However, when his own resources eventually became depleted, the businessmen of the city went to his assistance and were successful in their efforts to purchase the mission building for him. It is now given 2 per cent of the annual community chest funds of the city.

Mr. P., in addition to his other good deeds, goes out of his way to look for people in trouble. A downtown street corner is where he is to be found daily, greeting friends and making arrangements to aid those who need help. No questions are asked of those who come to him for assistance, and he has helped people in every walk of life.

Although Mr. P. is now eighty-one years of age, he still makes daily visits to the police courts, jails, railroad stations, etc.

He does not believe in thrusting religion on anyone, but says, "God gave us two commandments: 'Love God, and Love Thy Neighbor.' And our neighbor is the one who is in need." "Kindness is the language that even the deaf can hear and the dumb can understand."

Although Mr. P. has been reduced to poverty, he has been happy in his work. His belief is:

"The breast is the temple; the earth is the altar; the heart the sacrifice—and you the priest. And you will have to settle your plan for salvation between here and the cemetery."

"No one can be saved for you, no one can die for you, and no one can be put in the grave for you."

Mrs. P.

Name: Mrs. P.

Sex: Female.

Age: Fifty-seven.

Race: White.

National extraction: English Canadian.

Religion: Episcopalian until she was twenty. Then Salvation Army, taken there by her husband.

Occupation: Maid while children growing up. At home now. Started as maid at age of seven.

Intelligence: Average. Perhaps above average, considering lack of intellectual advantages.

Political affiliation: None. "I don't understand politics; so I leave it alone. I don't like the fight between the two parties. I just don't like to fight. I suppose we have to have two parties, but it wouldn't be if everyone was a good Christian."
Mrs. P's son is a relatively powerful Republican.
She tends to have very liberal ideas on particular issues.

Education: None whatever. Never went to school. Neither she nor her husband could read or write in youth. With difficulty they learned to do so when their children went to school.

Economic status: Born in conditions of extreme poverty. Spent childhood in economic slavery. Went out to work for her board plus fifty cents a week at the age of seven. Came to this country with her husband at the age of twenty. Worked as maid until the children grew up and went to work. Many times the whole family went without meals. Husband worked at starvation wages driving trucks, cutting grass, taking care of furnaces, etc. Not much they could do, being illiterate.

APPENDIX A

Present economic status much higher. Live in ten-room, well-furnished house. Children send home much money. One is a lawyer. Mr. P. works part time. Mrs. P. does not work outside the home at all.

Social status: Twenty years ago were at the bottom of the scale. Now in remarkable transition. Sons marrying into lower-middle-class families. In a community in which the family was not known, sons would be completely accepted in middle-class circles.

Family: Mrs. P. has a husband and six children and several grandchildren.

Personal appearance: About average in attractiveness. Might be more attractive than the average if not so marred by work.

Evidences of sociality: It is hard to imagine anyone more sincerely kind and good than Mrs. P. She always helped the poor, even when she was not in an economic position to do so. She looks for the good in everyone and forgives all. She is equally kind to the rich, doing whatever she can for them with their individual problems. She is more than faithful and vigilant in her work with the Salvation Army. Her personal morals are absolutely above suspicion. She sets rigid standards for herself, yet readily forgives anyone else who lives in what she considers terrible sin.

Length of time person has been characterized by sociality: She has always wanted to be what she considers a good Christian as long as she can remember. She reports no particular incident that influenced her greatly. She can think of no person who taught her particularly. She developed her philosophy herself, later on, through reading the Bible. Gradually she discovered more and more things in the Bible which taught her how to be good.

Sociality of other members of family: Mrs. P. considers sociality, which is what she calls goodness, an individual thing, not a family thing. She thinks it helps to be born in a Christian family; but many good people come from the gutter, and many people go to the gutter from a good Christian family.

Mrs. P's mother always had family prayers read. However, Mrs. P. did not consider her a very good Christian. She said: "She had to read the prayers. She could not get them from her own heart. Of course, she did right to read them, at least. But if she had been a very Christian woman, the prayers would have been in her own heart."

Mrs. P's father was a fairly good man, but not remarkably so. Mrs. P's children are none of them as good as she is. She is very proud of them and their great progress, but worries because they do not have quite the spirit she wishes they had. One son remarked in front of me that we should go to war with the Russians immediately, before they got powerful and made war on us. Mrs. P. remarked that we should not have any more wars, particularly now that we have the atomic bomb. Her son said: "We're the only country that has it now. We should wipe all of Europe off the map while we have the chance, before they get the bomb. Then we'd be pretty safe in this country, unless the Coons come up from the South. I suppose we could drop a bomb down South." He then laughed, and his mother said very sadly that it wasn't funny.

Another son is a minister, and distinguished himself as a chaplain in the Army. But he dislikes Germans. He is tolerant of Negroes, but only because he thinks he should be. He does not really feel a sense of love for them.

The other children, so far as is known by me, are about average in sociality.

Person's own idea of what sociality is: In answer to the question, "What do you think a person has to be like in order to be a true Christian, a really good person?": "You have to have will power and faith in God. You have to stand on your own feet and not be carried away by others. Pride stands in the way. For instance, the Salvation Army uniform. Some of my friends look down on it. Sometimes it is a little hard for me to wear it. But you have to have will power to do what you know is right."

Hardships in life: Extreme poverty, near starvation in early life. Through a terrible struggle Mr. P. and his sons (then small children) built a house by their own labor, gradually buying the materials. After living in it a year, it burned down. There is no telling how many hardships they have had, as they do not complain.

Emotional security in childhood: Bad interviewing on this point. Not sure of situation. "There were ten of us. In all my childhood my mother gave me just one smack." She said that she did feel

APPENDIX A

loved, but I am not sure that she understood the question. She believes that being loved helps you to extend love to others.

Ideas on social organization: "I think the middle class is the happiest. The poor sometimes don't have enough to eat, and the rich have the temptation to forget what God has given them. They are not happy. It would be best if everyone were in the middle class. Everyone should have the same amount of money."

Ideas on teaching and developing sociality: "It should begin at home, with little children, and then spread out to all people."

Attitude toward son who is a lawyer: "I never thought I should have a son who would be a lawyer." At this point I thought she meant she had never expected anyone in her family to be that educated and advanced socially, but she went on to say: "I never believed in lawyers, because I think there are always two sides to a question. But my son says it's all right if you make sure that you are right before you start a case."

Mrs. W.

Name: Mrs. W.

Sex: Female.

Age: Forty-three.

Race: White.

National extraction: Dutch.

Religion: Dutch Reformed Church.

Occupation: Social worker.

Intelligence: Unusually high.

Political affiliation: Registered as a Republican. Usually votes Democratic. Has Communist convictions.

Education: Bryn Mawr and Columbia.

Economic status: Born into a wealthy family. Now apparently has very little left.

SAMPLE AMERICAN "GOOD NEIGHBORS"

Social status: Mrs. W's family are colonial Dutch stock, settled New York. Descendant of first white child born on Long Island. Her present social position is somewhat altered through moving from her family's own territory and losing her money.

Personal appearance: Generally considered above the average in attractiveness.

Evidences of sociality: Mrs. W. has apparently been kind to many people, as she was referred to interviewer more times than anyone else under consideration in this study. When I first went to interview her, she flatly refused to have anything to do with it, on the grounds that she was not a good person and that to be studied in such a project would be dishonest. She only allowed herself to be interviewed after I went back to her and told her who the other people were who were being studied. She said "Why, they are worse than I am."

Mrs. W. works toward the goal of solidarity, both in her kindness to individuals and in her striving for political reforms.

Length of time the person has been characterized by sociality: According to Mrs. W's father, her sociality was shown before she was old enough to talk. He said: "I have wondered why Elizabeth is a Bolshevik. I guess she was born that way. When she was a little girl, not yet old enough to talk, she had a book with a picture of a big bird in it, and the bird had a frog in its beak. Little Elizabeth used to look at that picture and cry, and hit the bird, trying to make it let the frog go. I showed the book to other children, to see whether they would have the same reaction; but they paid no more attention to that picture than any of the others, and didn't notice the frog at all."

Sociality of other members of the family: There was a high degree of solidarity in the family group, and all members of the family were taught to conform to it. If they had antisocial feelings, they were taught to control them. This, however, was not extended outside of the family group, except to individuals with whom they came into direct contact. It seemed to be considered impossible and dangerous to extend it to other groups.

Person's own idea of what sociality is: "It's an understanding of suffering. Some don't know what it is. If you know what it is, you will want to relieve it. If you know what you are doing by hurting others, you won't want to do it."

APPENDIX A

"Do you think your own suffering has increased your understanding?" "Yes. I think your own suffering increases understanding until it reaches the point where you become frightened yourself, and then you become ruthless in order to survive."

"How about the time you said it would be better for you to die than to make a mistake on one of your cases, sacrificing the client to your own safety?" "I didn't say I should die. I said that it would be better. Naturally, anyone knows that it would be better."

Degree of emotional security in childhood: "I think that the word 'secure' is very much overworked nowadays. I don't know what it means. I felt loved, yes. I didn't feel safe by any means; I considered the world full of menace—not so much for me as for people in general. Also, I didn't grow up in the typical American family of mother, father, sisters, and brothers. We had a much, much larger group, many generations, aunts, uncles, and cousins. Some were dead, but had been there before, and I knew them. And there were servants living in the back yard, and semi-dependent neighbors next door, all a part of the group. I don't know anything about the typical American family and reactions that come from that form of life."

"What do you mean by saying that 'some were dead' but that you knew them?" "I didn't really know them. They were dead before I was born, but they were real to me. I mean it was a continuous group. It was a matriarchal set-up. Aunt Mary was the head. She had the money."

Life story of thought: "From an early age, I was taught that I was supposed to give the utmost consideration to everybody. All overprivileged people are taught that from the beginning. (This is the reason why self-made men make such wretched army officers—they haven't been taught *noblesse oblige.*) Of course, that is a very negative thing. They are taught only to help individuals they come into contact with. They aren't taught to help the whole world.

"Living in the middle of the city, I used to watch the dreadfully unfortunate people go by. One day some children came to the house and asked for shoes. The poor used to come to ask for whatever thing they needed. The servants told them to come back when my mother was there. I told my mother about it, and she said they could have the shoes I was wearing, if they fit.

We used to wear sturdy Coward shoes. It happened that they did come back, and I went to the door. I took off my shoes, and they fitted all right; so they took them and went away. After they had gone, my mother asked me if I had got their address, so that she could go to see what else they needed. I hadn't done it. She told me that this should always be done when anyone came to the door. I was dreadfully worried and remorseful. There they were, lost in the city of millions of poor, impossible ever to find. And it was my fault.

"The worst of it was that I knew it was not right to single out individuals, to take care of those who happened to come to the door, and close your eyes to the millions like them around you. I knew that we should give everything we had until we had no more than anyone else. My mother told me when I was very little that it wouldn't do any good, because it would be only a drop in the bucket, the rest of the world wouldn't be any better off, and we shouldn't have anything either. So I early became convinced that it was hopeless. Now I no longer think it's hopeless, and that's why I'm angry—angry at the unsocial people in authority who have power and use it in the wrong way. Furthermore, I know that anger is sinful. Every man is his brother's keeper, definitely, and it is sinful to ever have a thought of anger toward another person. You're supposed to forgive to the point where you don't even feel it necessary to forgive. That's plain Christian ethics, and any fool can read it in the Bible. Nobody does it. And what's more, anybody that tries to do it is going to meet the same fate that Jesus did—be crucified.

"I think that to speak unkindly of anyone is sinful, and that's something I've never lived up to. But my uncle did, and he died when I was five. I think that I felt that's why he died—because he was good.

"When I was a child, I used to worry about the starving millions in China—really worry about them dreadfully. Finally I decided that I should not worry about them, because I couldn't do anything about them and I couldn't worry about them any more—that's all. I think that's what most people do through life, which is wrong.

"I always noticed from early childhood that people have great solidarity within the family group, and I always thought it was very unjust. I am of the opinion that if the whole world treated each other as one family, there would be no trouble. I noticed that if a man outside the family killed someone, he was a murderer, a criminal, and should be hanged. If someone in the family did it, it was a terrible tragedy which had befallen him, and he was protected in every way.

"I always thought it was a very sad and tragic thing that the most unfortunate people were the cruelest to each other, observing how they acted on the street, beating their children and horses.

"From my Aunt C. I learned what Jesus said. She tried very hard to be good, but she very often felt like being bad. But even if she hadn't told me, I should have found out when I went to Sunday school. When I heard those things, I knew they were right—there was no other way.

"I could never reconcile Christian ethics with the way Christians behaved. Christ forgave the thief on the cross, and we put thieves in prison. When I heard that story and others like it, I was struck dumb by the contrast between what we professed and what we practiced.

"I know what good is, and I've never done it yet. I haven't got any idea of doing it, either. I know that it's complete sharing. <u>Christ said that you should give your property away</u>, and I haven't done it.

"I used to worry a lot about God—how could he possibly be all good and all powerful, both? Impossible! And I think that Satan, in whom I was taught to believe as a child, truly is constantly whispering to us to do bad things. Even if you don't call it Satan, it is certainly a good symbol of our evil impulses. The conflict between God and Satan, both after our soul, is surely a good symbolic way to put it.

"I used to think when I was a child that when the children grew up, everything would be different. I thought grown people were cruel and hypocritical, and I didn't think people my age were. But then I found out that it isn't cruelty and hypocrisy—it's just inability. I found out that it wouldn't be different, because everyone is incapable."

History of sociality: "There were periods when I became self-centered—periods when in love and when having little children."

Hardships in life: Mrs. W's husband went insane and then died. Two of her children were killed in an automobile accident. But perhaps the most calamitous thing in her life has been the death of her culture. She said, "I should like to go home, but home isn't there any more." "I understand what they mean by 'Lo, the poor Indian, his people are no more.'"

Although Mrs. W. has lost her way of life through social change, she seems to be truly glad it happened, because the world as a whole is better off. She has, in fact, done everything she could do to bring about the downfall of her own class.

"When I first heard that phrase 'From each according to his ability, to each according to his needs,' I thought I had never in my life believed anything more sincerely. Furthermore, that's the way we always did inside the family group. I could not understand why everyone didn't want to extend that to all people."

Mrs. W. has been in touch with me throughout this study and has been interested in it. Also, about this time she read Mr. Sorokin's *The Sociology of Revolution*. She says that at this point she is not angry; on the contrary, she suddenly feels peaceful and more encouraged to work constructively. While I, myself, was reading this book, an incident took place in the social-work office. Collectors came around for contributions to the Community Chest Fund. Mrs. W. and Mrs. D., who are leaders of thought in the office, made more or less revolutionary remarks adverse to the Community Chest system. However, both of these workers contributed, although no one else in the entire office did. The fact that the others carried their destructive criticism into action beyond what Mrs. W. and Mrs. D. had intended impressed them both very much and was frightening as an illustration. Neither of these two would try to destroy the old, no matter how bad and inadequate, until something new could be established to take its place.

Mrs. W. is of the opinion that we seem to be headed for a terrible revolution in this country in about twenty-five years. She says: "I am not intelligent enough to think further ahead than twenty-five years. But I have noticed that opinions I had, considered 'crazy' at the time, are more or less commonly held in twenty-five years. It would certainly be worth while now to definitely work on developing feelings of solidarity throughout the country, in the hope of being able to change conditions in a constructive way rather than by destructive revolution."

APPENDIX A

Dr. X.

The subject of this report is a practicing female physician. She is a short, stocky woman of fifty-six, has gray hair, dresses in a normally neat and attractive fashion, is extremely active in all her movements, and speaks clearly and decisively, without any apparent belligerence. She is a white woman, born in the United States of Irish descent.

Dr. X. did her medical studies and took her degree at a large Eastern medical school, finished her internship, and practiced medicine a little over a year before getting married. She has had four children, three girls and a boy, two of whom are still in college. Her husband is still living, but has no remunerative occupation. In religion she and the family are devout Catholics, all the children having attended Catholic schools and colleges.

Our first conversation lasted less than a half hour. I determined to interview her several times more to check on the high praise I had heard concerning her. I thought it very interesting that in our first meeting she had said nothing of the activities which had earned her such a high reputation.

Briefly, her reputation was that of a most remarkable woman who was, at all times, ready to help other people. She was active in public movements, working with the blind, the destitute, and unfortunates of all kinds. I was not particularly impressed by the reports concerning this public work; for there were several other prospective interviewees who had similar reputations. But I did start to take careful notice when I heard of other quiet and unobtrusive activities indicating that the doctor was not simply motivated by the glamor and acclaim that might be attached to public charities.

When I explained to people just what sort of a person I was looking for to exemplify solidarity, they invariably said that Dr. X. undoubtedly fitted the description. This was admitted also by several women who thought that she was too "officious," too anxious and ready "to move in and take over," not "pliable enough."

I shall not attempt to describe each interview completely and in its chronological order. In speaking with her I had the following questions in mind, and I was able to obtain fairly adequate answers to them: Is she solidaristic in accordance with the description of solidarity given in our seminar papers? By what activities does she demonstrate this solidarity? Has she any definite plan or purpose to explain it? Is there any event in her past life that could account for such activity? Does she exhibit any non-solidaristic characteristics?

The first time I went to call upon her with a companion, we were greeted at the door by a man of about forty-five. He held the door open for my associate and then almost closed it before I could put my hand out. He apologized cheerfully, and then announced to the doctor that there were two people here, not one. My first question to the doctor was: "Why did he try to shut me out?" She laughed and said, "Don't mind that; he's practically blind and didn't see you."

Naturally I wanted to know more about the man, who he was, what he was doing in her home, and so forth. The answer to these questions was indicative of the kind of action that gave the doctor a reputation for goodness and charity. About a year ago, she was called in on the case of a man who had attempted suicide. She really saved his life, but he was unwilling to go on living. For several years he had been gradually going blind; he lost his job, his wife left him, and he had become more and more despondent until, finally, he tried to take his own life. Dr. X. cheered him up, got him well enough to be moved, and invited him to live at her home as long as he wanted to. He had been there ever since and declares that he is perfectly happy doing little jobs around the house.

On another occasion the florist delivered a large bouquet while I was there. "Who's your friend?" I asked. She said this was the third birthday of a child she had delivered, and that the mother always remembered by sending flowers. That seemed a reversal of the usual procedure until she informed me that she had "done the job for nothing" and that the mother was simply trying to show her appreciation. I asked her whether she often did her medical work for nothing, and she said that about 60 per cent of her cases used to be entirely gratis but that now she gets paid for some of them through various federal and state agencies.

Numerous people who had worked with her informed me that she never made any inquiries concerning the patients' ability to pay or the source of payment. Her primary interest was in the patient, and in many cases where poverty was obvious, she simply left the prescription at the local drugstore and had the bill sent to her. There were so many instances of this kind, and there were so many different people who reported them, that there can be no doubt about the existence of such activities. She is the personal

APPENDIX A

physician for many of the religious nuns in this vicinity and never accepts any remuneration for such work. She takes care of several orphanages and a home for the blind, and also refuses pay for this.

Aside from her professional work, Dr. X. is also very active in general religious, social, and welfare activities. I had been told that any committee having her as a member was sure of success, whether it was the sponsoring of a drive, a card or theater party, a testimonial dinner, or any other activity. Besides this, she found time to attend concerts and to carry on as a member of several literary and discussion groups.

The question arises in the mind of a social investigator whether there was a cleavage between this woman's "public" life and her private domestic life. Was she building up a career, getting a reputation for solidaristic activities outside the home at the expense of the solidaric relationships of her family? This is, of course, the first suspicion one directs toward a woman who attempts to mix an outside career with the career of a wife and mother. I felt that this would be the test of her genuine solidarity.

The relationships between Dr. X. and her children appeared to be typically those of a solid familial group. From what I could observe and from what I had heard through others, the daughters were particularly proud of their mother and very affectionate toward her. They seemed to be inspired by her example and were very active in similar affairs, one of them studying to be a professional social worker. The son has been away from home, in the armed services; so I had no opportunity to talk with him. However, it seems that his reactions are about the same as those of his sisters.

The question of Dr. X's husband was one that seemed to be kept in the background most of the time, and the story concerning him was one I had to piece together from interviews with the doctor, with him, and with their friends. As mentioned above, the doctor married after about one year of medical practice. She had come from a fairly wealthy family and had a modest fortune in her own right when she married. Her husband, several years older than she, was already a successful businessman, and he took over her money to expand the business. She settled down to a career of domesticity and having babies. But before the fourth child was born, her husband had lost most of the money in business, and was fast dissipating the rest in an unbusinesslike manner. He had a physical breakdown and has never worked since then.

It was at this time that the doctor decided to start treating patients again, at least for several hours a day in an office in her own home. Some sort of income was necessary, and, as she said, "there was always enough to keep us going and to give the children a good Catholic education." This medical work always threatened to absorb more and more of her time, and she had to keep it in check in order to give sufficient time and attention to her growing children. People who knew the family during this trying period declare that the children were always her first concern, and that she represented a kind of model mother in their estimation. The children themselves say: "She used to be tough on us when we were growing up. All the other kids could go to the motion pictures, and we couldn't. We had to know our lessons; we had to be home on time; we had to behave ourselves around the house." There appeared to be no resentment in these remarks.

The husband is a quiet, soft-spoken man, who has been physically unable to support the family, and is apparently emotionally incapable of taking his place as the authoritative member of the family. The doctor defers to him in important decisions, but he seems disinclined to take responsibility and has fitted himself into a comfortable groove of dependence. He blames himself for having failed earlier in life, and makes no complaint whatever about his wife's activities. Rather, he speaks proudly of her achievements.

The evidence given above indicates that Dr. X. could be termed a solidaristic person in the correct sense. She is a force for social cohesion both in society at large and in smaller family units. She is a person who is constantly giving of her time and talents to others without selfish motivations and without discrimination. People are attracted to her; they say they would like to imitate her; they admire the positive virtues she practices.

Now the important question arises: Why is she this way? When I asked her about this, she slowly replied, "For the same reasons that you do good wherever you can." This was not very definite, but I suspected that she was trying to explain it all through some sort of religious motivation. So I asked her whether she helped people because she liked them and because she enjoyed helping them. "Yes, but there's more to it than that. It makes you feel good to be doing things for others, but I think it's more basic than that. When I was a little girl my mother impressed me very much with the idea of service for God. For quite a while I didn't catch on to what she meant; in fact, it was only when I was well on into adolescence and started to think for myself that I understood fully.

She kept giving me innumerable variations of the Gospel story of the master who gave money to his servants and then praised the profitable servants and blamed the unprofitable one. My mother kept pointing out that <u>we are on earth only temporarily, that we're really working for God</u>, we're using implements that belong to Him, and the whole test of living is whether we are profitable to Him."

I checked with other people to see whether they had ever heard Dr. X. give reasons for her actions. Several had, in private conversations, and a number of others had heard her explain her ideas but in a less personal fashion—in a public address. Hence I accept her explanation as a fairly adequate statement of her motives.

I asked whether any kind of a chart could be developed of her activities throughout her lifetime, whether there were any bursts of intense activity, and, if so, what the explanation for these could be. She reflected for quite a while before answering this series of questions. She said that there were definitely times when she did more than at other times, but felt that these were periods when more people needed help, or when she herself was in a more energetic mood, or when there were fewer family and personal duties to perform.

She did not recall that any crisis in her life had changed her habits or inspired her to socialize her activities. I asked her whether her husband's collapse wasn't such a crisis. She said that, of course, it was a crisis for the whole family and necessitated certain external arrangements and actions, but that it had no definite effect in forming her notions about life and solidarity in general. "My ideas and attitudes along that line had been formed long before I was married."

She said that besides the teachings of her mother concerning the advantage of working for others, she had also had the good example of both father and mother in their charitable activities. Both did a great deal of personal "poor relief" through the parish groups, Vincent de Paul societies, sodalities, and so forth. Her father sometimes took the trouble to explain why we must help the unfortunate, and he always kept his explanations on a high spiritual plane—"They were never as clear or as effective as mother's."

She also stressed the fact that at times in her life she felt "quite lazy" and at other times she was very "selfish." I tried to get some examples explaining this latter remark; and she said that when she looks back at her college days, she realizes that she spent an awful lot of time and money on herself and on her own pleasures. She does not have any feelings of remorse or regret over this because "there's nothing I can do about it now anyway."

I asked her whether she took on all of this social activity as a duty that she had to perform in conscience. The answer to this question was not given all at once, but it was approximately this: She did not really think of it as a duty in the strict sense of the word. She knows she has certain obligations to society in general, quite aside from the particular obligations to relatives and friends and smaller social groups. To neglect her children on any point would have bothered her conscience, but she feels that she could refuse to pay a poor person's medicine bill without feeling guilty. "But it isn't just a question of right and wrong. Let's say that I'm happier in doing things that I really haven't any obligation to do. The people I work with seem to be happier then, too, and everything seems to go more smoothly."

One concluding remark is this: Dr. X. does not hesitate to express openly her disapproval of many things in our "modern society," as she calls it. She is angry about poor school systems, inefficient politicians, broken homes, the lack of discipline for children, lack of medical attention for the poor, and so forth. I once asked her whether these things discouraged her from working with others. Her answer was: "No, I suppose that's all the more reason for trying to do something about it. The situation won't get cleared up by itself. People, after all, have to do it."

APPENDIX B

RUSSIAN–ORTHODOX SAINTS [1]

The main characteristics of the Russian saints as a statistical group are essentially similar to those of the Christian-Catholic saints.

Of 415 saints, 398 (95.9 per cent) are men and only 17 (4.1 per cent) are women. Thus among the Russian saints the proportion of women is still lower than among the Christian-Catholic saints (16.8 per cent). Among the latter the proportion of women saints tended to increase during the eighteenth, nineteenth, and twentieth centuries. No such trend is noticeable among the Russian saints; we do not find a single woman saint in these centuries, partly because there are no saints in the nineteenth and twentieth centuries aside from one male saint who died in 1833.

On *duration of life*: the Russian saints display an extraordinary longevity, similar to that of the Christian-Catholic saints. Out of 132 Russian saints whose age at death is known, 5.3 per cent died

---

[1] Desirous to find out to what extent the main results of the above study of Christian-Catholic saints are applicable to the saints of other Christian denominations, I asked an eminent historian of Russia, Dr. S. G. Pushkarev, to make an investigation of the saints of the Russian-Orthodox Church of Russia along the lines of the preceding study. In this appendix, I shall state the main results of Dr. Pushkarev's research. The chief sources were: E. Golubinsky, *Historia kanonizatzii sviatykh Russkoi Tzerkvi* (A History of Canonization of the Saints of the Russian Church), (Moscow, 1903); G. P. Fedotov, *Sviatyie drevney Russi* (The Saints of Ancient Russia), (Paris, 1931); V. O. Klutchevsky, *Drevnerusskyia Jytyia sviatykh* (Ancient Russian Lives of the Saints), (Moscow, 1871); N. Barsukov, *Istochniki Russkoi agiographii* (The Sources of Russian Hagiography), (St. Petersburg, 1882); *Russkyi Biographichesky Slovar* (Russian Biographic Dictionary, 25 Vols.), (St. Petersburg); M. V. Tolstoi, *Kniga glagolemaia opisanyie o Rossyiskikh sviatykh* (A Book of Descriptions of Russian Saints), (Moscow, 1887); M. Victorova, *Kievo-Petcherskyi Paterik* (Kiev-Petchersky Saints), (Kiev, 1870); taking only the saints officially canonized by the Russian Church, Dr. Pushkarev collected a group of 415 Russian saints. All the results of the study are based upon the lives of these 415 saints. Though the fluctuations of each general result are studied from the tenth to the nineteenth century, the relatively small number of saints make the trends and fluctuations less clear here than in the preceding study of more than 3,000 Christian-Catholic saints.

when less than 15 years of age, 9.1 per cent between 16 and 40 years of age, 28 per cent between 41 and 70 years of age, and 57.6 per cent at an age of 71 and above. Thus the longevity of both groups of saints is greater even than that of the present population of the United States. The data strongly suggest the existence of a causal connection between sainthood and longevity. Whether the longevity is due to the modes of life and thought of the saints, or to the appointment to sainthood of mainly long-living persons, or to both these factors, is a question that remains unanswered. However, the saints' ways of living, thinking, feeling, and acting, especially their deep and real love for God and for their neighbors, appears to be an important factor in their life duration. It seemingly overcomes all conditions that are adverse to good health and long life, such as their asceticism, lack of elementary necessities, and the many physical and mental hardships to which they are exposed. This should be kept in mind by health specialists and by all those who are interested in living a long life. Sainthood seems to be one of the surest ways to accomplish this result. There is no clear trend of either increase or decrease in the longevity of Russian saints (the same having been true for the Christian-Catholic saints).

The socio-economic position of the parental families of the Russian saints is also similar to that of the Christian-Catholic saints. Out of 147 parental families of saints whose economic position is more or less known, 76.2 per cent were rich, 7.5 per cent were poor, and 16.3 per cent occupied intermediary positions. The proportion of saints from poor parental families tends to increase from zero in the tenth, eleventh and twelfth centuries, to 3 and 4 per cent in the thirteenth and fourteenth centuries, and to 20 and 25 per cent in the seventeenth and eighteenth centuries. These results resemble the findings for the Christian-Catholic saints.

The data on *the socio-legal position of the parental families of the saints*, on the basis of 172 families, are as follows:

- 20.3 per cent (35 saints) were foreigners who immigrated into Russia (12 from Greece; 2 each from southern Slavic countries, Scandinavia and Hungary; 4 each from Byzantium and Lithuania; 6 were Tartars; and 3 others consisted of "a foreign merchant," a Bulgarian, and a Livonian);
- 26.8 per cent came from princely families;
- 14.5 per cent from the aristocracy (boyars);

APPENDIX B

12.2 per cent from the middle official class;
4.1 per cent from the clergy;
5.2 per cent from the merchant class;
1.2 per cent from the artisan and the city labor class;
15.7 per cent from the peasant class.

As was the case with the Christian-Catholic saints, most of the Russian saints came from the upper and middle classes. Among the lower classes, in both cases, the peasants contributed far more saints (in absolute number) than the urban labor, artisan, and small commercial strata combined.

The trend of a decreasing contribution of saints from the upper classes and an increasing quota from the lower classes between the first and the twentieth centuries, which held true for the Christian-Catholic saints, is also partly confirmed by the findings for the Russian saints. Thus, the stratum of princes ceased its contribution of saints after the sixteenth century; the stratum of the aristocracy (the boyars), after the seventeenth century; and the stratum of peasants increased its contribution from zero, 7, 3, and 4 per cent in the eleventh, twelfth, thirteenth, and fourteenth centuries respectively, to 27 and 43 per cent in the sixteenth and seventeenth centuries. However, in the eighteenth century and the nineteenth (1 saint), the saints stemmed from the middle official class (3), from the small merchant class (1), and from the clergy (1).

These results essentially agree with those obtained for the Christian-Catholic saints. The reasons for these results are essentially the same.

The social position and activities of the saints that led to their sainthood are shown in Table 44.

Among the Christian-Catholic saints 75 to 90 per cent were directly or indirectly members of the clergy, and similarly 80 to 84 per cent of the Russian saints were clergymen and monks. About 30 per cent of the Christian-Catholic saints were high Church dignitaries; 15 to 48 per cent of the Russian saints belonged to that category.

The princes (11.8 per cent) occupy a notably larger place among the Russian saints than they do among the Christian-Catholic saints (about 2 per cent). This difference is undoubtedly due to the fact that in Russia the Christian-Orthodox religion was the official religion of the Russian state. It was introduced and somewhat coercively propagated by the Russian princes (St. Vladimir and others),

Table 44

		Number	Percentage
Princes:	Missionaries	5	
	Protectors and defenders of Christian faith	15	
	Patrons of the Church	5	
	Hermits and monks	12	
	Martyrs	12	
		49	11.8
Clergy:	High hierarchy of the Church	64	15.4
	Founders of monasteries	139	33.5
	Missionaries, apostles, preachers	14	3.4
	Hermits, ascetics, monks	103	24.8
		320	77.1
God's Fools:		17	4.1
Patrons:	Secular Christians, etc	29	7.0
	Total	415	100.0

and became the national religion of Russia, inseparably bound with its historical destiny in the past. In contrast to this the Christian-Catholic saints frequently came from countries that were ruled by pagan princes and kings who were inimical to the Christian religion. Even many non-Catholic Christian princes and rulers were antagonistic to the Catholic Church. These reasons make evident why the proportion of royalty among the Christian-Catholic saints was notably lower than among the Russian saints.

A uniquely Russian group of saints are the "God's Fools" (*Christa-rady jurodivyie*). Tested by contemporary mental, psychological, and psychiatric tests, some of these "Fools for the sake of Christ" are likely to be classified as abnormal, moronish, and otherwise stupid persons. In a few cases, perhaps, some of them were. But their bulk is made up of persons who had some prophetic vision, untutored wisdom, and a deep love of God and of their neighbors. Because of various specific conditions, they often expressed themselves in intentionally "foolish" forms and deliberately behaved like "fools." Ordinary people intuitively perceived the

APPENDIX B

golden nuggets under their foolish wrappings and built up their prestige and sainthood. This is an interesting type of saint that needs to be studied in detail.

By and large the data obtained for the Russian and the Christian-Catholic saints in these particulars are essentially the same.

The historical trends in the position and activities of the Russian-Orthodox saints from the tenth to the nineteenth centuries indicate that royalty and missionary saints disappear after the sixteenth century, that "God's Fools" disappear after the seventeenth century, as do the patron saints and those who founded monasteries in order to attain sainthood. Only a few saints from the high hierarchy of the Church, the hermits, ascetics, and monks, remain in the eighteenth and nineteenth centuries. The reasons for these trends are similar to those pointed out in the case of the Christian-Catholic saints.

Among the Christian-Catholic saints about 37 per cent are martyrs, whereas there are only 15.4 per cent among the Russian saints. This lower percentage is due to several reasons. First, the missionary activities of the Russian saints outside of Russia, among pagan peoples and powers, were less extensive than those of Christian saints in general and of Catholic saints in particular. Russian saints and missionaries worked mainly amidst Christians and were protected by the Russian government; this is in contrast to the Christian saints of the first five centuries who heroically went out into the inimical pagan world, producing thereby a high rate of martyrs among their leaders and saints. Second, after the twelfth century and especially after the Reformation, the Western Christian denominations engaged more frequently in religious wars than did the Russian Church. As we have seen, these centuries of religious wars produced a large number of martyrs in the West. The Russian Church had only one religious war—a relatively mild one —throughout its history, a war between the "Old Believers" and the "Nikonians," and thus it did not shed the blood of martyrs to the extent that the Western Christian Church did. These reasons make the lower percentage of martyrs among the Russians more comprehensible. They also explain why there are no martyr-saints in Russia after the seventeenth century.

The communist government murdered and persecuted a large number of religious leaders and pious Christians in Russia. These, however, have not had time to be canonized. Therefore they do not enter into the study of the Russian saints. The large number of Christian martyrs who perished at the hand of the Soviet government (some of whom will eventually be canonized) corroborates some of the generalizations made previously with regard to the Christian-Catholic saints.

Out of the 113 saints of whose background we have some knowledge, 69.9 per cent belong to the "fortunate" type and 30.1 per cent to the "converted" type. Salvation from an imminent danger, loss of a close relative (wife, husband, child), a miraculous vision, or unexpected kindness were the events that precipitated the conversion of some of these saints.

Among the Christian-Catholic saints we find that almost the same percentage (68 per cent) belong to the "fortunate" type, 17.5 per cent to the "converted-catastrophic" type, and the remaining 14.5 per cent to the "intermediary" type (a type which was not identifiable among the Russian saints). On the whole, the data on the Russian and the Christian-Catholic saints agree in this respect.

Among the Russian saints, 84.1 per cent used a *moderate technique of self-control, free from extreme self-immolation and self-mortification.* Only 15.9 per cent used the technique of self-torture and self-mortification. Consequently the Russian saints provide a somewhat lower percentage of self-immolators than do the Christian-Catholic saints (38 per cent belong to this category). After the seventeenth century the self-torturer saints disappear altogether from the Russian scene. Here again the two sets of data essentially agree with each other.

Lastly, the figures of Table 45 show the total number of Russian saints produced by each century.

The year 988 A.D. is considered to be the year of the official conversion of Kievan Russia to Christianity, a conversion which was initiated by Prince Vladimir and imposed upon the Russians in a semi-compulsory manner. The latter part of this century had already produced four saints. Subsequently, with the growth of the Russian Church, the number of its saints rapidly increased in the eleventh century, remained at a high level during the twelfth, thirteenth, and fourteenth centuries, and then the number doubled and reached its highest mark in the fifteenth and sixteenth centuries, after the overthrow of the Tartar yoke by Muscovy. Beginning with the seventeenth century, a rapid decline in the number of saints set in, a decline which reached the zero point at the start of the nineteenth century. The last 150 years have not produced

APPENDIX B

Table 45

Century	Number of saints	Percentage
X	4	1.0
XI	42	10.1
XII	50	12.1
XIII	45	10.8
XIV	49	11.8
XV	96	23.0
XVI	84	20.2
XVII	37	9.0
XVIII	7	1.7
XIX [2]	1	0.3
Total	415	100.0

a single saint in the Russian Church (except Serafim of Sarov mentioned in footnote 2).

The curve of "production" of Russian saints is essentially similar to that of the Christian-Catholic saints; from the beginning of the seventeenth to the twentieth century, the two curves become almost identical. In both the Christian-Catholic and the Russian-Orthodox Churches the "production" of saints declines sharply; in the Russian Church it reaches a zero point as early as the nineteenth century. The reasons for the growth and decline in the number of Russian saints, and especially for the rapid decline after the sixteenth century, are essentially the same as those indicated in the case of the Christian-Catholic saints from the tenth through the twentieth centuries. The Russian-Orthodox Church displays an even more catastrophic decline of the grace of saintliness, of spiritual creativity, and of religious and moral vigor during the last three centuries than does the Christian-Catholic Church. Perhaps the ordeal of communist persecution will awaken these qualities in the twentieth century. Indeed, there are some signs that such an awakening is taking place. Otherwise the Russian-Orthodox Church can consider itself the dead shell of what was previously a full vessel animated by the creative Holy Spirit.

The above discussion delineates the main characteristics of the

---

[2] This saint was Serafim of Sarov, who died in 1833 and who lived the greater part of his life in the eighteenth century. There were no other canonized saints in the nineteenth or twentieth centuries.

Russian-Orthodox saints taken as a statistical or nominal group. These characteristics have turned out to be very similar to those obtained for a much larger group of Christian-Catholic saints. The agreement of the results obtained in the study of both groups strongly suggests their rough validity, and indicates that the saints as a nominal group indeed possessed the characteristics discussed.

INDEX

Abbess, abbott, as saint, 155
Absolute, union with, 153
Accident, and conversion, 60, 61, 147
Activities of: "good neighbors," 11–15; saints, 154–56, 242–43
Actor, as saint, 155
Adams, C. W., 23
Adjustment, types of, 169–171, 207
Adolescents, as recipients of help, 67
Affiliations of "good neighbors": political, 50–51; religious, 41–42; welfare, 51
Affiliative tendencies, 41, 51–52
Africa, 108, 111
Agape, v
Age of: criminals, 23; "good neighbors," 22; martyrs, 157–58; men of genius, 23; monarchs, 23; saints, 100, 198–99, 240; scientists, 15–16
Aged, the, as recipients of help, 64–66
Agencies, welfare, 11, 12
Aggression, and frustration, 61–62, 210–211
Agnostics, among altruists, 12, 42–44; reasons for, 44–47, 206, 207
Agricultural occupation of: "good neighbors," 36; saints, 122–23, 133–34, 241–42
Albania, 108
Al Hallaj, 81
Allport, G. W., 43
Alpert, Marcia L., vii
Altruism: and antagonism, 81, 150; and intelligence, 39; and peace of mind, v, vii, 77–78; and vitality, 100–104; characteristics of, 17–18; factors of, 56–59, 61, 138–40, 146–47; irreligious, 44–48; opinions on, 17–18. See also "Good neighbor," Love

Altruistic person: as deviant, 81–82, 208–209; characteristics of, 17–18; life duration of, v, 22, 100–104; types of, 146–49, 185–87, 212. See also "Good neighbor," Saints
American Catholics, 112
American family, size of, 25
Americas, 108–115, 118–20
Antagonism, and altruism, 81, 150
Apostle, 155
Arabia, 108
Aristocracy, and saints, 133, 155, 203–04, 241–42
Aristotle, 80
Asceticism, and sainthood, 177–78, 208
Asia, 108–09
Atheism, and altruism, 12, 42–44, 47, 206, 207
Athletes of God, 103
Attitude: affiliative, 39–40; parental, toward sainthood, 136–37
Augustine, Saint, 61, 111, 113
Aurobindo, Sri, 59, 80, 81, 152, 153
Austria, 108–111

Baltic countries, 108, 110
Barsukov, N., 240
Beethoven, L. van, 61
Belgian, Belgium, 38, 110
Berardinis, L. de, 107
Betts, G., 44
"Biographies" group, 7, 8, 26, 31, 35, 39
Birthplace of saints, 108–110
Bishops, as saints, 155–56
Boccaccio, G., 61
Boldrini, M., 107
Books: influence of, 54–55, 57–58, 60, 211; liked by "good neighbors," 55

248

INDEX

Boredom, in American life, 13–14
Bourget, Paul, 61
Bowerman, W. G., 20
Brahmans, 103
Breneman, Tom, 6
British: genius, 20, 82; Isles, 108, 109, 113–116
Buddha, Buddhism, 44, 45, 47–48, 61, 81, 103
Bulgaria, 108
Bureaucracy, in agencies, 13
Burgess, E., 25
Butler, Alban, 92, 112

Calamity. See Catastrophe
Canadian "good neighbors," 38
Canonization: months of, 106–07; procedure of, 92, 93
Cardinals, as saints, 155, 162
Catastrophe, rôle in conversion of, 57–59, 159, 186–88
Catastrophic type: of "good neighbors," 57–59; of saints, 147–48, 185–90, 209–10
Catholic Church, 92–93, 96, 97, 98, 102, 111, 112, 119, 127, 148, 149, 155, 156, 162, 166–67, 179–184, 189, 204
Catholic "good neighbors," 42
Catholic popes, 101, 156, 157, 164, 165, 166
Catholic saints. See Saints
Cattel, J. McKeen, 20
Chastity, and sainthood, 151–155, 160–61
Chaytania, 61
Children, as martyrs, 157
Children, number of, in "good neighbor" families, 25, 31
China, 108–10, 118
Christ, Jesus, 17, 37, 60, 61
Christian, Christianity, 10, 45, 46, 47. See also Catholic, Russian-Orthodox, Atheism
Clarke, E. L., 20
Class, social: of "good neighbors," 35–37; of saints, 122–35, 241–42
Clergy and saints, 154–57, 162–67, 205, 243

Compulsory marriage of saints, 151, 152
Confessors, as saints, 155, 157, 158, 163–66
Confucianism, 34, 81
Creativity, altruism and sainthood as, v, vi, 9, 23, 94, 95, 184, 198
Crespi, L. P., 43
Crime, as topic, 3
Criminals, 19, 24, 208–09
Crisis, and type of saints, 158–59, 162–65, 183–84, 186–89, 209. See also Catastrophe
Culture: dominant, 185–86; idealistic, ideational, sensate, 181–89
Culture type, and type of saints, 158–59, 162–65, 181–82, 186–89
Culture, Western, negativism of, 3–4
Curé d'Ars, 178
Czech: "good neighbors," 38; saints, 108–10

Dearest persons: children as, 71; kinsfolk as, 69, 70; parents as, 71; similarity and dissimilarity of, 74–75; spouses as, 71
Death place, of saints, 117–20
Debunking interpretations, 3–4
Decline of number of saints: Catholic, 179–80, 181, 184, 208; Russian-Orthodox, 246
Decline of upper and middle-class saints, 127, 129, 132, 133
Dedication of saints by parents, 138–39
Delehaye, H., 93, 94, 95, 160, 162, 181
Democratization of saints, 167–68
De Musset, A., 61
Denmark, 108
De Sanctis, S., 147
Desert Fathers, 61
Deviants and criminals, altruists and saints as, 81–82, 208–09
Dharma, 44
Dissimilarity, and friendship, 74–76
Distribution, geographic, of saints: by birth, 108–09; by death, 117–19
Dollard, J., 62
Dostoievsky, F., 61

249

INDEX

Economic position of: "good neighbors," 35–36; saints, 122–23, 127, 128, 130–33, 241
Education of "good neighbors," 39–40
Ego-transcendence, v, vi, 78–79
Egypt, 108, 118, 119
Ellis, H., 20, 81, 82
English "good neighbors," 38. See also British
Environmental factors of altruism, 26–28, 29, 32, 41, 136–37
Environment of saints, types of, 169–73
Eremitic isolation of saints, 169–71
Eros, v
Estonia, 108
Ethical creativity, v, vi, 9, 23, 94, 95, 184
Europe, 108, 109, 111, 114, 116
Existentialists, 58, 211
Experience, personal, 58, 211

Factors in: altruism, 56–59, 61, 138–40, 211; decline of number of saints, 178–181, 184, 246; saintliness, 138–40, 146–47, 159, 186–88, 211
Family of "good neighbors": happiness and integration of, 31–32; size of, 30–31
Family, parental, of "good neighbors": harmony in, 26–27; size of, 25; troubles of, 27
Family, parental, of saints, 136–37, 139, 140–41
Father, influence and popularity of, 27–28
Fedotov, G. P., 48, 78, 79, 240
Female: "good neighbors," 19; saints, 94–99
Fichter, J., vii
Fishermen, as saints, 122–23
Fortunate: "good neighbors," 59–60; saints, 146–47, 149
France, 108
Francis, Saint, of Assisi, 61
Freud, (S.), Freudians, 26–28, 62, 201
Friendship. See Altruism, Love

Frustration, effects of, 61, 62, 210–11
Fry, L., 44

Gandhi, M., 51, 147, 152, 153, 207
Genius, v, vi, 9, 23, 94–95, 184
Geographic distribution of saints. See Distribution, geographic
Germany, 108–110
Gillespie, J. M., 43
Gini, C., 107
"God's Fools," 243–44
Golden Rule, 17–18, 45
Golubinsky, E., 240
"Good neighbor," vii, 6, 7, 9, 10, 17–18, 77–78. See also Altruism, Altruistic person, Love
Gowin, E. B., 23
Great Britain, 108–10. See also British
Greece, 108–09

Happiness, of altruists, v, vi, 77–78
Harmonious family, 26–27, 31–32, 136–37
Harvard Research Center in Altruistic Integration and Creativity, v, 201
Harvard students, religiosity of, 43, 44
Heine, H., 61
Hentig, H. von, 19, 24
Heredity factor, v, 26–28, 32, 41, 100–104
Hermit saints, 155, 165–68, 169
Hero, saint as, 95
Hierarchy, Catholic, and saints, 154–57, 162–67, 243
Hildegard, Saint, 61
Hinduism, 33, 45
Hobbies of "good neighbors," 54, 55
Holland, 108–10
Hugo, Victor, 60
Hungary, 108

Idealistic culture, and types of saints, 158–65, 181–89
Ideational culture, and types of saints, 158–59, 180, 182–89
Ideological atheism and religiosity, 42, 43, 45, 46
Ignatius, Loyola, 61
India, 108–110

INDEX

Integration of: family, 31–32; personality, v, vi, 77–78
Intelligence, and altruism, 39
Isolation, eremitic, 155, 169–71
Italy, 108–110

Jainism, 45
James, W., 146, 147
Japan, 108
Jerusalem, 108
Jessup, M. F., 44
Jesus. See Christ
Judaism, 45
Judges, 35–36

Karma, 45
Kenyon & Eckhardt, Inc., 6
Kinsfolk, as dearest ones, 69–71
Kiser, C. V., 25, 31
Klutchevsky, V., 240

Ladies' Home Journal, 43, 46
Lag in production of saints: by lower classes, 132, 134; by peasant class, 132
Landon, Herbert, 6
Law, conflict of altruists with, 35–36, 81–82, 208–09
Law of polarization, 61–62, 131, 148, 159, 210–11
Lawrence, Brother, 61
Lawyers, 35–36
Lehman, H. S., 23
Leuba, J. H., 44
Life span: of men of genius, 100–103; of saints, 100–103, 240–41
Lithuania, 108
Locke, H., 25
Longevity. See Life span
Love, v, vi, 74–75, 213. See also Altruism, Altruistic person, "Good neighbor"
Lower classes, increasing number of saints from, 132–35

Maddox, H. J., vii
Male: "good neighbors," 19; saints, 94–99
Malzberg, B., 20
Manfredi, J., vii

Manifold Infinity, vi
Marital status of "good neighbors," 30–32
Marriage: happy, 26–27, 31–32; involuntary, 151; preferences in, 32–34; voluntary, 151–52
Martyrs, 148–49, 157–59, 163–67, 185–90, 209
Materialism. See Agnostics, Atheism
Mayr, G., 107
Merchants, as saints, 161, 242
Middle classes: "Good neighbors" from, 35; saints from, 122–25, 131
Millionaires, American, longevity of, 102
Mohammed, 81
Monarchs, longevity of, 101
Monastery, as special environment, 169–70
Months of death of saints, 106
Mortification of self, 177–78
Mother, influence and popularity of, 27–28
Music liked by "good neighbors," 55

Nationality: of "good neighbors," 38; of saints, 108–110
Negativistic character of our culture, 3–4
Newman, Cardinal, 61
Nobility, saints from, 133, 155, 203–04, 241–42
Norms, legal and superlegal, 81–82, 208
Norway, 108
Number of saints, by centuries: Catholic, 179–84; Russian-Orthodox, 246

Occupational status of: "good neighbors," 35–36; parental families, 35, 122–32, 241; saints, 155–64, 243
Ogburn, W., 25, 31, 44
Origen, 111, 112

Palestine, 108–10, 118–19
Parental: attitude towards saints, 136–37; families of "good neighbors," 25–27; families of saints, 136–37, 139, 140; influence, 27–28, 201

INDEX

Pascal, Blaise, 61
Pathological character, in our culture, 3–4
Paul, Saint, 61
Peace of mind, and altruism, v, vi, 77–78
Peasant class, saints from, 122–25, 241–42
Persia, 108
Plato, 81
Poland, 108
Polarization, law of. See Law of polarization
Political affiliation of "good neighbors," 50–51
Popes, Catholic. See Catholic popes
Portugal, 108
Preference, racial and religious, in marriage, 32–34
Pushkarev, S. G., vii, 240

Race preference in marriage, 32–34
Radcliffe students, religion of, 43, 44
Recipients of help, 65–67
Reckless, W. C., 24
Reformation, 111, 112
Religion: of "good neighbors," 41–44, 47, 207; of intellectuals, 43–44; of students, 43–44
Religious dissimilarity, and love, 76
Religious wars, and martyrs, 115, 186–90
Rôle: of "good neighbors," 12–16, 85, 97; of saints, 94, 95, 197
Rumania, 108
Rural-urban distribution of "good neighbors," 38
Russia, 108–110
Russian-Orthodox saints, 198, 199, 203, 205, 240–46

Saints: activities and functions of, 94–95, 197; age of, 100, 198–99, 240; birth and death place of, 108–10, 116–18; decline of number of, 178–84, 208, 246; environmental adjustment of, 169–75; facilitating factors of, 136–41; marital status of, 151–52; parental social classes of, 122–27; sex of, 94–99; social position of, 154–55; types of, 146–50. See also Altruistic person
Scandinavian countries, 108, 111–12
Scheinfeld, A., 20
School education, and altruism, 54–58
Schweitzer, A., 147, 207
Self-consecration of saints, 138–40
Self-control of saints, types of, 177–79, 245
Self-determination of altruists, 58, 211–12
Self-mortification, 177–79, 245
Sensate culture: and sainthood, 191; and types of saints, 138, 191–93
Serfs, as saints, 122–26
Servants, as saints, 122, 126
Sex-satisfaction, and sainthood, 152–53
Sex of: "good neighbors," 19; persons of genius, 19–20; saints, 94–99
Shapleigh, G. S., 43
Similarity in religion, and friendship, 74–76
Slaves, as saints, 122, 126
Social class. See Class, social
Socrates, 81
Solovyev, V., 91
Spain, 108–10
Special environment of saints, 169–70
Starbuck, E. D., 147
Sweden, 108, 111
Switzerland, 108
Syria, 108

Taoism, 45
Teresa, Saint, 61
Tertullian, 111, 112
Thurston, S. J., 92, 112
Tolstoi, M. V., 240
Toynbee, A. J., 62
Trends, declining: in number of saints, 179–84, 208, 246; in proportion of saints from upper and middle classes, 127, 129, 132, 133; in proportion of self-consecration and dedication, 138–40; in quota of hermit-saints, 169–71; in self-mortificators, 177–79, 245
Trends, increasing: of saints from the

252

lower classes, 132–35; of women saints, 94–99
Turkey, 108
Tychon, Saint, 78

Underwood, A, C., 147

Vallière, Madame de la, 61
Victorova, M., 240
Virgins, as saints, 151–55, 160–61
Vital force, love as, v, vi, 74–75, 213
Vitality of eminent persons and saints, 100–103

Wanderer saints, 170–72
Wars, religious, and martyr-saints, 162–63
Whelpton, P. K., 25, 31
Woodson, C., vii

Yelchaninov, Father, 146, 159
Young, J., 43

Zimmerman, C. C., 20
Zingali, G., 107